HAMMOND

Family Reference

WORLD ATLAS

DOUBLEDAY & COMPANY, INC.

GARDEN CITY   NEW YORK

Contents

GAZETTEER-INDEX OF THE WORLD

ABBREVIATIONS

Aust.	—Australian	I.	—Island	Prot.	—Protectorate
Br.	—British	Is.	—Islands	Rep.	—Republic
Cond.	—Condominium	It.	—Italian or Italy	S.	—South
Den.	—Danish or Denmark	N.	—North	S. Afr.	—South Africa
E.	—East	Neth.	—Netherlands	Sp.	—Spain or Spanish
Eq. Guin.	—Equatorial Guinea	N.Z.	—New Zealand	sq. mi.	—square miles
Fr.	—France or French	pen.	—peninsula	S.S.R.	—Soviet Socialist Republic
Fr. Poly.	—French Polynesia	Port.	—Portugal or Portuguese	Trust.	—Trust Territory

U.K. —United Kingdom
U.S.A. —United States of America
U.S.S.R. —Union of Soviet Socialist Republics
W. —West

Country	Area (Square Miles)	Population	Index Ref.	Plate No.
Afars and Issas, Terr. of....	8,498	89,000	P 9	63
Afghanistan	250,000	17,480,000	A 2	48
Africa	11,682,000	365,000,000		62–65
Alabama, U.S.A.	51,609	3,444,165		104–105
Alaska, U.S.A.	586,412	302,173		106–107
Albania	11,100	2,154,000	E 5	35
Alberta, Canada	255,285	1,627,874		96–97
Algeria	919,595	14,083,000	G 5	62
American Samoa	76	27,159	K 7	56
Andaman & Nicobar Is., India	3,215	115,092	G6–7	49
Andorra	175	15,000	G 1	27
Angola (Port.)	481,351	5,800,000	K14	64
Antarctica	5,500,000			11
Antigua and Dependencies (Br.)	171	64,000	G 3	77
Argentina	1,072,162	24,384,000		70
Arizona, U.S.A.	113,909	1,772,482		108–109
Arkansas, U.S.A.	53,104	1,923,295		110–111
Armenian S.S.R., U.S.S.R.	11,500	2,493,000	F 6	37
Ascension I., St. Helena....	34	1,266	D13	64
Asia	17,032,000	2,203,964,000		42–43
Australia	2,967,741	12,881,100		58–59
Australian Capital Terr.	939	150,600	H 7	59
Austria	32,374	7,443,809	B 3	32
Azerbaidzhan S.S.R., U.S.S.R.	33,436	5,111,000	G 6	37
Azores, Portugal	893	291,028	B 4	62
Bahamas	4,404	175,192	C 1	76
Bahrain	231	216,078	F 4	44
Balearic Islands, Spain	1,936	451,343	H 3	27
Bangladesh	55,126	70,000,000	G 4	48
Barbados	166	253,620	G 4	77
Belgium	11,779	9,690,991	C 6	20
Belize	8,866	119,645	B 1	78
Bermuda (Br.)	20	54,000	G 2	77
Bhutan	18,000	880,000	G 3	48
Bismarck Arch., Terr. New Guinea	18,770	209,051	E 6	56
Bolivia	424,164	5,063,000	G 7	68
Botswana	219,815	630,000	L16	65
Brazil	3,284,426	93,204,379		69,71
British Columbia, Canada....	366,255	2,184,621		98–99
British Indian Ocean Terr.	30	2,000	L10	43
Brunei	2,226	135,665	E 4	54
Bulgaria	42,829	8,515,000	G 4	34
Burma	261,789	27,900,000	A 2	53
Burundi	10,747	3,624,000	N12	65
California, U.S.A.	158,693	19,953,134		112–113
Cambodia	69,898	6,928,000	D 4	53
Cameroon	183,568	5,871,000	J10	62
Canada	3,851,809	21,815,978		84–85
Canal Zone (U.S.A.)	647	44,198	E 3	79
Canary Islands, Spain........	2,808	1,017,361	B 4	26
Cape of Good Hope, South Africa	262,079	3,936,306	L18	65

Country	Area (Square Miles)	Population	Index Ref.	Plate No.
Cape Verde Islands (Port.)	1,557	272,071	N 5	9
Caroline Is., Terr. of the Pacific Islands......	267	47,202	E 5	56
Cayman Is. (Br.)	100	10,652	B 3	76
Celebes, Indonesia	72,986	7,665,000	G 6	55
Central African Republic ..	240,534	1,624,000	K10	63
Central America	196,928	17,015,000		78–79
Ceylon (Sri Lanka)	25,332	12,747,755	E 7	49
Chad	495,753	3,751,000	K 8	63
Channel Is. (Br.)	75	126,020	E 6	17
Chatham Is., N. Z.	372	520	J10	56
Chile	292,258	9,432,000		70
China (mainland)	3,691,506	759,619,000		50–51
China (Taiwan)	13,948	14,907,000	K 7	51
Christmas I., Aust.	52	3,439	O11	43
Cocos Is., Aust.	5.4	607	N11	43
Colombia	439,737	21,772,000	F 3	68
Colorado, U.S.A.	104,247	2,207,259		114–115
Comoro Is. (Fr.)	838	280,000	P14	65
Congo	132,046	1,200,000	J12	64
Connecticut, U.S.A.	5,009	3,032,217		116–117
Cook Is., (N.Z.)	93	22,000	K 7	56
Corsica, France	3,368	269,831	A 6	25
Costa Rica	19,576	1,777,000	E 5	79
Crete, Greece	3,218	483,075	G 8	35
Cuba	44,218	8,589,000	B 2	76
Curaçao, Netherlands Antilles	182	145,455	E 4	77
Cyprus	3,473	640,000	E 5	46
Czechoslovakia	49,370	14,500,000	D 2	32
Dahomey	44,290	2,531,000	G10	62
Daito Is., Japan	17	3,896	M 6	51
Delaware, U.S.A.	2,057	548,104		139
Denmark	16,625	4,950,598	E 9	19
District of Columbia, U.S.A.	67	756,510	B 5	138
Dominica (Br.)	290	70,302	G 4	77
Dominican Republic	18,816	4,188,000	D 3	77
Ecuador	109,483	6,194,000	E 4	68
Egypt	386,100	34,350,000	M 6	63
El Salvador	8,260	3,480,000	C 4	78
England, U.K.	50,327	46,089,820		17
Equatorial Guinea	10,832	292,000	H11	62,64
Estonian S.S.R., U.S.S.R. ..	17,413	1,357,000	C 3	36
Ethiopia	471,776	25,543,000	O 9	63
Europe	4,063,000	647,641,000		14–15
Faeröe Is., Den.	540	39,000	D 2	14
Falkland Is. (Br.)	4,618	3,000	H14	71
Fiji	7,015	531,000	H 7	56
Finland	130,128	4,686,000	O 5	18
Florida, U.S.A.	58,560	6,789,443		118–119
France	212,841	51,500,000		24–25
French Guiana	35,135	51,000	K 3	69
French Polynesia	1,544	119,168	M 7	56

GAZETTEER-INDEX OF THE WORLD

Country	Area (Square Miles)	Population	Index Ref.	Plate No.
Gabon	103,346	483,000	J12	64
Gambia	4,003	366,000	C 9	62
Georgia, U.S.A.	58,876	4,589,575		120–121
Georgian S.S.R., U.S.S.R.	26,911	4,688,000	F 6	37
Germany, East (German Democratic Republic)	41,814	17,040,926		22–23
Germany, West (Federal Republic of)	95,959	61,846,000		22–23
Ghana	91,843	8,545,561	F10	62
Gibraltar (Br.)	2	27,965	D 4	26
Gilbert & Ellice Islands (Br.)	369	57,000	H 6	56
Great Britain & Northern Ireland (United Kingdom)	94,214	55,346,551		16–17
Greece	50,548	8,986,000	F 6	35
Greenland (Den.)	840,000	46,331	B12	10
Grenada	133	94,500	G 6	77
Guadeloupe and Dependencies (Fr.)	687	332,000	F 3	77
Guam (U.S.A.)	209	84,996	E 4	56
Guatemala	42,042	5,348,000	B 3	78
Guinea	94,925	3,967,000	D 9	62
Guyana	83,000	714,000	J 2	69
Haiti	10,694	4,969,000	D 3	76
Hawaii, U.S.A.	6,450	769,913		122
Holland (Netherlands)	13,958	13,234,000	E 4	20
Honduras	43,277	2,751,000	D 3	78
Hong Kong (Br.)	398	4,045,000	J 7	51
Hungary	35,915	10,378,000	E 3	33
Iceland	39,768	204,578	C 2	14
Idaho, U.S.A.	83,557	713,008		123
Illinois, U.S.A.	56,400	11,113,976		124–125
India	1,261,483	547,572,686		48–49
Indiana, U.S.A.	36,291	5,193,669		126–127
Indonesia	735,264	121,386,000		54–55
Iowa, U.S.A.	56,290	2,825,041		128–129
Iran	636,293	30,159,000	F 3	45
Iraq	167,924	9,750,000	D 3	44
Ireland	26,600	2,971,230	B 4	17
Israel	7,993	3,002,000		47
Italy	116,303	54,908,000		28–29
Ivory Coast	124,503	4,369,000	E10	62
Jamaica	4,232	1,989,000	C 3	76
Japan	143,622	105,710,000		52
Java, Indonesia	48,842	69,323,000	K 2	55
Jordan	37,297	2,383,000		47
Kansas, U.S.A.	82,264	2,249,071		130–131
Kazakh S.S.R., U.S.S.R.	1,048,301	12,850,000	G 5	38
Kentucky, U.S.A.	40,395	3,219,311		132–133
Kenya	224,902	11,467,000	O11	65
Kirgiz S.S.R., U.S.S.R.	76,641	2,933,000	H 5	38
Korea, North	46,540	14,356,000	C 2	52
Korea, South	38,452	32,635,000	C 3	52
Kuwait	8,000	747,000	E 4	44
Laos	91,459	3,033,000	D 3	53
Latvian S.S.R., U.S.S.R.	24,595	2,365,000	B 3	36
Lebanon	4,015	2,787,000	F 6	46
Lesotho	11,716	937,000	M17	65
Liberia	43,000	1,207,000	E10	62
Libya	679,359	1,937,000	K 6	62–63
Liechtenstein	61	21,078	J 3	31
Lithuanian S.S.R., U.S.S.R.	25,174	3,129,000	B 3	36
Louisiana, U.S.A.	48,523	3,643,180		134–135
Luxembourg	999	339,848	H 8	20
Macao (Port.)	6.2	-263,000	H 7	51
Madeira Is., Portugal	308	253,220	A 2	26
Maine, U.S.A.	33,215	993,663		136–137
Malagasy Republic	226,657	7,400,000	R15	65
Malawi	45,483	4,400,000	N14	65
Malaya, Malaysia	50,670	8,801,399	C 7	53
Malaysia	128,308	10,434,034	C-F 4	54
Maldives	115	113,000	L 9	43
Mali	463,948	5,152,000	E 9	62
Malta	122	324,000	E 7	29
Man, Isle of (Br.)	227	56,248	D 3	17
Manitoba, Canada	251,000	988,247		92–93
Mariana Is., Terr. of the Pacific Islands	184	9,640	E 4	56
Marquesas Is., Fr. Poly.	492	5,593	N 6	56
Marshall Is., Terr. Pac. Is.	70	22,888	H 4	56
Martinique (Fr.)	425	341,000	G 4	77
Maryland, U.S.A.	10,577	3,922,399		138–139
Massachusetts, U.S.A.	8,257	5,689,170		140–141
Mauritania	397,954	1,200,000	D 8	62
Mauritius & Dependencies..	787	817,000	S19	65
Mexico	761,604	50,900,000		80–81
Michigan, U.S.A.	58,216	8,875,083		142–143
Midway Is. (U.S.A.)	2	2,220	H 3	56
Minnesota, U.S.A.	84,068	3,805,069		144–145
Mississippi U.S.A.	47,716	2,216,912		146–147
Missouri, U.S.A.	69,686	4,677,399		148–149
Moldavian S.S.R., U.S.S.R.	13,012	3,572,000	C 5	37
Monaco	368 acres	23,610	G 6	25
Mongolia	604,090	1,265,000	E-H 2	50–51
Montana, U.S.A.	147,138	694,409		150–151
Montserrat (Br.)	38	12,302	G 3	77
Morocco	172,413	15,379,259	E 5	62
Mozambique (Port.)	302,328	7,790,000	O15	65
Natal, S. Afr.	33,578	2,979,920	N17	65
Nauru	8.2	7,000	G 6	56
Nebraska, U.S.A.	77,227	1,438,791		152–153
Nepal	54,362	11,383,000	E-F 3	49
Netherlands	13,958	13,234,000	E 4	20
Netherlands Antilles	961	223,558	E 4	77
Nevada, U.S.A.	110,540	488,738		154
New Britain, Terr. New Guinea	14,098	138,689	F 6	56
New Brunswick, Canada	28,354	634,557	C 3	86
New Caledonia & Dependencies (Fr.)	8,548	101,000	G 8	56
Newfoundland, Canada	156,185	522,104	J 4	86
New Guinea, Terr. of (Aust. Trust.)	92,160	1,793,036	E-F 6	56
New Hampshire, U.S.A.	9,304	737,681		155
New Hebrides (Br.-Fr. Cond.)	5,700	86,000	G 7	56
New Jersey, U.S.A.	7,836	7,168,164		156–157
New Mexico, U.S.A.	121,666	1,016,000		158–159
New South Wales, Aust.	309,433	4,641,000	H 6	59
New York, U.S.A.	49,576	18,241,266		160–161
New Zealand	103,736	2,860,475	M 7	59
Nicaragua	50,193	1,947,000	E 4	78
Niger	489,189	4,634,000	H 8	62
Nigeria	356,669	55,367,000	H10	62
Niue (N. Z.)	100	4,988	K 7	56
Norfolk I., Aust.	13.3	1,377	G 8	56
North America	9,363,000	320,512,000		74–75
North Carolina, U.S.A.	52,586	5,082,059		162–163
North Dakota, U.S.A.	70,665	617,761		164–165
Northern Ireland, U.K.	5,459	1,534,000	G 3	17
Northern Territory, Aust. ..	520,280	87,400	E 3	58
Northwest Territories, Canada	1,304,903	34,807	E-J 3	84–85
Norway	125,181	3,914,000	F 6	18
Nova Scotia, Canada	21,425	788,960		86–87
Ohio, U.S.A.	41,222	10,652,017		166–167
Oklahoma, U.S.A.	69,919	2,559,253		168–169
Oman	82,000	667,000	G 5	45
Ontario, Canada	412,582	7,703,106		90–91
Orange Free State, S. Afr.	49,866	1,386,547	M17	65
Oregon, U.S.A.	96,981	2,091,385		170–171
Orkney Is., Scotland	376	17,254	E 1	16
Pacific Is., Terr. of the (U.S. Trust)	687	102,000	D-G 5	56
Pakistan	310,403	60,000,000	B 3	48
Palau Is., Terr. Pac. Is.	179	11,210	D 5	56
Panama	29,208	1,444,000	G 6	79
Papua (Aust.)	86,100	654,441	B 7	54
Paraguay	157,047	2,340,000	J 8	69,71
Pennsylvania, U.S.A.	45,333	11,793,909		172–173
Persia (Iran)	636,293	30,159,000	F 3	45
Peru	496,224	14,029,000	E 5	68
Philippines	115,707	38,728,000	H 4	55
Pitcairn Is. (Br.)	18	82	O 8	56
Poland	120,702	32,834,000		21
Portugal	35,510	9,711,000	B 3	26
Portuguese Guinea	13,948	487,448	C 9	62
Portuguese Timor	5,762	610,541	H 7	55
Prince Edward I., Canada..	2,184	111,641	F 3	87
Puerto Rico	3,435	2,732,000	G 2	77
Qatar	8,500	80,000	F 4	45
Québec, Canada	594,860	6,027,764		88–89
Queensland, Aust.	667,000	1,848,600	G 4	59

Country	Area (Square Miles)	Population	Index Ref.	Plate No.
Réunion (Fr.)	969	453,000	R20	65
Rhode Island, U.S.A.	1,214	949,723	.....	141
Rhodesia	150,332	5,500,000	M15	65
Rumania	91,699	20,373,000	G 3	34
Russian S.F.S.R., U.S.S.R.	6,592,819	130,090,000	D–R 4	38–39
Rwanda	10,169	3,641,000	N12	65
Ryukyu Is., Japan	848	950,000	G 4	52
Sabah, Malaysia	29,388	655,622	F 4–5	54–55
St. Christopher-Nevis-Anguilla (Br.)	138	62,000	F 3	77
St. Croix, Virgin Is. (U.S.A.)	80	31,779	H 2	77
St. Helena & Dependencies (Br.)	47	6,541	E15	64
St. John, Virgin Is. (U.S.A.)	20	1,729	H 1	77
St. Lucia (Br.)	238	101,100	G 4	77
St-Pierre & Miquelon (Fr.)	93.5	5,235	H 6	87
St. Thomas, Virgin Is. (U.S.A.)	32	28,960	G 1	77
St. Vincent (Br.)	150	89,129	G 4	77
Sakhalin, U.S.S.R.	28,215	600,000	P 4	39
San Marino	23.4	19,000	D 2	28
São Tomé e Príncipe (Port.)	372	73,811	H11	64
Sarawak, Malaysia	48,250	977,013	E 5	54
Sardinia, Italy	9,301	1,419,362	B 4	29
Saskatchewan, Canada	251,700	926,242	.....	94–95
Saudi Arabia	920,000	7,740,000	D 4	44
Scotland, U.K.	30,411	5,227,706	D 2	16
Senegal	75,750	3,900,000	D 9	62
Seychelles (Br.)	91	52,437	T 6	9
Shetland Is., Scotland	551	17,567	G 1	16
Siam (Thailand)	198,456	38,136,000	C 3	53
Sicily, Italy	9,926	4,721,001	D 6	29
Sierra Leone	27,925	2,681,000	D10	62
Singapore	226	2,093,000	E 6	53
Society Is., Fr. Poly.	646	84,552	L 7	56
Solomon Is., Terr. New Guinea	4,080	72,661	F 6	56
Solomon Is. Prot. (Br.)	11,500	164,000	G 6	56
Somalia	246,200	2,823,000	R11	63,65
South Africa	471,663	21,621,000	L18	65
South America	6,875,000	276,500,000	.....	68–71
South Australia, Aust.	380,070	1,184,600	E 5	58
South Carolina, U.S.A.	31,055	2,590,516	.....	174–175
South Dakota, U.S.A.	77,047	666,257	.....	176–177
South-West Africa (South Africa)	317,838	634,000	K16	64–65
Spain	194,896	34,134,000	.....	26–27
Spanish Sahara, Spain	102,702	76,425	D 6	62
Sri Lanka	25,332	12,747,755	E 7	49
Sudan	967,495	15,965,000	M 9	63
Sumatra, Indonesia	163,265	17,345,000	C 6	54
Surinam (Neth.)	55,144	410,000	J 3	69
Svalbard, Norway	23,958	2,808	C 2	18
Swaziland	6,704	408,000	N17	65
Sweden	173,665	8,116,000	J 6	19
Switzerland	15,941	6,300,000	.....	30–31
Syria	71,498	6,451,000	G 5	46
Tadzhik S.S.R., U.S.S.R.	55,251	2,900,000	G 6	38
Tahiti, Fr. Poly.	402	79,494	M 7	56
Taiwan, China	13,948	14,907,000	K 7	51
Tanzania	362,819	13,478,000	N13	65

Country	Area (Square Miles)	Population	Index Ref.	Plate No.
Tasmania, Aust.	26,215	392,500	J 8	59
Tennessee, U.S.A.	42,244	3,924,164	.....	178–179
Texas, U.S.A.	267,339	11,196,730	.....	180–181
Thailand	198,456	38,136,000	C 3	53
Tibet, China	471,660	1,270,000	C 5	50
Togo	21,853	1,991,000	G10	62
Tokelau Is. (N. Z.)	3.9	2,000	J 6	56
Tonga	270	87,400	J 7	56
Transkei, S. Afr.	16,675	1,439,195	M18	65
Transvaal, S. Afr.	109,621	6,273,477	N17	65
Trinidad & Tobago	1,979	945,210	G 5	77
Tristan da Cunha, St. Helena	40	275	O 7	9
Tuamotu Arch., Fr. Poly.	343	8,226	M 7	56
Tunisia	63,378	5,291,000	H 5	62
Turkey	301,381	36,162,000	.....	46
Turkmen S.S.R., U.S.S.R.	188,456	2,158,000	F 6	38
Turks & Caicos Is. (Br.)	166	5,500	D 2	76
Uganda	92,674	9,904,000	N11	65
Ukrainian S.S.R., U.S.S.R.	232,046	47,496,000	D 5	37
Union of Soviet Socialist Republics	8,649,498	243,900,000	.....	36–39
United Arab Emirates	32,278	196,000	F 5	45
United Kingdom	94,214	55,346,551	.....	16–17
United States of America .... land	3,536,855			
.... land and water	3,615,123	203,235,298	.....	102–103
Upper Volta	105,841	5,438.000	F 9	62
Uruguay	72,172	2,909,000	J10	71
Utah, U.S.A.	84,916	1,059,273	.....	182
Uzbek S.S.R., U.S.S.R.	173,591	11,963,000	G 5	38
Vatican City	109 acres	1,000	B 6	29
Venezuela	352,144	10,572,000	G 2	68
Vermont, U.S.A.	9,609	444,732	.....	183
Victoria, Aust.	87,884	3,530,700	G 7	59
Vietnam, North	61,293	21,154,000	D 3	53
Vietnam, South	66,263	18,570,000	E 4	53
Virginia, U.S.A.	40,817	4,648,494	.....	184–185
Virgin Is. (Br.)	59	10,484	H 1	77
Virgin Is. (U.S.A.)	132	62,468	H 1	77
Wake I. (U.S.A.)	2.5	1,647	G 4	56
Wales, U.K.	8,017	2,725,180	E 4	17
Wallis & Futuna (Fr.)	106	9,000	H–J 7	56
Washington, U.S.A.	68,192	3,409,169	.....	186–187
Western Australia, Aust.	975,920	1,045,800	C 4	58
Western Samoa	1,133	146,000	J 7	56
West Virginia, U.S.A.	24,181	1,744,237	.....	188–189
White Russian S.R.R. U.S.S.R.	80,154	9,074,000	C 4	37
Wisconsin, U.S.A.	56,154	4,417,933	.....	190–191
World	52,422,640	3,734,000,000	.....	8–9
Wyoming, U.S.A.	97,914	332,416	.....	192
Yemen Arab Republic	75,000	5,817,000	D 7	44
Yemen, Peoples Democratic Republic of	111,075	1,299,000	E 7	44
Yugoslavia	98,766	20,514,516	C 3	34
Yukon Territory, Canada	207,076	18,388	C 3	84
Zaire	905,563	21,637,876	L12	65
Zambia	290,586	4,215,000	M14	65

THE SOLAR SYSTEM

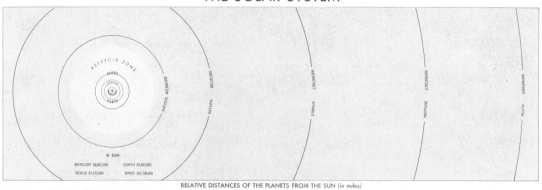

RELATIVE DISTANCES OF THE PLANETS FROM THE SUN (in miles)

ASTEROID ZONE
MARS
VENUS
EARTH
MERCURY
JUPITER 483,880,000
SATURN 887,180,000
URANUS 1,782,000,000
NEPTUNE 2,792,000,000
PLUTO 3,684,000,000

* SUN

MERCURY 36,001,000   EARTH 93,003,000
VENUS 67,272,000   MARS 141,708,000

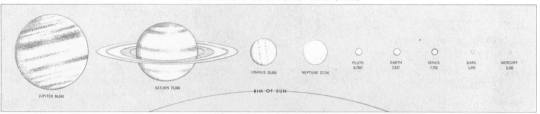

RELATIVE DIAMETERS OF THE PLANETS (in miles)

JUPITER 88,698
SATURN 75,060
URANUS 29,200
NEPTUNE 27,740
RIM OF SUN
PLUTO 6,700?
EARTH 7,927
VENUS 7,700
MARS 4,200
MERCURY 3,100

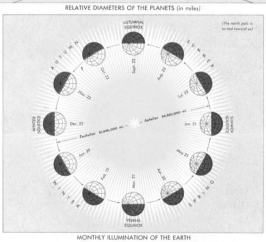

MOON'S UMBRA
MOON'S PENUMBRA
MOON'S PENUMBRA
EARTH

TOTAL ECLIPSE OF THE SUN

AUTUMNAL EQUINOX
(The north pole is turned toward us)
AUTUMN
SUMMER
Oct. 23
Sept. 23
Aug. 23
Jul. 23
Nov. 22
WINTER SOLSTICE
Dec. 22
Perihelion 91,446,000 mi.
Aphelion 94,560,000 mi.
SUMMER SOLSTICE
Jun. 21
Jan. 20
May 21
Feb. 19
WINTER
Mar. 21
Apr. 20
SPRING
VERNAL EQUINOX

MONTHLY ILLUMINATION OF THE EARTH

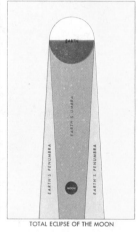

EARTH
EARTH'S UMBRA
MOON
EARTH'S PENUMBRA
EARTH'S PENUMBRA

TOTAL ECLIPSE OF THE MOON

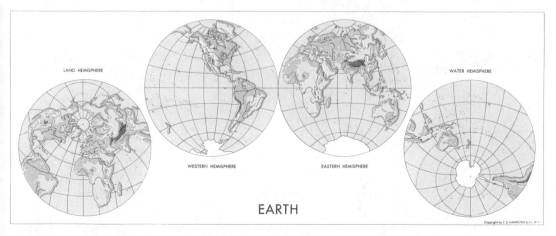

LAND HEMISPHERE
WESTERN HEMISPHERE
EASTERN HEMISPHERE
WATER HEMISPHERE

EARTH

ARCTIC

OCEAN

Komsomolets I.
SEVERNAYA
ZEMLYA
(NORTH LAND)
October Revolution I.
Bol'shevik I.

Borden I.
SVERDRU
QUEEN ELIZ
ISLAND
Pr. Patrick I.
N. MAG. POLE
Lands End
Melville I.
Bathurst
M'Clure Str.
Vis. Melville Sd.
Banks I.
Som
Pr. of
Wales

C. Chelyuskin
TAYMYR
PEN.
LAPTEV SEA
L. Taymyr
Nordvik
NEW
SIBERIAN IS.
DeLong
Is.
BEAUFORT
SEA
Victoria I.
Amundsen Gulf
Mackenzie
Great
Bear Lake

Khatanga
EAST SIBERIAN SEA
Bear Is.
Wrangel I.
Barrow
Pt. Barrow
N O R T

Verkhoyansk
Srednekolymsk
Arctic Circle
CHUKCHI PEN.
Pt. Hope
UNITED STATES
Ft. Yukon
Great
Slave Lake
Dawson
A L

Oymyakon
Gizhiga
Anadyr
Bering Str.
Nome
Yukon
Fairbanks
ALASKA
Anchorage
Whitehorse
Athabasca
Churchill
C A N

Olekminsk
UNION OF SOVIET
KAMCHATKA PEN.
(U.S. Trust Terr.)
BERING SEA
Lawrence I.
Pribilof
Is.
Gulf of Alaska
Kodiak I.
Juneau
Sitka
Peace
Edmonton
Saskatoon
A M E R I

SOCIALIST REPUBLICS
Krasnoyarsk
SEA OF
OKHOTSK
Komandorskiye
Is.
Attu
QUEEN
CHARLOTTE
IS.
Pr. of Wales I.
Prince
Rupert
Calgary
Regina
Winn

Irkutsk
Ulan-Ude
Baykal
Chita
Shilka
Nikolayevsk
Komsomol'sk
Khabarovsk
Sakhalin
Petropavlovsk-
Kamchatskiy
Cape
Lopatka
ALEUTIAN ISLANDS
Vancouver I.
Vancouver
Seattle
Portland
Boise
Salt
Lake City
Minneapolis
St.

Ulan Bator
MONGOLIA
GOBI (Desert)
Paotow
Harbin
Changchun
Mukden
Vladivostok
Hokkaido
KURIL IS.
NORTH PACIFIC
OCEAN
San Francisco
Los Angeles
C. Mendocino
Denver
Colorado
UNITED S
Kansas
El Paso
Dallas
Housto

Peking
(Peiping)
Tientsin
Lanchow
Tsinan
N. KOREA
Seoul
S. KOREA
YELLOW
SEA
Nagoya
Honshu
JAPAN
Tokyo
Yokohama
SEA OF
JAPAN
Midway Is.
(U.S.)
UNITED STATES
HAWAII
Honolulu
Hawaii
Tropic of Cancer
Guadalupe
(Mex.)
C. San Lucas
Guadalajara
MEXICO
Monterrey
Mexico City
CEN
AM

CHINA
Chengtu
Chungking
Changsha
Kunming
Nanking
Wuhan
Foochow
Canton
Yangtze Kiang
Shanghai
EAST
CHINA
SEA
Kyushu
Shikoku
Osaka
Ryukyu Is.
Bonin Is.
(Jap.)
Wake I.
(U.S.)
Johnston Atoll
(U.S.)
Revillagigedo Is.
(Mex.)
Clipperton I.
(Fr.)

BURMA
Rangoon
THAIL'D
Bangkok
INDIA
Hanoi
N. VIETNAM
S. VIETNAM
MACAO
(Port.)
Hainan
HONG KONG
(Br.)
Taipei
Taiwan (Formosa)
MARIANA
IS.
Guam
MARSHALL
IS.
Palmyra I.
(U.S.)
Fanning I.
Washington I. (Br.)
Christmas I. (U.S.& Br.)
Equator
GALÁPAGOS
(Ec.)

G. of
Siam
CAMB.
SOUTH
CHINA
SEA
Saigon
MALAYSIA (Br.)
SABAH
SARAWAK
BRUNEI
Luzon
Manila
PHILIPPINES
Mindanao
CAROLINE IS.
Palau
Is.
TERRITORY OF THE PACIFIC ISLANDS
(U.S. Trust Terr.)
NAURU
Howland I.(U.S.& Br.)
Baker I.(U.S.)
Canton I.(U.S.)
GILBERT
IS. (Br.)
Jarvis I.(U.S.)
Malden I.(U.S.& Br.)
Starbuck I.(U.S.& Br.)
PHOENIX IS.
(U.S.& Br.)

Sumatra
SINGAPORE
INDONESIA
Borneo
Celebes
New
Guinea
TERR. OF
NEW GUINEA
(Austr.)
NEW
GUINEA
BISMARCK
ARCH.(Austr.)
SOLOMON IS.
(Br.)
ELLICE IS.
(Br.)
MARQUESAS IS.
(Fr.)
TUAMOTU
ARCH.

Cocos Is.
(Austr.)
Christmas I.
(Austr.)
Djakarta
Java
SUNDA ISLANDS
Timor
PAPUA
ARAFURA SEA
C. York
Sta. Cruz
Is. (Br.)
Rotuma I.
(Br.)
W. SAMOA
Tutuila (U.S.)
SOCIETY IS.
(Fr.)
Tahiti
Papeete
SOUTH PACIFIC

Port Hedland
Darwin
CORAL
SEA
NEW
HEBRIDES
(Br. & Fr.)
FIJI
TONGA
COOK IS.
(N.Z.)
OCEAN

INDIAN
OCEAN
AUSTRALIA
Townsville
Rockhampton
New
Caledonia
(Fr.)
Loyalty Is.
(Fr.)
AUSTRALES IS.
(Tubuai) (Fr.)
Tropic of Capricorn
Pitcairn I.
(Br.)
Ducie I.
(Br.)
Easter I.
(Chile)
Sala y Góme
(Chile)

Perth
Kalgoorlie
Brisbane
Norfolk I.
(Austr.)
Kermadec Is.
(N.Z.)

Fremantle
Albany
C. Leeuwin
Adelaide
Murray
Bass Str.
Sydney
Canberra
Melbourne
TASMAN
SEA
Lord Howe I.
(Austr.)
Newcastle
North Cape
North I.
NEW
ZEALAND
Auckland
Wellington
Christchurch
SOUTH PACIFIC
OCEAN

Tasmania
Hobart
South I.
Dunedin
Chatham Is.
(N.Z.)

Stewart I.
Bounty Is.
(N.Z.)
Auckland Is.
(N.Z.)
Antipodes Is.
(N.Z.)
Campbell I.
(N.Z.)

Macquarie I.
(Austr.)

Balleny Is.
Scott I.

ANTARCTICA

THE WORLD
MERCATOR PROJECTION
EQUATORIAL SCALES
MILES
0   500   1000   1500   2000   2500
KILOMETRES
0   500 1000 1500 2000 2500
Capitals of Countries .... ◉
© C.S. HAMMOND & Co., Maplewood, N.J.

Antarctic Circle

8

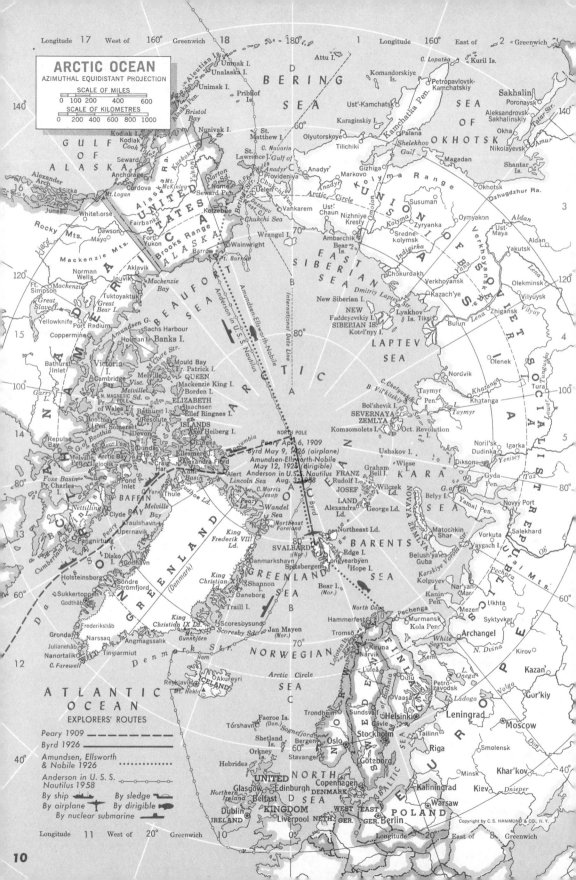

ARCTIC OCEAN
AZIMUTHAL EQUIDISTANT PROJECTION

SCALE OF MILES
0 100 200 400 600

SCALE OF KILOMETRES
0 200 400 600 800 1000

ATLANTIC OCEAN

EXPLORERS' ROUTES

Peary 1909
Byrd 1926
Amundsen, Ellsworth & Nobile 1926
Anderson in U.S.S. Nautilus 1958

By ship   By sledge
By airplane   By dirigible
By nuclear submarine

Copyright by C. S. HAMMOND & CO., N. Y.

10

ANTARCTICA
AZIMUTHAL EQUIDISTANT PROJECTION

SCALE OF MILES
0 200 400 600 800

SCALE OF KILOMETRES
0 200 400 600 800 1000

© C. S. HAMMOND & Co., N. Y.

EXPLORERS' ROUTES

Palmer 1820 +—+—+—+—+
Amundsen 1910-12 •••••••••••••
Scott 1910-13 ——————————
Byrd 1928-30 — — — — — —
Fuchs 1957-58 ooooooooooooooo

By ship 🚢   By sledge 🛷   By airplane ✈
By snow tractor 🚜

ATLANTIC OCEAN

INDIAN OCEAN

PACIFIC OCEAN

WEDDELL SEA

SCOTIA SEA

ROSS SEA

BELLINGSHAUSEN SEA

Amundsen Sea

Queen Maud Land

New Schwabenland

Enderby Land

Wilkes Land

Marie Byrd Land

Victoria Land

South Polar Plateau

SOUTH POLE
Amundsen-Scott Sta.

Amundsen Dec. 14, 1911
Scott Jan. 17, 1912
Byrd Nov. 29, 1929 (airplane)
Fuchs Jan. 20, 1958

AREA OF POLE OF INACCESSIBILITY

Antarctic Circle

SOUTH AMERICA

NEW ZEALAND

AUSTRALIA
Hobart
Tasmania
Melbourne
King I.
Furneaux Gr.

Tasman Sea

Dunedin
Stewart I.
Auckland Is. (N.Z.)
Campbell I. (N.Z.)
Antipodes Is. (N.Z.)
Bounty Is. (N.Z.)
Macquarie I. (Australia)
Balleny Is.

Dumont d'Urville
ADÉLIE COAST
CLARIE COAST
C. Keltie
C. Goodenough
BANZARE COAST
SABRINA COAST
BUDD COAST
KNOX COAST
Vincennes Bay
Shackleton Ice Shelf
Farr Bay
Davis Sea
West Ice Shelf
Mirnyy
Mt. Barr Smith 4,318
QUEEN MARY COAST
Gaussberg
WILHELM II COAST
Davis
American Highland
Prydz Bay
Amery Ice Shelf
MacKenzie Bay
C. Darnley
MAC-ROBERTSON COAST
C. Daly
Mawson
Edward VIII Bay
KEMP COAST
C. Batterbee
Amundsen Bay
C. Norvegia
PRINCE OLAV COAST
Lützow-Holm Bay
Riiser-Larsen Pen.
PRINCESS RAGNHILD COAST
PRINCESS ASTRID COAST
PRINCESS MARTHA COAST
Sanae
Lazarev
Bouvet I. (Nor.)
Prince Edward Is. (S. Afr.)

South Sandwich Is. (Br.)
Grytviken
South Georgia (Br.)
South Orkney Is. (Br.)
Coronation I.
Stanley
Falkland Is. (Br.)
Elephant I.
King George I.
Joinville I.
Hope Bay
James Ross I.
Biscoe Is.
Adelaide I.
Marguerite Bay
Charcot I.
Alexander I.
Peter I I. (Nor.)
Thurston I.
Palmer Arch.
Palmer Sta.
Larsen Ice Shelf
Hearst I.
Hilton Inlet
FILCHNER ICE SHELF
Ronne Entrance
ROB'T ENGLISH COAST
Berkner I.
LUITPOLD COAST
LAIRD COAST
Edith Ronne Land
Vinson Massif 15,970
EIGHTS COAST
Ellsworth Mts.
Queen Maud Ra.
Byrd Sta.
Executive Comm. Ra. 10,371
Mt. Sidley 12,008
Sible Comm. Ra.
C. Dart
Getz Ice Shelf
HOBBS COAST
RUPPERT COAST
Edsel Ford Ra.
SAUNDERS COAST
Sulzberger Bay
WALGREEN COAST
Hollick-Kenyon Plateau
Roosevelt I.
Little America
KAINAN COAST
Kainan Bay
Ross Ice Shelf
Beardmore Glacier
Mt. Kirkpatrick 14,600
Mt. Markham 15,098
Mt. Lister 12,762
Mt. Nansen 8,789
SOUTH MAGNETIC POLE AREA
GEORGE V COAST
OATES COAST
Ninnis Glacier Tongue
Mertz Glacier Tongue
C. Adare
Mt. Sabine 10,000
McMurdo Sd.
Scott Base
Ross I.
Drake Passage
C. Horn
South Shetland Is.
Limit of Drift Ice

Scott Route 1957-58
Fuchs

17 20° Longitude West 18 of Greenwich 0° Longitude East of Greenwich 20° 2
40°
16 60°
15 80°
14
13
12
11 160° Longitude West 180° Longitude East of Greenwich 160° 8
40°
60°
80°
3
4
5
6
7
140°

13

Map of
EUROPE
SCALE OF MILES
0 100 200 300 400

⬠ Capitals of Countries
• Cities
▬▬▬ Boundaries of Countries
▪▪▪▪ Other Boundaries
▲ Mountain Peaks

Mountains Highlands Lowlands Depression Water

40° 30° 20° 10° 0° 10°

ARC

NORWEGIAN SEA

Reykjavik ICELAND

Faeroe Islands (Danish)

Shetland Islands (British)

Trondheim

Bergen

Oslo

50°

ATLANTIC OCEAN

Hebrides

Orkney Islands

Scotland

Northern Ireland Glasgow

British Isles GREAT

IRELAND IRISH SEA Liverpool

Dublin

BRITAIN

Wales England

London

Greenwich

English Channel

NORTH SEA

Skagerrak Kattegat Göteborg

DENMARK
Copenhagen

Hamburg

NETHER-LANDS EAST Berlin

The Hague Amsterdam WEST Oder

Brussels BELGIUM Bonn GERMANY

Le Havre LUXEM-BOURG

Seine River GERMANY Frankfurt CZECHO

Nantes Paris R. Prague

Loire River Rhine R. Danube

FRANCE Munich Vienna

40°

Bay of Biscay

Bilbao

Bordeaux

Lyon R. SWITZER-LAND Bern AUSTRIA

LIECHT. Milan Trieste Zagreb

Mt. Blanc Po River Venice YUG

Genoa MONACO ADRIATIC

Oporto PYRENEES Marseille

Iberian ANDORRA Corsica (French)

Lisbon PORTUGAL SPAIN Peninsula Barcelona San Marino

Madrid Rome ITALY

Cape St. Vincent Valencia Balearic Islands (Spanish) VATICAN CITY

Seville Sardinia (Italian) Naples

GIBRALTAR (British)
Strait of Gibraltar Palermo
Tangier Ceuta (Spanish)

Rabat Melilla (Spanish) Algiers MEDITERRANE Sicily (Italian)

MOROCCO ALGERIA Tunis

AFRICA TUNISIA MALTA

30°
10° Longitude West of Greenwich 0° 10°

C O C E A N
20°   North Cape   30°   40°   BARENTS   50°   60°   70°   80°
msö   SEA   Arctic Circle   URAL   Ob'   River   Irtysh River   60°
Murmansk   A   S
White Sea   Archangel   50°
Luleå   Northern Dvina R.   Sverdlovsk
FINLAND
Oulu
Lake Onega   UNION OF SOVIET   I
Lake Ladoga   A
Helsinki   Leningrad   River   Kazan
Stockholm   Gulf of Finland   Volga   Gor'kiy   SOCIALIST REPUBLICS   50°
Tallinn   Moscow   Kuybyshev
Estonia   (RUSSIA)   A
Riga   Western Dvina R.   River   Ural   River   Aral Sea
Latvia
Lithuania   Saratov
zig   White   Minsk   Don   Volga
Russia   River
Vistula   Warsaw   Astrakhan
OLAND   Dnieper   Khar'kov   ine   Volgograd   CASPIAN
Cracow   L'vov   U   River   (Stalingrad)
CARPATHIAN MOUNTAINS   Dniester River   Kiev   Rostov   40°
VAKIA   R.   Budapest   Sea of   CAUCASUS MOUNTAINS   SEA
UNGARY   Cluj   Odessa   Azov   Mt.
RUMANIA   Crimea   El'brus   Tbilisi   Baku
Belgrade   Bucharest   River   BLACK SEA   A
SLAVIA   Danube   Balkan   BULGARIA   Bosporus   Tehran
Tiranë   Sofia   Istanbul   Ankara   IRAN
ea   Peninsula   T U R K E Y   Tigris R.
Salonika   AEGEAN   Dardanelles   Euphrates   River   Baghdad
Athens   SEA   SYRIA   IRA
Crete   CYPRUS   LEBANON   40°   Longitude East of Greenwich   50°
(Greek)
A   20°N   30°   S E A   13

The government of the United States has not recognized the incorporation of Estonia, Latvia and Lithuania into the Soviet Union, nor does it recognize as final the de facto western limit of Polish administration in Germany (the Oder-Neisse line).

Longitude West of Greenwich

Longitude East of Greenwich

A T L A N T I C   O C E A N

ICELAND

Reykjavik

Arctic Circle

N O R W E G I A N

Jan Mayen
(Nor.)

Vesterålen
Lofoten Is.
Senja

Vestfjorden

S E A

Faeroe Is.
(Den.)
Tórshavn

Shetland Is.

Rockall

Trondheimsfjorden

Namsos

Kristiansund

Ålesund

Trondheim

Sognefjord

Bergen

Hardangerfjord

Haugesund

Stavanger

Oslo

Drammen

Fredrikstad

Larvik

Arendal

Kristiansand

Lillehammer

Hamar

Ørsta

Sundsvall

Falun

Uppsala

Västerås

N O R W E G I A N

Lerwick

Orkney Is.
Kirkwall
Pentland Firth

Hebrides

SCOTLAND

Moray Firth
Inverness
Aberdeen
Dundee

Glasgow
Edinburgh

BRITISH

NO. IRELAND
Belfast

IRELAND
Donegal Bay
Dundalk
Galway
Limerick
(Luimneach)
Dublin
IRISH SEA
Waterford
Cork
(Corcaigh)
Cobh
C. Clear

Newcastle
upon Tyne
Carlisle

UNITED
ISLES

NORTH SEA

KINGDOM

Leeds
Manchester
Liverpool
Sheffield
Hull
The Wash

WALES
Birmingham
ENGLAND
Cardiff
LONDON
Bristol
Swansea
Southampton
Portsmouth
Plymouth
Land's End

DENMARK

Ålborg
Kattegat
Århus
Esbjerg
Odense
Copenhagen

Flensburg
Kiel

BALTIC

Helsingborg
Lund
Malmö

Bornholm

Göteborg
Borås
Jönköping

Vänern

Vättern

Öland

NORTH SEA

Helgoland

Frisian Is.
Helder
Amsterdam
The Hague
NETHER-
LANDS
Utrecht
Rotterdam
Antwerp
BELGIUM
Brussels

Stralsund
Rostock
Lübeck
Hamburg
Bremen
Elbe
Hannover

EAST
BERLIN

Stettin
(Szczecin)

Poznań
PO

English Channel
Channel Is.
(Br.)

Cherbourg
Le Havre
Calais
Boulogne
Dunkirk
Lille
Amiens
Rouen
Seine
Brest
Rennes
Angers
St-Nazaire
Nantes

F R A N C E

Versailles
PARIS
Orléans
Tours
Loire

La Rochelle
I. d'Oléron
Limoges
Vichy
Clermont-Ferrand

Bordeaux

Bay of Biscay

Essen
Dortmund
Düsseldorf
Cologne
Bonn
Liège
LUX.
Mainz
Wiesbaden
Frankfurt
Saarbrücken
Mannheim
Nuremberg
Karlsruhe
Stuttgart
Strasbourg
Freiburg
Mulhouse
Basel
Nancy
Dijon
Bern
Geneva
SWITZER-
LAND

Brunswick
Magdeburg
Halle
Leipzig
Dresden
GERMANY
Erfurt
Plauen
Karl-Marx-
Stadt
Plzeň
Prague
(Praha)

C Z E C H O S L O

Brno

Regensburg
Augsburg
Munich
Linz
Salzburg
Innsbruck
VIENNA
(Wien)

Danube

A U S T R I A

Graz

H U N

Bratislava
Győr

St-Étienne
Lyon
Grenoble
Valence
Nîmes
Montpellier
G. of Lions
Marseille
Toulon
Montauban
Toulouse

Montélimar

Mont Blanc
Turin
(Torino)
Milan
Brescia
Verona
Venice
(Venezia)
Padua
Bologna
Ferrara
Genoa
Parma
Modena
La Spezia
Florence
(Firenze)
I T A L Y

Trento
Bolzano
Trieste
Rijeka
(Fiume)
Ljubljana
Zagreb

Y U G O S L A V

Banja Luka
Drava
Zadar
(Zara)
Sarajevo
Split

A T L A N T I C

C. Finisterre
La Coruña
El Ferrol
Gijón
Oviedo
Vigo
Miño
Braga
Oporto
(Porto)
Coimbra
Douro

Santander
Bilbao
San Sebastián
Biarritz
Bayonne
Pyrenees
ANDORRA

León
Valladolid
Burgos
Saragossa
Ebro
Salamanca
(Duero)

SPAIN

MADRID
Toledo
Guadiana

Zaragoza

Tarragona
Barcelona

Balearic Is.
Minorca
Palma
Majorca
(Mallorca)
Ibiza

Corsica
(Corse)
Ajaccio
Elba

MONACO
Nice
Leghorn
(Livorno)
Siena
Perúgia
Ancona

SAN
MARINO

Tiber
ROME

A D R I A T I C

Pescara

PORTUGAL

Lisbon
(Lisboa)
Setúbal
Évora
(Tejo)
Tagus
(Tejo)

Sa. de Guadarrama

Sierra Morena
Córdoba
Guadalquivir
Seville
Jerez
Badajoz
Albacete
Granada
Sa. Nevada
Málaga
Almería
Cartagena
Murcia
Lorca
Alicante
Valencia

Sassari
Sardinia
(Sardegna)
Iglesias
Cagliari

VATICAN
CITY

Foggia
Naples
(Napoli)
Vesuvius
Bari

Taranto

G. of
Taranto

T Y R R H E N I A N

SEA

Catanzaro

I O N I A N

SEA

C. St. Vincent

G. of Cádiz
Cádiz
Str. of Gibraltar
GIBRALTAR
Ceuta
(Sp.)
Tangier

Kénitra
Rabat
Casablanca
Meknès
Fez

Marrakech

MOROCCO

Melilla
(Sp.)
Oran

Algiers
(Alger)

Skikda

Constantine

Biskra

A L G E R I A

Bizerte
Tunis

TUNISIA
Sousse

Pantelleria

M E D I T E R R A N E A N

Palermo
Messina
Reggio
Sicily
(Sicilia)
Etna
Catania
Syracuse

MALTA
Valletta

Annaba

C. Bon

14

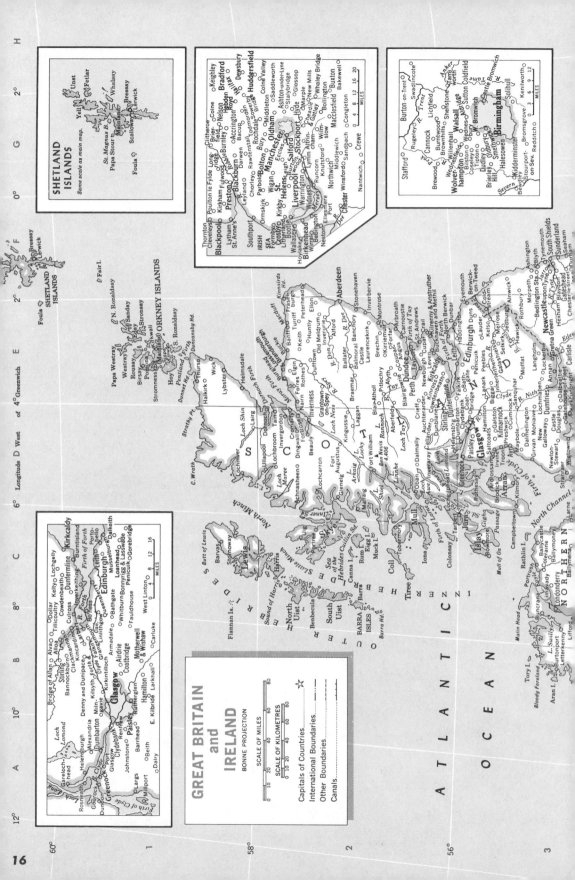

NORWAY, SWEDEN FINLAND and DENMARK

CONIC PROJECTION

SCALE OF MILES

SCALE OF KILOMETRES

Capitals of Countries
Administrative Centers
International Boundaries
Internal Boundaries
Canals

SUBDIVISIONS
Indicated by Numbers
Fylker in NORWAY
1 Akershus   G6
2 Vestfold   G7
3 Østfold   G7
4 Oslo   G7
5 Bergen   D6

Oslo is the administrative center for Akershus and Oslo Fylker; Bergen for Hordaland and Bergen Fylker.

Lan in SWEDEN
6 Göteborg och   G7
   Bohus
7 Västmanland   K7
8 Södermanland   K7
9 Östergötland   J7
10 Malmöhus   H9
11 Kristianstad   J8

Copyright by C. S. Hammond & Co., N.Y.

19

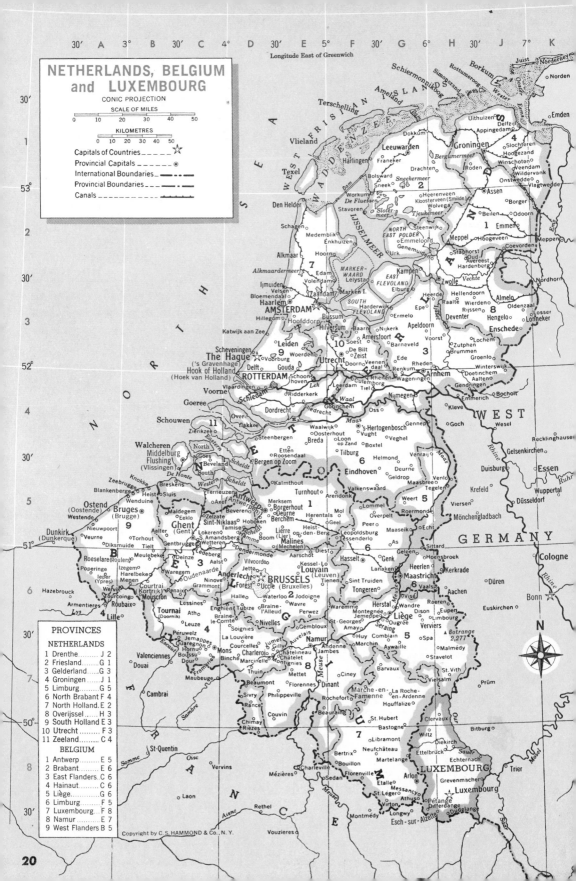

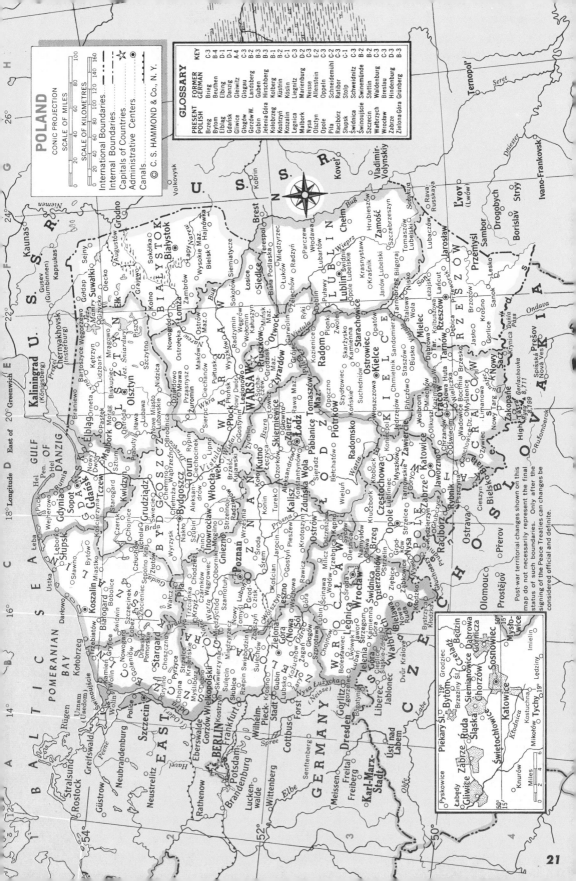

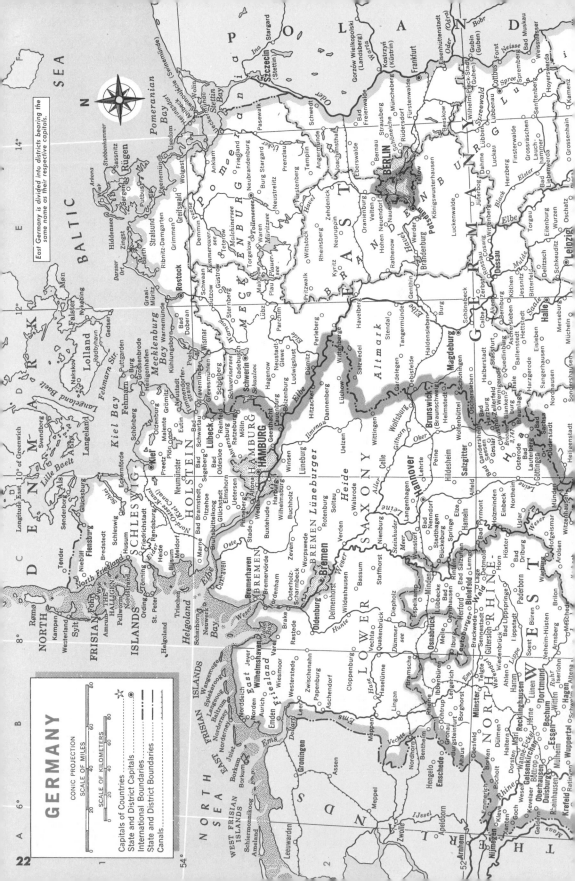

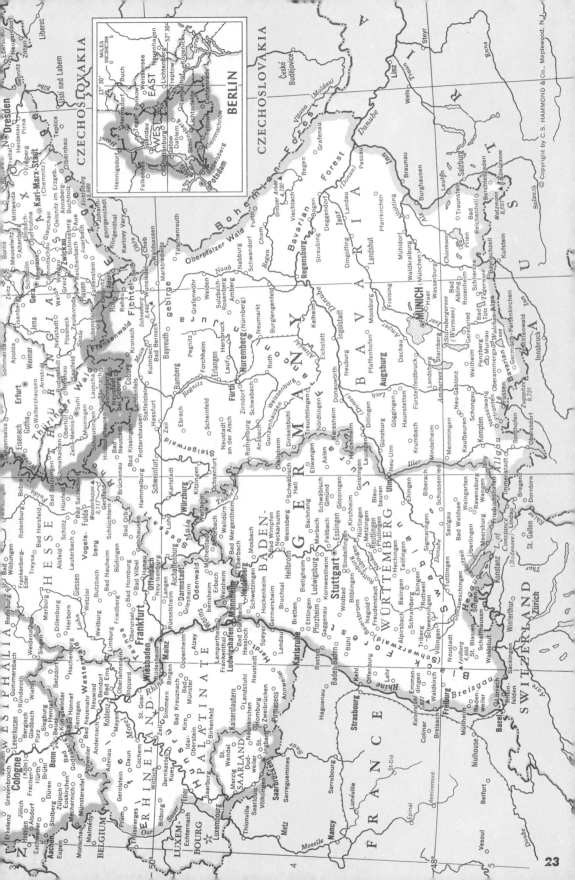

BERLIN

MILES

EAST

WEST

Potsdam

CZECHOSLOVAKIA

Dresden

Karl-Marx-Stadt
(Chemnitz)

Zwickau

Erfurt

T H U R I N G I A

H E S S E

Frankfurt

Wiesbaden

Mainz

R H I N E L A N D

Bonn

Cologne
(Köln)

Aachen

BELGIUM

LUXEM-
BOURG

Luxembourg

SAARLAND

Saarbrücken

R H E I N P F A L Z (P A L A T I N A T E)

W E S T P H A L I A

F R A N C E

Nancy

Metz

Strasbourg

Karlsruhe

Ludwigshafen

Mannheim

Heidelberg

Darmstadt

Offenbach

B A D E N -
W Ü R T T E M B E R G

Stuttgart

Ulm

B L A C K F O R E S T
(Schwarzwald)

Freiburg

Basel

SWITZERLAND

Zürich

L. of Constance
(Bodensee)

B A V A R I A

Nuremberg

Fürth

Regensburg

MUNICH
(München)

Augsburg

Bavarian Alps

Innsbruck

A U S T R I A

Salzburg

Linz

Danube

G E R M A N Y

Bohmen-
Forest

Fichtel-
gebirge

B o h e m i a n F o r e s t

23

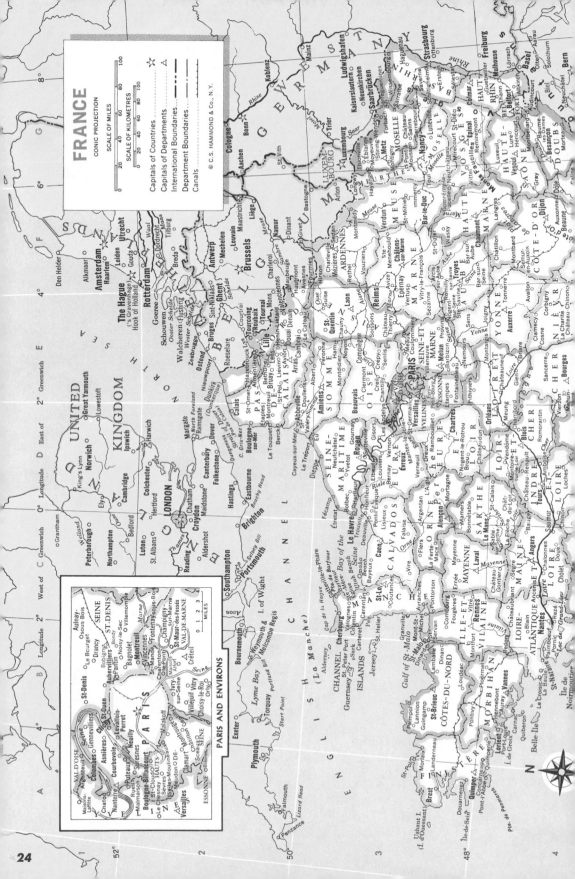

FRANCE

CONIC PROJECTION

SCALE OF MILES

SCALE OF KILOMETRES

Capitals of Countries .... ✪
Capitals of Departments .... △
International Boundaries ....
Department Boundaries ....
Canals ....

© C.S. HAMMOND & CO., N.Y.

PARIS AND ENVIRONS

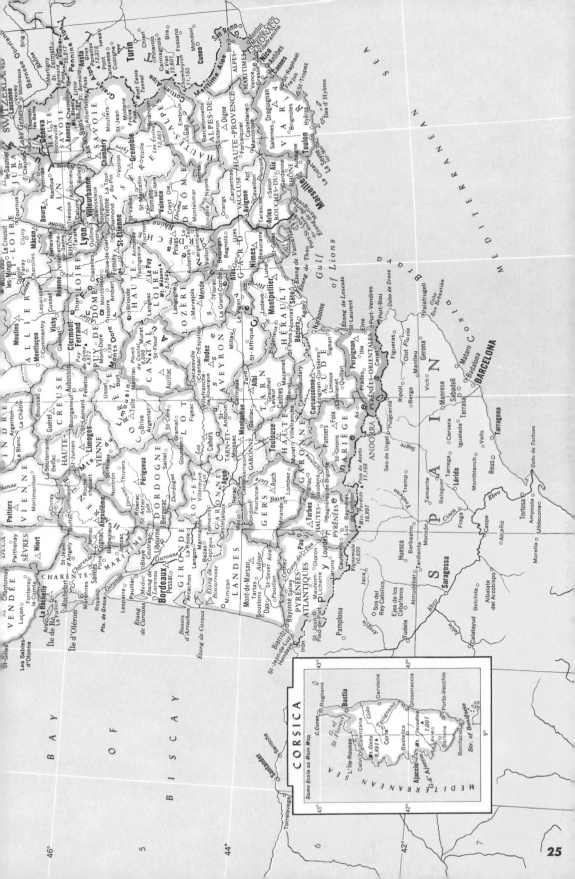

SWITZERLAND

Brig

Oberalppass

Martigny

Zermatt

15,217

Pennine Alps

St. Bernard

Little St. Bernard

12,601

Aosta

Gran Paradiso

13,323

Cuorgne

Canavese

Ivrea

Biella

Chieri

Bra

Fossano

Mondovi

TURIN

Cuneo

San Remo

Menton

Monaco

Ventimiglia

Monte Carlo

Villefranche

NICE

Antibes

Cannes

St-Raphael

Fréjus

St-Tropez

Îles d'Hyères

Hyères

TOULON

La Seyne

MARSEILLE

Aubagne

Aix

Gardanne

Salon

Arles

BOUCHES-DU-RHÔNE

Tarascon

St-Gilles

Beaucaire

Gard

NÎMES

Lunel

Étang de Vaccarès

Étang de Thau

Sète

Agde

MEDITERRANEAN SEA

Gulf of Lions

Cabo de Creus

Palafrugell

San Sebastian

Gerona

Mataro

BARCELONA

Badalona

Manresa

Sabadell

Tarrasa

Igualada

Tárrega

Cervera

Vich

Manlleu

Ripoll

Berga

SPAIN

Tarragona

Reus

Valls

Montblanch

Tortosa

Cabo de Tortosa

Amposta

Ulldecona

Caspe

Ebro

Fraga

Lérida

Balaguer

Tamarite

Barbastro

Huesca

Monzón

Cinca

Alcañiz

Beceite

Albalate del Arzobispo

Belchite

Calatayud

Morella

SARAGOSSA

Tudela

Almudébar

Tardienta

Sos del Rey Catolico

Ejea de los Caballeros

Tudela

Pamplona

Jaca

Canfranc

ANDORRA

Seo de Urgel

Puigcerda

Prades

Céret

PYRÉNÉES-ORIENTALES

Port-Vendres

Port-Bou

Figueras

Olot

Fluvia

Ter

Segre

AUDE

PERPIGNAN

Elne

Ille

Étang de Leucate

Quillan

Limoux

Carcassonne

Castelnaudary

Lézignan-Corbières

Sigean

Étang de Sigean

NARBONNE

Béziers

HÉRAULT

St-Pons

Pézenas

Lodève

MONTPELLIER

Bédarieux

Mazamet

Castres

TARN

ALBI

Graulhet

Gaillac

Lavaur

Carmaux

AVEYRON

Rodez

Espalion

Decazeville

Cransac

Villefranche-de-Rouergue

Millau

St-Affrique

LOZÈRE

Mende

Marvejols

Langogne

Florac

Le Vigan

Ganges

St-Girons

ARIÈGE

FOIX

Ax

Tarascon

Pamiers

Lavelanet

St-Gaudens

HAUTE-GARONNE

Muret

TOULOUSE

GERS

AUCH

Condom

Fleurance

Lombez

Mirande

HAUTES-PYRÉNÉES

TARBES

Bagnères-de-Bigorre

Luchon

Vignemale

10,820

Mt. Perdido

11,168

Pico de Aneto

11,055

Pico de Anie

8,217

Laruns

Oloron

PYRÉNÉES-ATLANTIQUES

PAU

Orthez

Lourdes

Argelès

Cauterets

St-Jean-Pied-de-Port

Mauléon

Bayonne

Biarritz

St-Jean-de-Luz

Hendaye

Irún

GERS

GARONNE

Gramont

Lectoure

Nérac

Agen

LOT-ET-GARONNE

Marmande

Villeneuve

Tonneins

Casteljaloux

Langon

Bazas

LANDES

MONT-DE-MARSAN

Tartas

Dax

St-Sever

Aire

Soustons

Mimizan

Étang de Biscarrosse

Étang de Cazaux

Bassin d'Arcachon

Arcachon

GIRONDE

La Teste

Pessac

BORDEAUX

Libourne

Bergerac

DORDOGNE

Périgueux

Sarlat

Riberac

St-Astier

Nontron

Thiviers

Brantôme

Terrasson

Gourdon

LOT

Cahors

Figeac

St-Céré

CANTAL

Aurillac

St-Flour

Murat

Mauriac

Plomb du Cantal

6,096

Bort

Ussel

Tulle

CORRÈZE

Brive

Argentat

Uzerche

HAUTE-VIENNE

LIMOGES

St-Léonard

St-Junien

Rochechouart

Bellac

La Souterraine

CREUSE

GUÉRET

Aubusson

Boussac

PUY-DE-DÔME

CLERMONT-FERRAND

Mont-Dore

Monts Dore

6,188

Puy de Sancy

Thiers

Ambert

Issoire

Brioude

HAUTE-LOIRE

Le Puy

Langeac

St-Étienne

LOIRE

Roanne

Montbrison

Feurs

Rive-de-Gier

St-Chamond

Firminy

ALLIER

MOULINS

Montluçon

Commentry

Gannat

VICHY

Lapalisse

St-Pourçain

Cusset

Yzeure

Mont Mézenc

5,764

RHÔNE

LYON

Villefranche

Givors

Vienne

ISÈRE

Voiron

GRENOBLE

Vizille

Bourgoin

La Tour-du-Pin

DRÔME

VALENCE

Romans

St-Vallier

Crest

Die

Montélimar

Donzère

Nyons

VAUCLUSE

Orange

Carpentras

AVIGNON

Cavaillon

Apt

Manosque

ALPES-DE-HAUTE-PROVENCE

Digne

Sisteron

Castellane

Forcalquier

BASSES-ALPES

Barcelonnette

HAUTES-ALPES

GAP

Embrun

Briançon

Les Écrins

13,461

ALPES-MARITIMES

Grasse

Vence

Draguignan

VAR

Brignoles

St-Maximin

Salernes

Aups

AIN

BOURG

Belley

Nantua

Oyonnax

Ambérieu

Trévoux

JURA

Lons-le-Saunier

St-Claude

Dole

SAÔNE-ET-LOIRE

MÂCON

Charolles

Digoin

Paray-le-Monial

Le Creusot

Montceau-les-Mines

Tournus

Chalon

Louhans

SAVOIE

CHAMBÉRY

St-Jean-de-Maurienne

Moûtiers

Modane

Mont Cenis Tunnel

Aiguille

Lanslebourg

HAUTE-SAVOIE

ANNECY

Aix-les-Bains

Thonon-les-Bains

Évian

Bonneville

Chamonix

Mont Blanc

15,781

Megève

St-Gervais

Albertville

GENEVA

Lake Geneva

Villeneuve

Montreux

Vevey

Ugine

Graian Alps

Cottian Alps

Maritime Alps

M. Viso

12,609

Mont Genèvre

Col de Larche

Maritime Alps

Monte Argentera

10,794

Chartreuse

Belledonne

Vercors

Col du Lautaret

Pelvoux

VIENNE

POITIERS

Châtellerault

Montmorillon

Civray

Confolens

CHARENTE

Angoulême

Cognac

Jarnac

Barbezieux

Ruffec

CHARENTE-MARITIME

La Rochelle

La Pallice

Rochefort

Saintes

St-Jean-d'Angély

Royan

Marennes

Île d'Oléron

Île de Ré

DEUX-SÈVRES

NIORT

Parthenay

Bressuire

Thouars

Melle

Chef-Boutonne

St-Maixent

VENDÉE

La Roche-sur-Yon

Fontenay-le-Comte

Luçon

Les Sables-d'Olonne

St-Gilles-Croix-de-Vie

Chantonnay

INDRE

Argenton

Le Blanc

La Châtre

Châteauroux

Le Dorat

Vienne

Sèvre

Gironde

Dordogne

Lot

Tarn

Aveyron

Garonne

Adour

Gave de Pau

Gave d'Oloron

Ariège

Aude

Hérault

Rhône

Durance

Isère

Saône

Allier

Loire

Creuse

Indre

Charente

BAY OF BISCAY

46°

5

44°

6

42°

7

43°

42°

3°

4°

5°

6°

7°

8°

9°

CORSICA

Same Scale as Main Map.

C. Corse

Rogliano

Bastia

Cervione

Ghisonaccia

Porto-Vecchio

Bonifacio

Str. of Bonifacio

Sartène

Mt. l'Incudine

7,007

Ghisoni

Corte

Vizzavona

Mt. d'Oro

7,845

Calvi

L'Île-Rousse

Calenzana

Mt. Cinto

8,891

G. of Ajaccio

AJACCIO

G. of St-Florent

Golo

Tavignano

MEDITERRANEAN SEA

9°

43°

42°

Torrelavega

Santander

25

SPAIN and PORTUGAL

CONIC PROJECTION

SCALE OF MILES
0   20   40   60   80   100

SCALE OF KILOMETRES
0   20   40   60   80   100

Capitals of Countries _____ ☆
Provincial Capitals _____ △
International Boundaries _____
Provincial Boundaries _____

© Copyright by C.S. HAMMOND & Co., Maplewood, N.J.

27

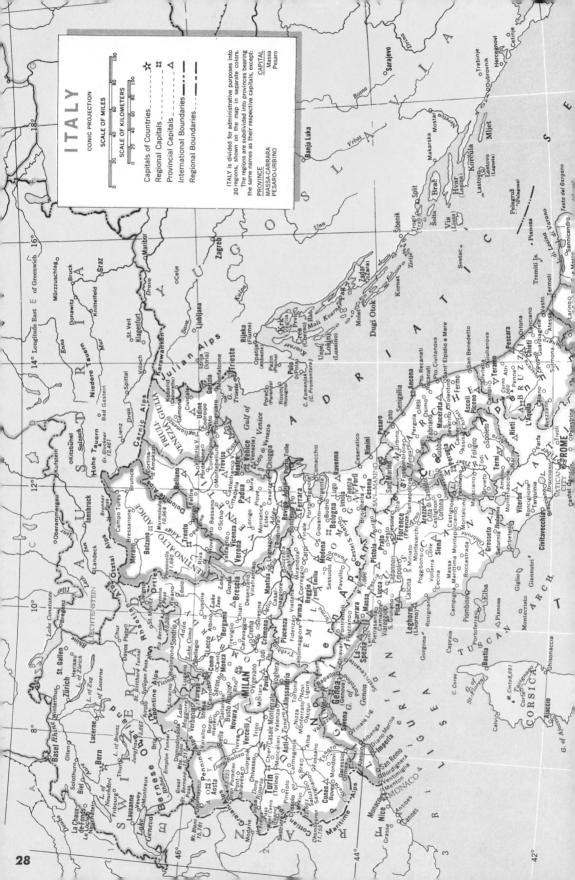

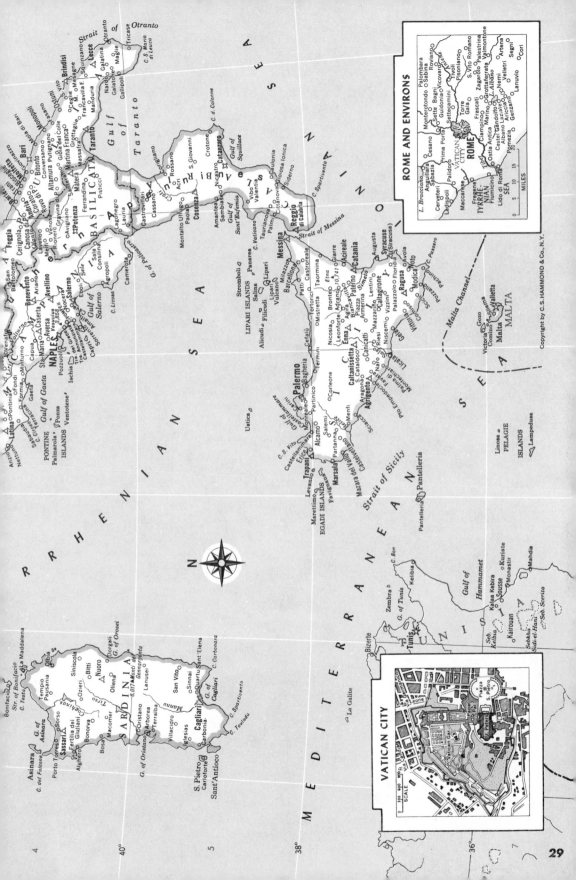

Strait of Otranto
Tricase S. Maria di Leuca
Lecce
Galatina Maglie
Brindisi
C. S. Maria di Leuca
Gallipoli Nardo Galatone
Mesagne
Francavilla F. Manduria
Martina Franca
Massafra Pulsano
Ginosa Castellaneta
Taranto
Foggia
Bari
Bitonto
Conversano
Monopoli
Mola di Bari
Canosa di P.
Altamura
Gravina di P.
Matera
Pisticci
Gulf of Taranto
Basilicata
Potenza
Ferrandina
Calabria
Metaponto
Policoro
Nova Siri
Rocca Imperiale
Trebisacce
Cassano
Corigliano
Rossano
S. Giovanni
Crotone
C. Colonne
Cosenza
Acri
Paola
Amantea
Gulf of Sant'Eufemia
Nicastro
Catanzaro
Gulf of Squillace
Sambiase
Soverato
Gioiosa Ionica
Stilo
Siderno
C. Spartivento
Palmi
Reggio di Calabria
Strait of Messina
Messina
Milazzo
Patti
Castroreale
Taormina
Giarre
Acireale
Catania
Augusta
Syracuse (Siracusa)
Floridia
Noto
Avola
Vizzini
C. Passero
Niscemi
Gela
Vittoria
Modica
Ragusa
Comiso
Scicli
Pozzallo
C. Scalambri
Licata
Malta Channel
Victoria Gozo
Comino
Valletta
Malta
MALTA

Lipari Islands
Stromboli
Panarea
Salina
Lipari
Vulcano
Filicudi
Alicudi

Palermo
Bagheria
Termini
Cefalù
Nicosia
Leonforte
Agira
Enna
Piazza Armerina
Caltagirone
Caltanissetta
Canicatti
Aragona
Agrigento
Porto Empedocle

Ustica

Gulf of Castellammare
Castellammare del Golfo
C.S. Vito
Alcamo
Monreale
Partinico
Corleone
Salemi
Menfi
Sciacca
Trapani
Erice
Marsala
Partanna
Castelvetrano
Mazara del Vallo
Levanzo
Marettimo
Favignana
Egadi Islands
Pantelleria

Strait of Sicily
Pantelleria

Linosa
Lampedusa
PELAGIE ISLANDS

TYRRHENIAN SEA

Copyright by C.S. HAMMOND & Co., N.Y.

Vesuvius
Naples
Salerno
Gulf of Salerno
Capri
Sorrento
Amalfi
Avellino
Benevento
Caserta
Capua
Aversa
Pozzuoli
Ischia

Pontine Islands
Ponza
Ventotene
Gaeta
Gulf of Gaeta
Formia
Latina
Anzio
Nettuno

MEDITERRANEAN SEA

N

RHENIAN SEA

SARDINIA
Sassari
Asinara
G. of Asinara
Alghero
Bosa
Macomer
Oristano
G. of Oristano
Iglesias
Carbonia
Cagliari
G. of Cagliari
S. Pietro
Sant'Antioco
Carloforte
Nuoro
Olbia
Str. of Bonifacio
La Maddalena
Tempio Pausania
Ozieri
Bitti
Siniscola
Orosei
G. of Orosei
Dorgali
Monti del Gennargentu
6,017
Lanusei
Tortolì
C. Carbonara
Quartu Sant'Elena

Gulf of Hammamet
C. Bon
Kelibia
Zembra
G. of Tunis
Bizerte
Tunis
TUNISIA
Kalaa Kebira
Sousse
Monastir
Kuriate
Mahdia
Kairouan
La Galite

ROME AND ENVIRONS

Palombara
Monterotondo
Sabina
Montecelio
S. Vito Romano
Cesano
Sette Bagni
Vicovaro
Tivoli
Pisoniano
Prima Porta
Guidonia
Settebagni
S. Vito Romano
Palestrina
Zagarolo
Grottaferrata
Valmontone
Frascati
Artena
Segni
Cori
ROME
VATICAN CITY
Ciampino
Marino
Castel Gandolfo
Albano
Ariccia
Velletri
Lanuvio
Nemi
Genzano
Ostia Antica
Acilia
NIAN
FREGENE
Fiumicino
Lido di Roma
SEA
Maccarese
L. Bracciano
Anguillara
Cerveteri
Ladispoli
TYRRHE-
MILES
0   5   10   15   20

VATICAN CITY

Piazza S. Pietro
S. Pietro
Vaticano

SCALE
300 600

40°
38°
36°
4
5
6
7
29

SWITZERLAND and LIECHTENSTEIN

CONIC PROJECTION

SCALE OF MILES

0   5   10   20   30

SCALE OF KILOMETRES

0   5   10   20   30   40   50

Capitals of Countries .... ☆

Capitals of Cantons .... ◉

International Boundaries .... — · · — · ·

Canals ....

31

33

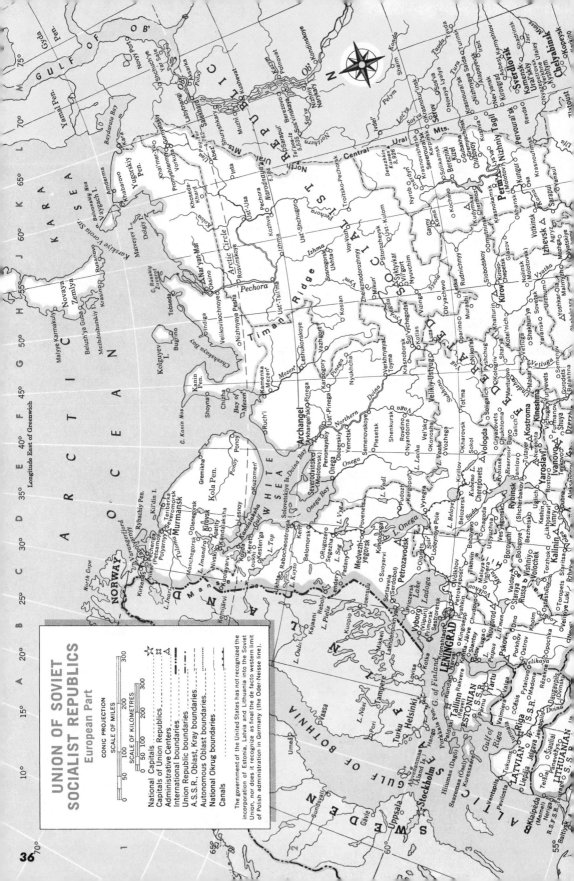

UNION OF SOVIET SOCIALIST REPUBLICS

European Part

CONIC PROJECTION

SCALE OF MILES

0   50   100   200   300

SCALE OF KILOMETRES

0 50 100   200   300

National Capitals..................☆ ⊠
Capitals of Union Republics..........⊛ ⊡
Administrative Centers..............△ ▲
International boundaries...........—·—·—
Union Republic boundaries..........—·—·—
A.S.S.R., Oblast, Kray boundaries....—··—··
Autonomous Oblast boundaries........—···—···
National Okrug boundaries...........—····—····
Canals.......................................

The government of the United States has not recognized the
incorporation of Estonia, Latvia and Lithuania into the Soviet
Union, nor does it recognize as final the de facto western limit
of Polish administration in Germany (the Oder-Neisse line).

Administrative Divisions bear same names as their respective Capitals or Centers, except:

Division	Capital/Center	Grid
Abkhaz A.S.S.R.	Sukhumi	F6
Adygey Aut. Oblast	Maykop	F6
Adzhar A.S.S.R.	Batumi	F6
Bashkir A.S.S.R.	Ufa	J4
Chechen-Ingush A.S.S.R.	Grozny	G6
Chuvash A.S.S.R.	Cheboksary	G3
Crimean Oblast	Simferopol'	D6
Dagestan A.S.S.R.	Makhachkala	G6
Kabardin-Balkar A.S.S.R.	Nal'chik	F6
Kalmuck A.S.S.R.	Elista	F5
Karachay-Cherkess Aut. Obl.	Cherkessk	F6
Karelian A.S.S.R.	Petrozavodsk	D2
Komi A.S.S.R.	Syktyvkar	H2
Komi-Permyak Nat'l Okrug	Kudymkar	H3
Mari A.S.S.R.	Yoshkar-Ola	G3
Mordvinian A.S.S.R.	Saransk	G4
Nagorno-Karabakh Aut. Obl.	Stepanakert	G7
Nenets Nat'l Okrug	Nar'yan-Mar	H1
North Ossetian A.S.S.R.	Ordzhonikidze	F6
South Ossetian Aut. Obl.	Tskhinvali	F6
Tatar A.S.S.R.	Kazan'	G3
Trans-Carpathian Oblast	Uzhgorod	B5
Udmurt A.S.S.R.	Izhevsk	H3
Volyn Oblast	Lutsk	C4

UNION OF SOVIET SOCIALIST REPUBLICS

CONIC PROJECTION

SCALE OF MILES

0 100 200 300 400 500 600

SCALE OF KILOMETRES

0 100 200 300 400 500 600

Capitals	Boundaries
☆ National	National
☆ Union Republic	Union Republic
◎ A.S.S.R.	A.S.S.R.
◎ Autonomous Oblast	Autonomous Oblast
◦ National Okrug	National Okrug

38

ARCTIC OCEAN

PACIFIC OCEAN

Aleutian Islands

BERING SEA

UNITED STATES
Alaska

Bering Strait

Anadyr'

Kamchatka Peninsula

SEA OF OKHOTSK

Kuril Islands
(to U.S.S.R.)

Sakhalin I.
(to U.S.S.R.)

Hokkaido
(to U.S.S.R.)

Tokyo
Osaka
Shikoku
Kyushu

Honshu

JAPAN

Khabarovsk

Vladivostok

SOUTH KOREA
Seoul

Pyongyang
NORTH KOREA

Dairen
Mukden
Harbin

Manchuria

Amur River

Chita

Ulan Bator

MONGOLIA

Gobi Desert

Peking
Tientsin

CHINA

Nanking
Shanghai

EAST CHINA SEA

YELLOW SEA

KOREA SEA

Tsingtao

Wuhan
Lanchow
Sian

Huang Ho (Yellow River)

Ryukyu Islands

Verkhoyansk

Yakutsk

Siberia

Lena River

Lena River

Irkutsk

Lake Baykal

ALTAI MOUNTAINS

TIEN SHAN

Sinkiang

KUNLUN MOUNTAINS

Urumchi

Kashgar

New Siberian Is.
(to U.S.S.R.)

Severnaya Zemlya
(U.S.S.R.)

North Pole

140° 160° 180° 160° 140°
120° 120°
100° 100°
80° 80°
60° 60°
40° 40°
20° 20°
0°

80°

Franz Josef Land
(to U.S.S.R.)

Svalbard
(Norwegian)

Novaya Zemlya
(to U.S.S.R.)

KARA SEA

GREENLAND
(Danish)

Igarka

Yenisey River

Novosibirsk

Ob' River

Irtysh River

Omsk

Sverdlovsk

URAL MOUNTAINS

SIBERIA

UNION OF SOVIET SOCIALIST REPUBLICS (RUSSIA)

Karaganda

Lake Balkhash

Alma-Ata

Syr-Dar'ya R.

Tashkent

Amu-Dar'ya

Aral Sea

Ashkhabad

KASHMIR
Islamabad

Kabul

AFGHANISTAN

Lake Balkhash

Arctic Circle

NORWAY

SWEDEN

FINLAND

Moscow

Volga River

Ural River

Ural R.

CASPIAN SEA

IRAN

Tehran

Tabriz

ATLANTIC OCEAN

ICELAND

IRELAND

GREAT BRITAIN

NORTH SEA

BALTIC SEA

DEN.

NETH.

BEL.

FRANCE

EAST GER.
WEST GER.

POLAND

CZECHO.

AUST.
SWITZ.

HUNG.

YUGOSLAVIA

ITALY

ALB.

RUMANIA

BULG.

GREECE

EUROPE

BLACK SEA

TURKEY
Asia Minor

Ankara

MEDITERRANEAN SEA

Crete (Greek)

CYPRUS

LEB.

SYRIA

ISRAEL

Jerusalem

Tigris R.

R. Euphrates R.

IRAQ
Baghdad

Basra

KUWAIT

SAUDI ARABIA

JORDAN

EGYPT

Suez Canal

Nile River

RED SEA

P

PHILIPPINES

Luzon Quezon City
Manila

Mindanao

Molucca Is.
CELEBES SEA
Celebes Is.
Flores
Timor

BANDA
SEA

HONG KONG (British)
Canton
Hainan
Kunming

SOUTH CHINA SEA

NORTH VIET-NAM
Hanoi
LAOS
THAILAND
Bangkok
Gulf of Siam
CAMBODIA
Saigon
SOUTH VIET-NAM

BRUNEI (British)
Sabah
Sarawak
MALAYSIA
Borneo

I N D O N E S I A

JAVA SEA
Bali
Java
Sumbawa
Sumba

AUSTRALIA

Mekong R.
BURMA
Salween
Irrawaddy River
Rangoon

Malaya Lumpur
Kuala Lumpur
MALAYSIA
SINGAPORE

Medan
Sumatra
Djakarta
Java

ANDAMAN SEA
Andaman Is. (Indian)

Nicobar Is. (Indian)

BAY OF BENGAL

Calcutta
Ganges
Mt. Everest
NEPAL
Kathmandu
BHUTAN
BANG.

Ahmadabad
Hyderabad
DECCAN PLATEAU
Madras

New Delhi
INDIA

SRI LANKA (CEYLON)
Colombo
Dondra Head
Cape Comorin

Equator

MALDIVES

Bombay
Karachi
Tropic of Cancer

I N D I A N   O C E A N

Laccadive Is. (Indian)

ARABIAN SEA

BRITISH INDIAN OCEAN TERR.

Tropic of Capricorn

Seychelles (British)

MAURITIUS

Réunion (French)

Madagascar

MALAGASY REP.

ARAB EMIR.
OMAN
Rub' al Khali Desert
Socotra (P.D.R. Yemen)
Gulf of Aden
YEMEN ARAB REP.
Sana
PEOP. DEM. REP. YEMEN
Aden
(Fr.)
ARABIA

SOMALIA
ETHIOPIA
A F R I C A

Indus
PAK

20°
30°
40°

0°
10°
20°
30°
40°

0°
10°

Map of
ASIA

SCALE OF MILES
0 200 400 600 800 1000

Capitals of Countries
Cities
Boundaries of Countries
Other Boundaries
Mountain Peaks
Canals

Water
Lowlands
Depression
Highlands
Mountains

Longitude 50° 60° 70° 80° 90° Greenwich 100° 110° 120° East of
Latitude

40° 30° 20° 10° 0° Tropic of Capricorn

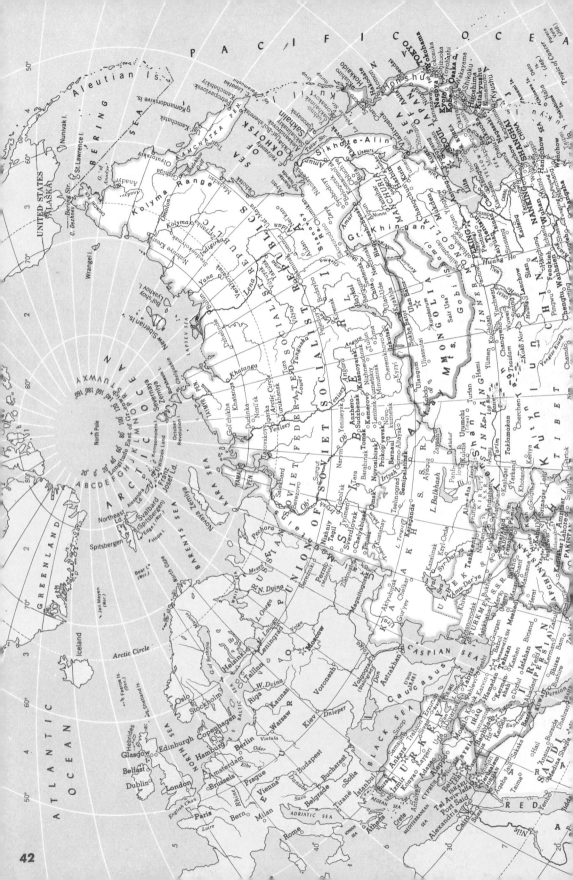

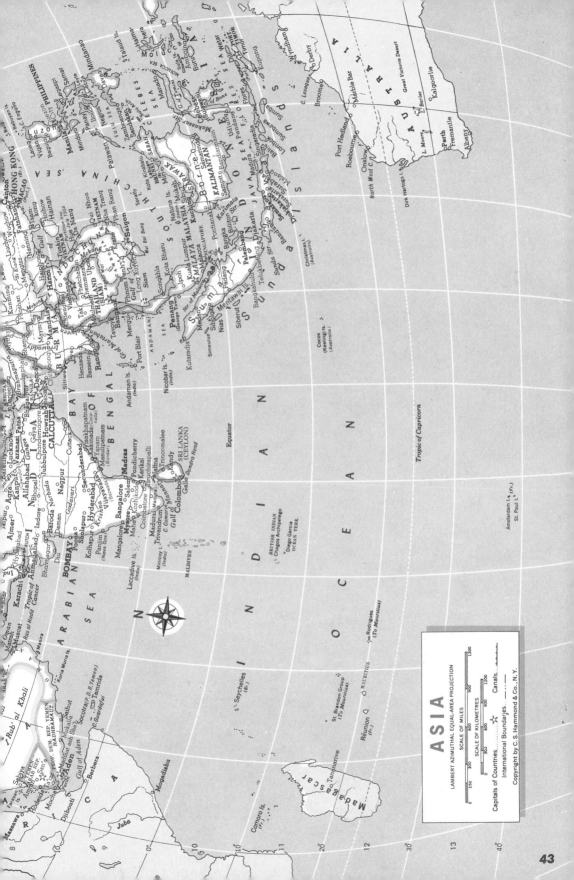

ASIA
LAMBERT AZIMUTHAL EQUAL-AREA PROJECTION

SCALE OF MILES

0   150   300   600   900   1200

SCALE OF KILOMETRES

0   150   300   600   900   1200

Capitals of Countries............ ✪ Canals........

International Boundaries............

43

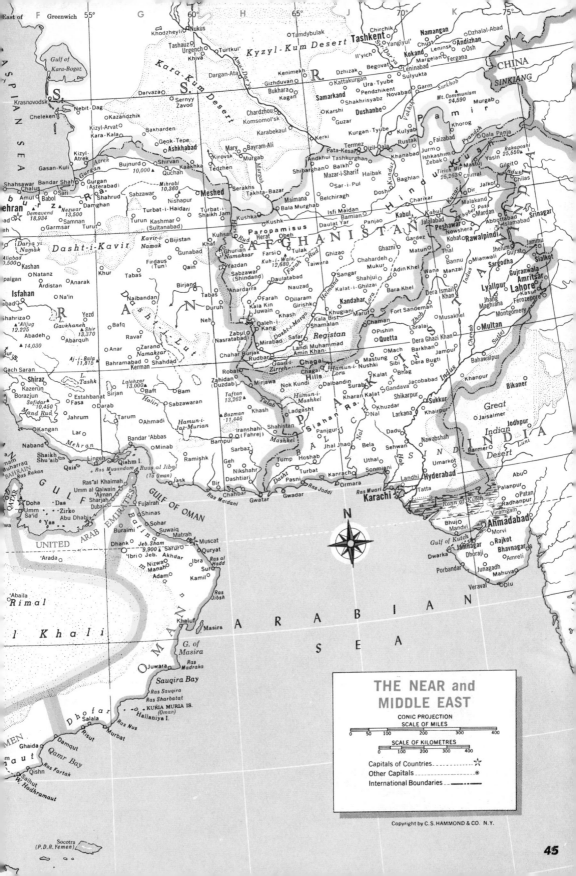

THE NEAR and MIDDLE EAST

CONIC PROJECTION
SCALE OF MILES

0 50 100 200 300 400

SCALE OF KILOMETRES

0 100 200 300 400

Capitals of Countries............☆
Other Capitals............◉
International Boundaries.........

Copyright by C.S. HAMMOND & CO. N.Y.

45

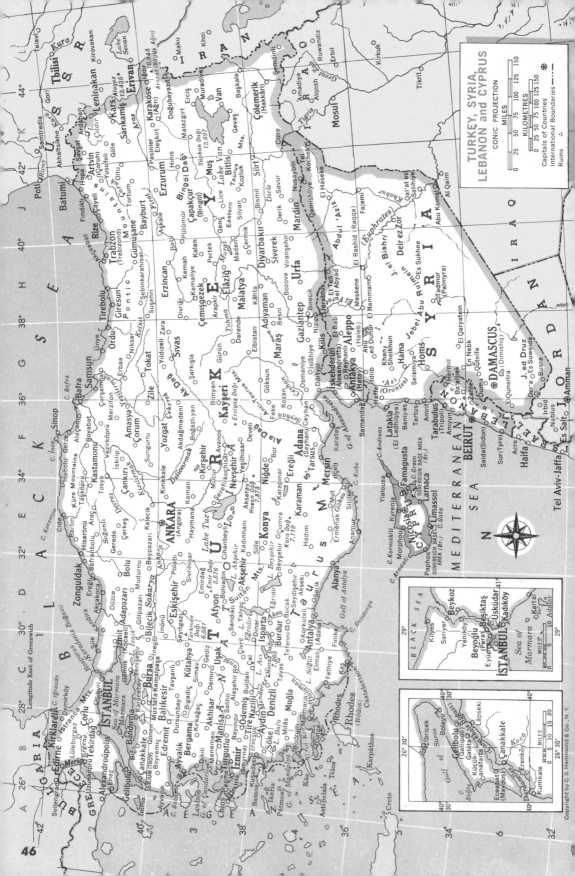

TURKEY, SYRIA, LEBANON and CYPRUS

CONIC PROJECTION

KILOMETRES
0   25   50   75   100 125 150

MILES
0   25   50   75   100 125 150

⊕ Capitals of Countries
International Boundaries ....
Ruins ....

BLACK SEA

MEDITERRANEAN SEA

SEA OF MARMARA

ISTANBUL

BLACK SEA

Sea of Marmara

MILES
0   5   10

İSTANBUL

MILES
0   5   10   15   20

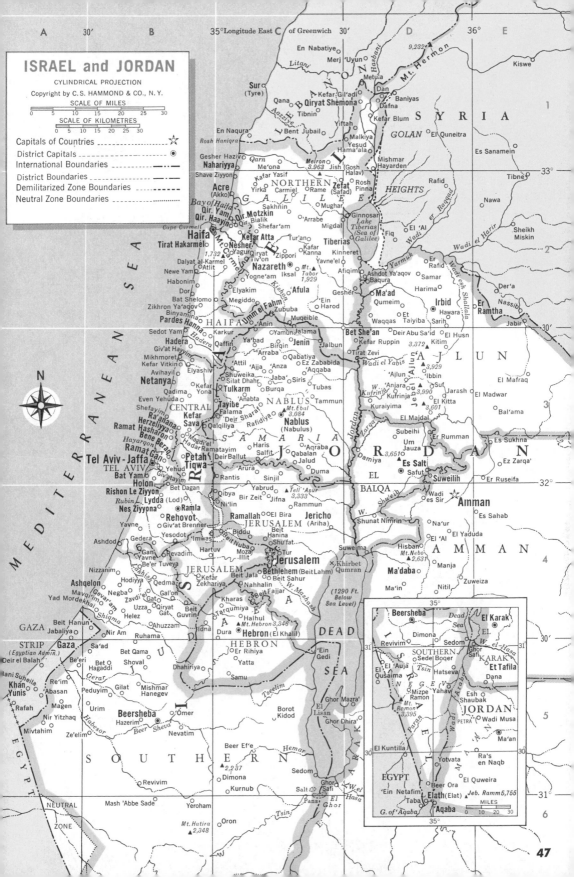

35° Longitude East   of Greenwich   30'   36°

En Nabatiye
Merj 'Uyun
Metula   Mt. Hermon 9,232
Dan   Kiswe
Qiryat Shemona   Baniyas
Sur   Kefar Gil'adi   Dafna
(Tyre)   Qana   Kefar Blum
Tibnin   Malkiya   El Quneitra   Es Sanamein
En Naqura   Bent Jubail Hama'ala   GOLAN
Rosh Haniqra Yiftah   Yesud Hama'ala
Naharriya   Qarn   Me'ona Meiron Jish (Gosh HEIGHTS
Shave Ziyyon   Kafar Yasif   3,963   Halav)
Acre   Yirka Carmiel Rame Zefat (Safad) Rosh Pinna
(Akko) Sakhnin   Mughar   Rafid
Bay of Haifa Shefar'am   Arrabe Migdal   Ginnosar
Qir. Yam   Qir. Motzkin Bialik   Lake   El 'Al
Qir. Haayin   Kefar Atta Tur'an Kafar   Tiberias   Fiq
Haifa   Nesher Zippori Kanna (Sea of
Tirat Hakarmel Yagur Qiryat Iksal Yavne'el Galilee)
1,732 Tiv'on   Mt. Kinneret   Afiqim   Samar
Dalyat al-Karmel Nazareth Tabor Ein Ashdot Ya'aqov
Newe Yam Atlit Yogne'am 1,929 Harod Baqura
Habonim Elyakim Afula Gesher   Ma'ad
Dor   Megiddo   Qumeim   Irbid
Bat Shelomo   Ein Harod   Et   Er
Zikhron Ya'aqov Zububa Muqeible Waqqas Taiyiba Ramtha
Binyamina   Anin Jenin Jalbun   Sarih   Er Nassib
Pardes Hanna Karkur   Ya'bad Kefar Ruppin Jabir
Hadera   Qaffin Arraba Ez Zababida Tirat Zevi 3,372 Kitim
Giv'at Hayyim 'Attil 'Ajja 'Anza Aqqaba Wadi el Yabis 3,929
Mikhmoret Kefar Vitkin Shuweika Jaba' Siris   'Ajlun Ibbin El Mafraq
Avihayil Elyashiv Silat Dhahr Burqa Tubas   Kufrinja 3,990
Netanya Kefar   Anabta Tammun   'Anjara   Suf Jarash El Madwar
Qadima Yona   Tulkarm   W. 3,601 El Kitta
Even Yehuda Taiybe Falama Mt. Ebal Kuraiyima Bal'ama
Shefayim CENTRAL Deir Sharaf 3,084 El Majdal
Ra'anana Kefar Qalqiliya Nablus
Herzliyya Sava   Rafidiya (Nablus)   Subeihi
Ramat Hasharon Magdi'el Aqraba Um Er Rumman Es Sukhna
Bene Beraq Hadar Ramatayim Haris Jauza 3,650 Ez Zarqa'
Ramat Hayarqon Deir Ballut Salfit   Damiya
Gan   Petah   Qabalan   Es Salt Er Ruseifa
Tel Aviv-Jaffa Tiqwa Arura Jalud Safut
TEL AVIV Yehud Rantis Sinjil Duma Suweilih
Bat Yam Giv'ataym Bet Dagan Yabrud EL Amman
Holon   Qibya Bir Zeit Jifna Tell 'Asur BALQA Es Sahab
Rishon Le Ziyyon Ni'lin 3,333 Wadi Na'ur
Nes Ziyyona Rubin Lydda (Lod) Rammun es Sir El Yaduda
Yavne Ramla Ramallah El Bira Jericho El 'Al
Rehovot Giv'at Brenner Biddu (Ariha) Shunat Nimrin
Giv'at Brenner Yesodot Imwas Beit Suweima Hisban Ma'daba
Ashdod Gedera Hartuv Hanina Mt. Nebo Manja
Nizzanim Revadim Moza Shu'fat 2,631 Nitil
Hodiyya Gan Et Tur X Khirbet Ma'in Zuweiza
Ashqelon Yavne JERUSALEM Qumran
Gevar'am Negba Jerusalem Ma'in
Yad Mordekhai Zavdi'el Gal'on Bethlehem (Beit Lahm)
Mavqi'im Qedma Kefar (1290 Ft.
Beit Hanun Uzza Gat Zekhariya Below
GAZA Jabaliya Qiryat Beit Nahhalin Sea Level) 'Ein Gedi
Gaza Na'im Gat Kharas Beit Fajjar
Bani Suheila Be'eri Ruhama Tarqumiya DEAD
Khan Sa'ad Bet Qama Halhul Ghor Mazra'
Yunis Re'im Bet Hagaddi Dura Hebron (El Khalil) El Lisan
Rafah Abasan Shoval Dhahiriya Er Rihiya SEA
Magen Gilat Mishmar Yatta Borot
Nir Yitzhaq Peduyim Hanegev Samu Kidod
Mivtahim Urim Beersheba Ghor Dhira'
Beersheba Hazerim 'Omer
Ze'elim Nevatim Ghor
Habesor Beer Sheva Safi
El Ghor

SYRIA

S Y R I A

Tibne
Nawa
Der'a

A J L U N

J O R D A N

A M M A N

D E A D   S E A

GAZA
STRIP
(Egyptian Admin.)
Deir el Balah

EGYPT

NEUTRAL
ZONE

SOUTHERN

2,237
Revivim   Dimona
Mash 'Abbe Sade Kurnub
Yeroham Sedom
Oron Mt. Hatira El Ghor
2,348   W. el Hasa
Tsin

(inset map, lower right)

35°
Beersheba   Dead   El Karak
Sea   EL
Revivim Dimona Sedom
Ghor
SOUTHERN Safi
El 'Auja Sede Boqer Hatseva KARAK
El Qusaima NEGEV Et Tafila
Tsin Dana
Yahav Esh
Mizpe Shaubak
Mt. Ramon Ramon
3,395 JORDAN
PETRA Wadi Musa
Paran Ma'an
El Kuntilla Ra's
Beer Ora en Naqb
EGYPT El Quweira
'Ein Netafim Elath (Elat) Jeb. Ramm 5,755
Taba Ma'an
Aqaba
G. of 'Aqaba MILES
0 10 20 30
35°

47

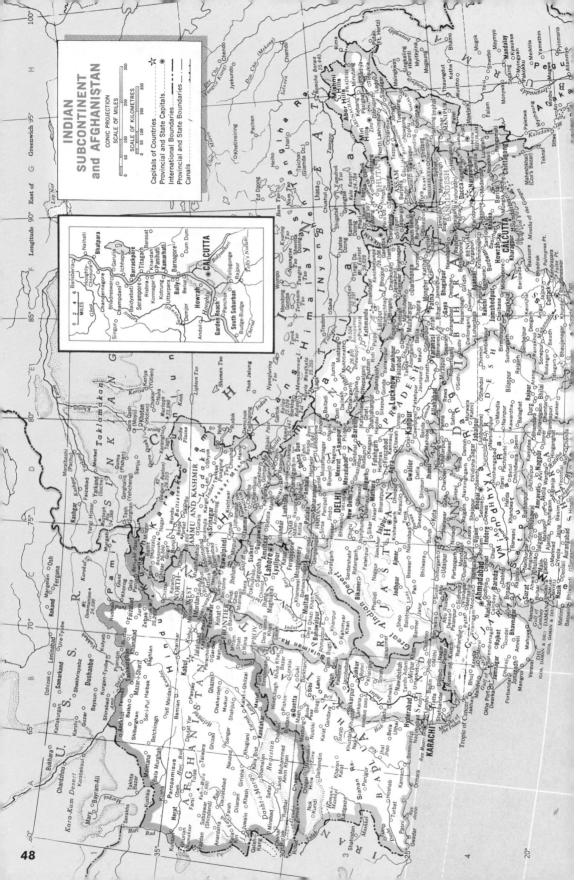

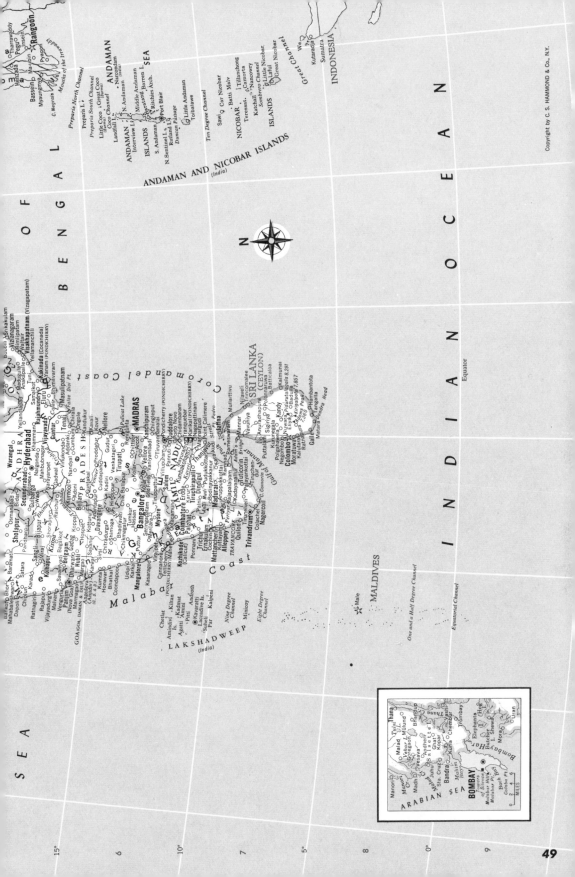

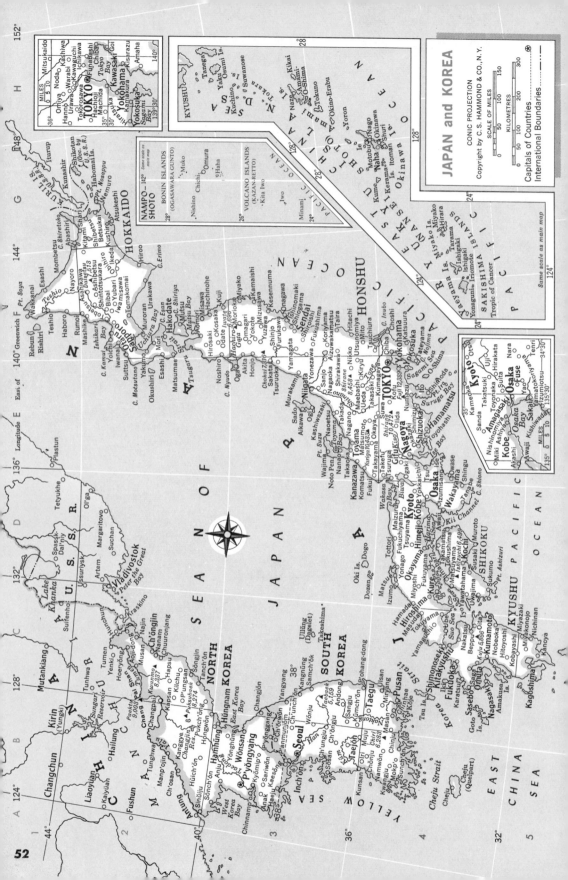

JAPAN and KOREA

CONIC PROJECTION

Copyright by C. S. HAMMOND & CO., N.Y.

SCALE OF MILES

MILES 0 50 100 150

KILOMETRES 0 50 100 200 300

Capitals of Countries ⊛
International Boundaries

TOKYO

MILES 0 5 10

KANSEI SHOTO

NAMPO SHOTO

BONIN ISLANDS (OGASAWARA GUNTO)

VOLCANO ISLANDS (KAZAN-RETTO)

Same scale as main map

Tropic of Cancer

KYOTO — OSAKA

MILES 0 5 10

HOKKAIDO

HONSHU

KYUSHU

SHIKOKU

PACIFIC OCEAN

SEA OF JAPAN

YELLOW SEA

EAST CHINA SEA

U. S. S. R.

M A N C H U R I A

NORTH KOREA

SOUTH KOREA

Seoul

Pyongyang

Tokyo

52

BURMA, THAILAND,
INDOCHINA and MALAYA

CONIC PROJECTION

SCALE OF MILES
0 50 100   200   300

SCALE OF KILOMETRES
0 50 100   200   300

Capitals of Countries .... ⊛
Capitals of States .... ⊙
International Boundaries ....

© C. S. HAMMOND & Co., Maplewood, N.J.

53

95°   100°   D   105°   E   110°   115°

BANGLA-   Mansshkhali Pakokku   CHINA   Kongmoon   HONG KONG
DESH   MACAO (Port.)
Sittwe   Luichow Pen.
BAY   Hoihow
                                    Hanoi   Haiphong
                                    Nam Dinh
                         NORTH
                    Thanh Hoa   VIETNAM   Hainan
OF   Vinh
                                        Luichow Pen.
              RANGOON
BENGAL   Bassein   Moulmein
Pegu
         Mouths of the   Hue   Da Nang
         Irrawaddy   PARACEL IS.
                                          (China)   AMPHITRITE
ANDAMAN   Tavoy   GROUP
North Andaman   Lincoln I.
Middle Andaman
ISLANDS (India) Mergui   BANGKOK   SOUTH
South Andaman   Qui Nhon
                                    VIETNAM
ANDAMAN   Mergui   Nha Trang
Little Andaman
                         Phnom
Ten Degree Channel   Penh   SAIGON
Car Nicobar   Chau Phu
SEA   Isthmus of Kra   SOUTH
NICOBAR   CHINA
Katchall Camorta
Sombrero Chan.
Little Nicobar   Phuket   MALAYSIA   SEA
Great Nicobar
ISLANDS   Nakhon Si Thammarat
(India)
                         Penang   Spratly I.
                         MALAYA   Natuna Islands
                         Kuala Lumpur   BRUNEI
                         Medan   SARAWAK
                         Malacca   Kuching   KALIMANTAN
                         SINGAPORE
Simeulue   RIAU ARCH.   Pontianak
BANJAK IS.   LINGGA
Nias   Padang
                         Palembang   Bandjarmasin
Equator   Martapura
                         Djambi
                         Djakarta (Batavia)
INDONESIA
                         Bandung   Semarang Surabaja
                         Jogjakarta Surakarta   Bali
5°   SCHOUTEN IS.
         TERR. OF NEW GUINEA
         (Australian Trusteeship)   JAVA SEA
                         P A P U A
         New Britain
         SOLOMON
         SEA
         TROBRIAND
         IS.
10°   Port Moresby   10°
         CORAL
         SEA
EASTERN NEW GUINEA
         MILES
         0 50 100   200
145°   150°   INDIAN OCEAN

54

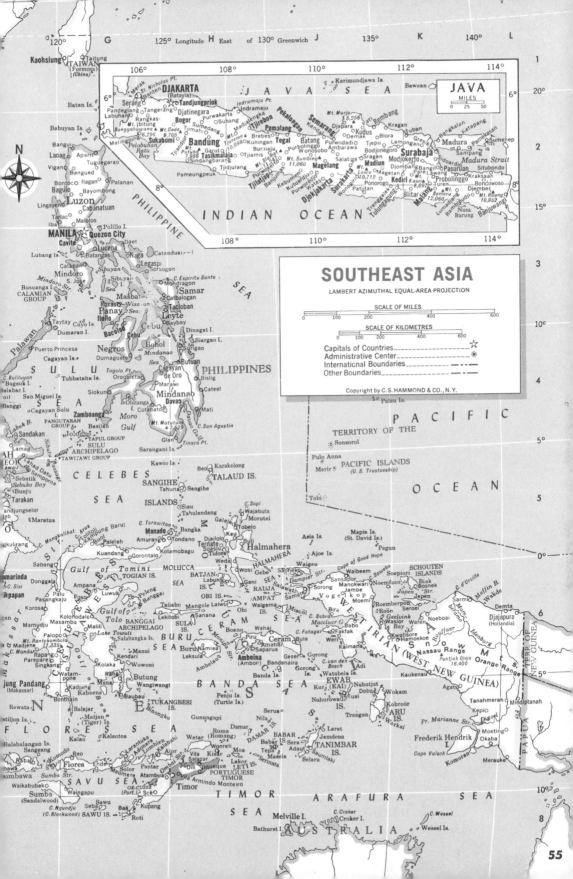

PACIFIC OCEAN

LAMBERT AZIMUTHAL EQUAL-AREA PROJECTION

NAUTICAL MILES

STATUTE MILES

KILOMETERS

Capitals of Countries
Other Capitals

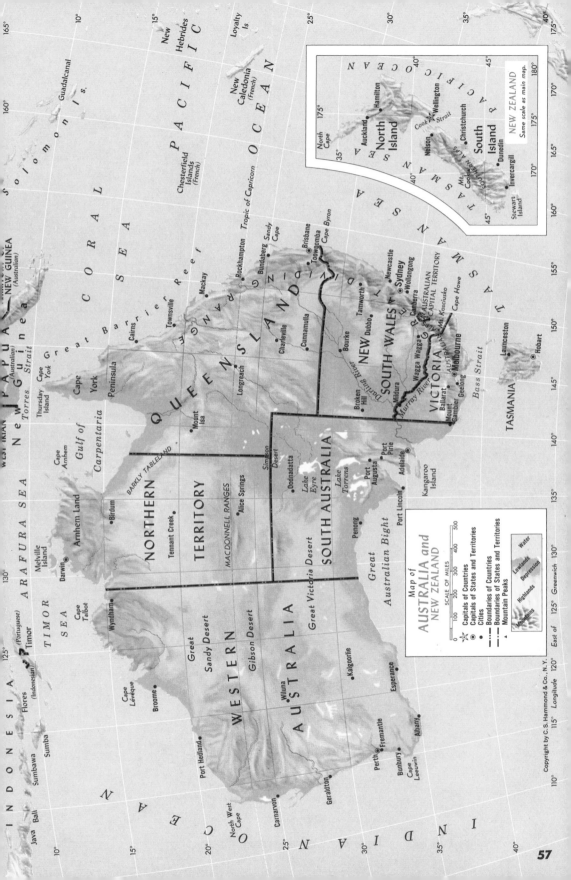

PACIFIC OCEAN

Guadalcanal
Solomon Is.
New Hebrides
Loyalty Is.
New Caledonia (French)

New Guinea (Australian)
PAPUA NEW GUINEA (Australian)

Chesterfield Islands (French)

CORAL SEA

Tropic of Capricorn

NEW ZEALAND
Same scale as main map.

PACIFIC OCEAN

North Cape
Auckland
Hamilton
North Island
Wellington
Cook Strait
Nelson
Christchurch
South Island
Southern Alps
Mt. Cook
Dunedin
Invercargill
Stewart Island

TASMAN SEA

WEST IRIAN
New Guinea
TIMOR (Portuguese)
Timor (Indonesian)
INDONESIA
Flores
Sumba
Sumbawa
Bali
Java

ARAFURA SEA
TIMOR SEA

Torres Strait
Thursday Island
Cape York
Cape York Peninsula

Great Barrier Reef

Cairns
Townsville
Mackay
Rockhampton
Bundaberg
Sandy Cape
Brisbane
Toowoomba
Cape Byron

QUEENSLAND
GREAT DIVIDING RANGE

Charleville
Cunnamulla
Bourke
Tamworth
Newcastle
Sydney
Wollongong
Dubbo
NEW SOUTH WALES
Canberra
AUSTRALIAN CAPITAL TERRITORY
Mt. Kosciusko
Cape Howe

Longreach
Mount Isa

BARKLY TABLELAND

Cape Arnhem
Gulf of Carpentaria

NORTHERN TERRITORY

Tennant Creek
MACDONNELL RANGES
Alice Springs
Simpson Desert

Oodnadatta
Lake Eyre
Lake Torrens

Broken Hill
Darling River
Mildura
Wagga Wagga
Murray River
Geelong
Melbourne
VICTORIA
Ballarat
Mount Gambier
Bass Strait
Launceston
Hobart
TASMANIA

Port Pirie
Port Augusta
Port Lincoln
Adelaide
SOUTH AUSTRALIA
Kangaroo Island

Penong
Great Australian Bight

Arnhem Land
Darwin
Melville Island
Birdum
Cape Talbot
Wyndham

Great Sandy Desert
Gibson Desert
Great Victoria Desert

WESTERN AUSTRALIA

Wiluna
Kalgoorlie
Esperance
Cape Leeuwin
Albany
Bunbury
Fremantle
Perth
Geraldton
North West Cape
Carnarvon
Port Hedland
Broome
Cape Lévèque

INDIAN OCEAN

Map of
AUSTRALIA and
NEW ZEALAND
SCALE OF MILES
0 100 200 300 400 500

Capitals of Countries
Capitals of States and Territories
Cities
Boundaries of Countries
Boundaries of States and Territories
Mountain Peaks

Water
Depression
Lowlands
Highlands
Mountains

East of 125° Greenwich 130°
Longitude 115° 120° 125°

57

INDONESIA

115° B 120° Longitude C East of 125° Greenwich D 130° E 135°

Wetar
Babar Is. Selaru
Frederik Hendrik I.

Flores Solor Alor Dili
Kupang OE.CUSSE PORTUGUESE TIMOR
SAWU SEA Roti

ARAFURA S

Cobourg Pen. Croker I. Miss.
Melville I. Dundas Str. Goulburn C.Wes.
C. Van Diemen Bathurst I. Croker I. Miss. Boucaut Bay Echo I. Wesse
Clarence Str. Van Diemen Gulf Goulburn
Darwin Rum Jungle ABORIGINAL Melvi
Adelaide River RESERVE C. A.
Pine Creek C. Grey

TIMOR SEA

TERR. OF ASHMORE
Ashmore Is. & CARTIER IS.
Cartier I.

C. Bougainville Long Reef C. Talbot C.Londonderry
Admiralty Gulf Montague Sound C. Ruthieres C. Fords
Joseph Bonaparte Gulf
Browse I. Katherine
Mataranka

Pt. Blaze Peron Is. Anson B.
RESERVE Coolibah
Larrimah

Borroloola
Rope
Urapunga Limmen Bight CAR
Sir Ed.

York Sound
Brunswick B. RESERVES Wyndham
Adele I. Collier B. Auvergne Victoria
Koolan Is. Victoria River Downs Daly Waters
Buccaneer Arch. Yampi Sound King Leopold Ra. Turkey Creek Newcastle Waters L.Woods Anthony
C. Leveque RESERVES Kimberley Plateau Nicholson Wave Hill Powell Creek Lagoon
Lacepede Is. King Sd. Fitzroy Crossing Ord R. Ord River Alexandria
Derby Halls Creek RES. Tanami Tabledand
C. Latouche Treville Roebuck B. St. George Ranges Desert Murchison Ra.
Dampier Land Broome Fitzroy R. Tanami Tennant Creek Hatches Creek
La Grange The Granites
Eighty Mile Beach RESERVE Barrow Creek
NORTHERN

Port Hedland Pardoo L. Mackay Mount Doreen
Thouin R. De Grey Great Sandy Desert Haris Range
Roebourne Mundabuliangana Bamboo Alice Springs
Monte Bello Is. Marble Bar RESERVE
Barrow I. Fortescue R. Nullagine Gibson Macdonnell Ranges Ewaninga
Muiron Is. Onslow Hamersley Ra. Wittenoom Gorge Desert Hermann= burg TERRITORY
Exmouth Gulf Mt. Bruce L. Macdonald Mission
North West C. WESTERN 4,024 L. Disappointment Hopkins L. L. Amadeus Rodinga
Learmonth Ashburton R. Finke Rumbalara
Exmouth Gulf Petermann Ayers Rock Charlotte Waters Simps
Pt. Cloates Ranges 2,845 OKulgera Deser
C. Farquhar AUSTRALIA Anabella
L. McLeod Lyons R. ABORIGINAL Musgrave Ranges The
C. Cuvier Gascoyne R. Mt. Woodroffe Alberga SOUTH
Geographe Chan. Robinson Ranges L. Carnegie RESERVE Mt. Woodroffe Oodnadatta
Bernier I. Carnarvon Mt. Hale Birksgate 4,970 Algebuckina
Dorre I. Wooramel R. 2,400 Range Warrina Lake
Naturaliste Chan. Meekatharra Eyre
Dirk Hartogs I. Shark B. Wiluna L. Wells Coober Pedy Anna
Steep Pt. Murchison R. Nannine Creek Range
Big Bell L. Carey Great Victoria Desert AUSTRAL Far
Cue Forrest Lakes L. Maurice
Ajana L. Austin Mt. Magnet Sandstone Moralana Penong
Yuna Mt. Margaret L. Raeside Wynbring C. Nuyts MT.Ga.
Northampton Yalgoo Miss. Leonora Rawlinna Forrest Reid Fisher Oodlea Kingoonya Woomera Eba Lake Torrens
Mullewa Youanmi Menzies Hughes Ooldea L. Everard L. Harris
Geraldton Morawa Leonora Nullarbor Plain Streaky B. L. Gairdner Port Haw
Houtman Abrolhos Mingenew Broad Arrow Madura Eucla Coduna Buckleboo Port
Dongara L. Moore Zanthus GREAT Penong Streaky Bay Iron Kn. Augusta
Dalwallinu Kalgoorlie Boulder Investigator Elliston Gawler Ra. Whyalla
Moora Mukinbudin L. Lefroy AUSTRALIAN Group Eyre Port Piri
Bulfinch Coolgardie Widgiemooltha Pen. Port Lincoln
Northam Merredin Norseman BIGHT Yorke Pen.
Perth York Southern Cross L. Cowan C. Spencer
Fremantle Bruce Rock L. Dundas Balladonia Investigator Str.
Kwinana Hyden Pt. Eyre Kangaroo I.
Corrigin Pt. Dover Kingscote
Bunbury Narrogin Salmon Gums Pt. Culver Edithburgh Victor
Collie Wagin Lake Grace Eyre Encoun
Geographe B. Katanning Newdegate Esperance
C. Naturaliste Bridgetown Ravensthorpe
Busselton Nannup Borden Hopetoun C. Arid
Augusta Northcliffe Archipelago
C. Leeuwin Albany of the Recherche
Flinders B. Bald Head Cap Le Grand
Pt. D'Entrecasteaux

INDIAN OCEAN

10°
2
3
20°
4
5
30°
6
7
35°
40°

WESTERN INSET (top left)

116°
0 10 20 30 40
MILES

Moore R.
Gingin
Goomalling
Muchea Toodyay
Swan R. Northam
Subiaco Midland Yorko
Nedlands Perth
Rottnest I. Avon R.
Fremantle Beverley
Garden I. Kwinana Mt. Dale 1,780
Rockingham Armadale
Peel Inlet Mandurah Jarrahdale Brookton
C. Bouvard Pinjarra Pingelly
Warpona
L. Preston Mt. Keats Hotham R.
Murray R. Williams R.
Williams
INDIAN OCEAN
32° 32°
116°

MAIN LEGEND (bottom left)

AUSTRALIA
and
NEW ZEALAND
BONNE PROJECTION

SCALE OF MILES
0 50 100 200 300 400 500

SCALE OF KILOMETRES
0 50 100 200 300 400 500

Capital of Country ✦ State and Territorial Capitals △

ADELAIDE INSET (bottom right)

138° 30'
Gawler
0 5 10 15
MILES
Williamstown
Gawler R.
Elizabeth
Outer Harbor Salisbury
Port Adelaide Mt. Pleasant
Woodville Gumeracha
Hindmarsh Adelaide Lobethal
West Torrens Kensington and Norwood Woodside
Marion Unley Mt. Lofty 2,304
Mitcham Nairne
Hahndorf
Reynella Mt. Barker
Onkaparinga R. Echunga
Noarlunga Strathalbyn
McLaren Vale R. Bremer
Gulf St. Vincent
35° 35°
138° 30'

NEW ZEALAND
Same scale as main map

CORAL SEA ISLANDS
TERRITORY

QUEENSLAND

NEW SOUTH WALES

VICTORIA

TASMANIA

NORTH ISLAND

SOUTH ISLAND

CORAL SEA

TASMAN SEA

PACIFIC OCEAN

MELBOURNE

SYDNEY

WOLLONGONG

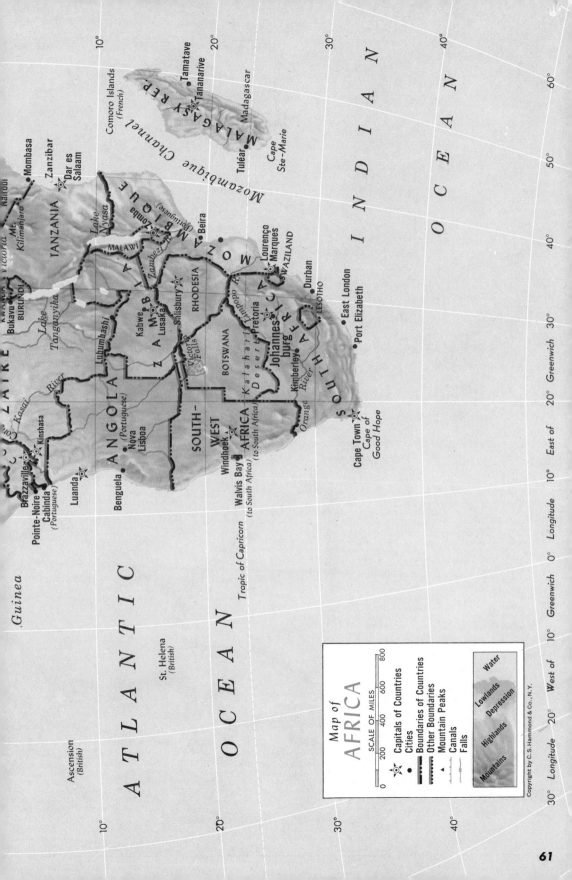

Nairobi
Mombasa
Zanzibar
Dar es Salaam

Comoro Islands (French)

Tamatave
Tananarive

MALAGASY REP.

Madagascar

Mozambique Channel

Cape Ste-Marie

Tuléar

INDIAN OCEAN

TANZANIA

Mt. Victoria
Mt. Kilimanjaro

RWANDA
BURUNDI
Bukavu
Lake Kivu

Lake Tanganyika

ZAIRE

Kinshasa
Brazzaville
Pointe-Noire
Cabinda (Portuguese)

Luanda

Benguela

ANGOLA (Portuguese)

Nova Lisboa

Kasai River

Lake Nyasa
Zomba

Lubumbashi

Z A M B I A

Kabwe
Lusaka

Kariba

Zambezi

MALAWI

M O Z A M B I Q U E (Portuguese)

Beira

RHODESIA

Salisbury

Victoria Falls

Limpopo R.

SOUTH-WEST AFRICA (to South Africa)

Windhoek

Walvis Bay (to South Africa)

Kalahari Desert

BOTSWANA

Kimberley

Pretoria
Johannesburg

Orange River

SOUTH AFRICA

Lourenço Marques
SWAZILAND
Durban
LESOTHO
East London
Port Elizabeth

Cape Town
Cape of Good Hope

INDIAN OCEAN

Guinea

ATLANTIC OCEAN

Tropic of Capricorn

St. Helena (British)

Ascension (British)

Map of AFRICA

SCALE OF MILES
0 200 400 600 800

Capitals of Countries
Cities
Boundaries of Countries
Other Boundaries
Mountain Peaks
Canals
Falls

Water
Lowlands
Depression
Highlands
Mountains

10° 20° 30° 40° 50° 60°

30° West of Greenwich 20° 10° 0° Longitude 10° East of Greenwich 20° Longitude 30° 40°

61

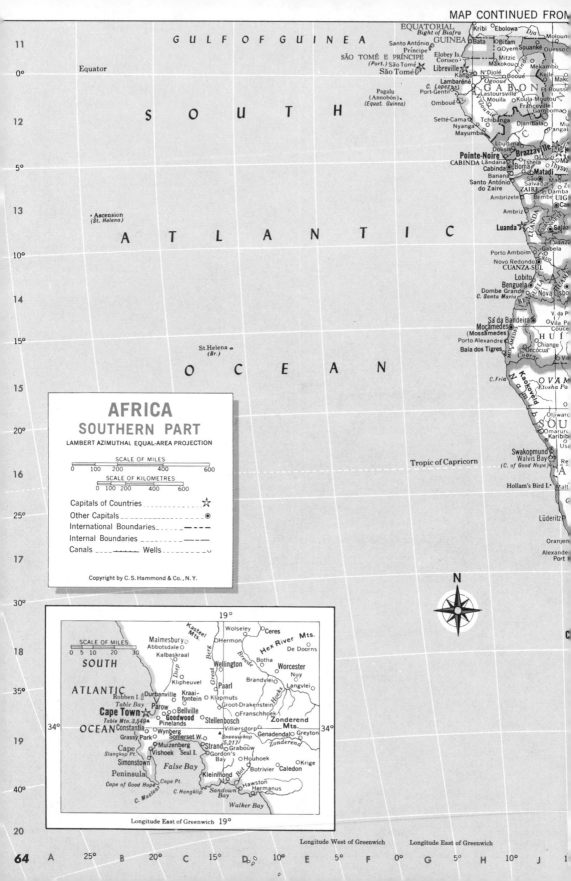

KENYA
Z A I R E
UGANDA
RWANDA
BURUNDI
KIVU
TANZANIA
KATANGA
ZAMBIA
ANGOLA
BOTSWANA
RHODESIA
MOÇAMBIQUE
ZAMBEZIA
MANICA
SOFALA
GAZA
NIASSA
CABO DELGADO
TETE
MADAGASCAR REPUBLIC
MADAGASCAR
COMORO IS.
SWAZILAND
LESOTHO
TRANSKEI
ORANGE FREE STATE
CAPE OF GOOD HOPE
Kalahari Desert
MOXICO
CUBANGO
CAPRIVI STRIP
BAROTSELAND

INDIAN OCEAN
INDIAN OCEAN

Equator
Tropic of Capricorn

Mogadishu
Nairobi
Mombasa
Zanzibar
Dar es Salaam
Dodoma
Tabora
Kigali
Bujumbura
Kisangani
Mbandaka
Luluabourg
Kindu
Bukavu
Lubumbashi
Ndola
Lusaka
Salisbury
Bulawayo
Gwelo
Beira
Quelimane
Nampula
Nacala
Porto Amélia
Vila Cabral
Diégo-Suarez
Majunga
Tananarive
Antsirabe
Fianarantsoa
Tuléar
Fort-Dauphin
Tamatave
Lourenço Marques
Johannesburg
Pretoria
Kimberley
Bloemfontein
Pietermaritzburg
Durban
Port Elizabeth
East London
Umtata
Maseru
Gaborone
Windhoek

Lake Victoria
L. Tanganyika
Lake Nyasa
L. Rukwa
L. Mweru
L. Bangweulu
L. Kivu
L. Edward
L. Albert
L. Kioga
Kariba Lake
Lake Ngami
L. Ngamiland
Makgadikgadi Salt Pan
Okavango Basin
Kalahari Desert

Zambezi
Limpopo
Kafue
Luangwa
Rovuma
Rufiji
Save

Kilimanjaro 19,340
Kenya 17,058
Inyanga 8,849
Milanje 9,843
Namuli 7,936

Mozambique Channel

Seychelles
Aldabra Is. (Br. Ind. Oc. Terr.)
Cosmoledo Is.
Providence I.
Assumption
Astove I.
Farquhar Is. (Br. Ind. Oc. Terr.)
Grand Comoro
Mohéli
Anjouan
Mayotte
Nossi-Bé
St. Pierre 'Cerf
Glorioso Is. (Fr.)
Réunion (Fr.)
Europa (Réunion)
Bassas da India (Réunion)

Mascarene Islands

INSET MAP:

SCALE OF MILES
0 25 50 100

I. aux Serpents
Round I.
Flat I.
Coin de Mire
Poudre d'Or
Poste de Flacq
Port Louis
Quatre Bornes
Curepipe
Black R. Mt.
Morne Brabant 2,711
Mahébourg
Souillac
MAURITIUS

La Possession
Le Port
St-Paul
St-Denis
St-André
St-Benoît
Piton des Neiges 10,069
Le Volcan 8,612
Étang-Salé
Le Tampon
St-Louis
St-Pierre
St-Joseph
St-Philippe
RÉUNION (Fr.)

INDIAN OCEAN

Longitude 56° East of Greenwich 57°
55°   56°   57°   58°
20°   21°

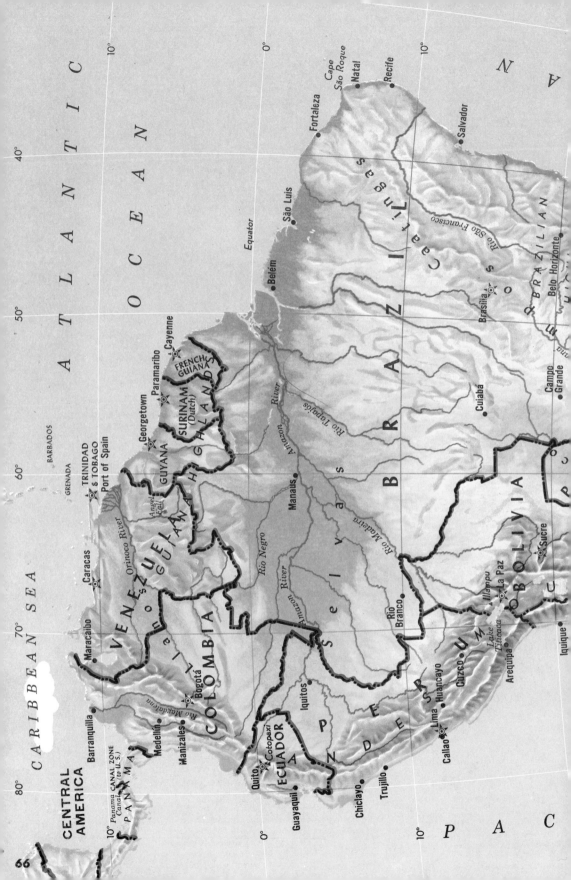

N

CENTRAL
AMERICA

CARIBBEAN SEA

80°

70°

PANAMA

10° Panama CANAL ZONE
Canal (to U.S.)

BARRADOS

GRENADA

TRINIDAD
& TOBAGO
Port of Spain

60°

A T L A N T I C

O C E A N

50°

40°

10°

0°

10°

Equator

Cape
São Roque
Natal
Recife

Fortaleza

Salvador

São Luis

Belém

Cayenne

FRENCH
GUIANA

Paramaribo

SURINAM
(Dutch)

Georgetown

GUYANA

GUIANA HIGHLANDS

Barranquilla

Maracaibo

Caracas

Angel
Fall

Orinoco River

VENEZUELA

L l a n o s

COLOMBIA

Rio Magdalena

Medellín

Manizales

Bogotá

Cotopaxi

Quito

ECUADOR

Guayaquil

Chiclayo

Trujillo

Iquitos

Amazon River

Rio Negro

Manaus

Amazon River

Rio Branco

Rio Madeira

Rio Tapajós

Amazon River

S e l v a s

P E R U

A N D E S

Callao
Lima
Huancayo

Cuzco

Arequipa

Iquique

Lake
Titicaca

Illampu
La Paz

BOLIVIA

Sucre

B R A Z I L

Caatingas

Rio São Francisco

BRAZILIAN

Belo Horizonte

Brasília

Cuiabá

Campo
Grande

P A C

0°

10°

66

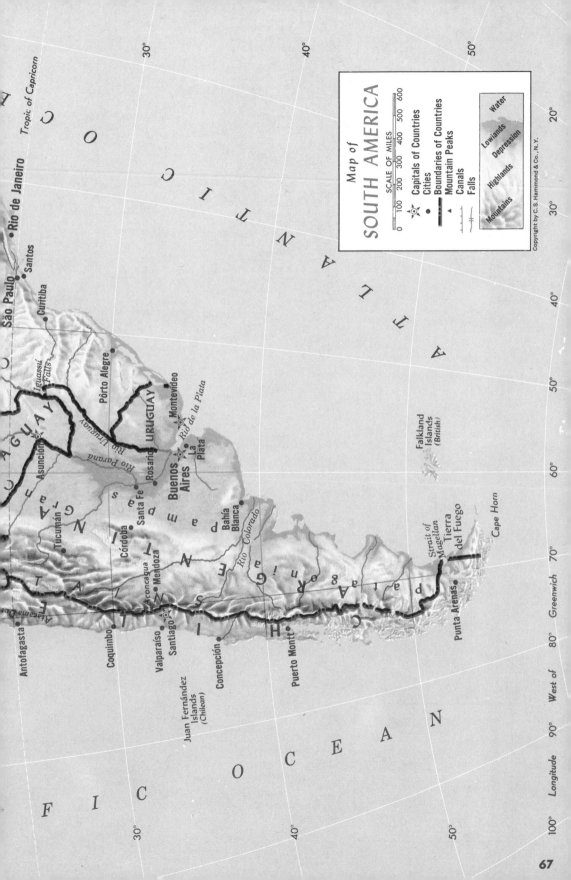

Map of
SOUTH AMERICA

SCALE OF MILES
0 100 200 300 400 500 600

Capitals of Countries
Cities
Boundaries of Countries
Mountain Peaks
Canals
Falls

Water
Lowlands
Depression
Highlands
Mountains

Copyright by C. S. Hammond & Co., N.Y.

Tropic of Capricorn

30°
40°
50°

20°
30°
40°
50°
60°
70°
80°

ATLANTIC OCEAN

Rio de Janeiro
Santos
São Paulo
Curitiba
Pôrto Alegre

Iguassú Falls

PARAGUAY
Asunción
Rio Paraguay
Rio Paraná
Rio Uruguay
URUGUAY
Montevideo
Rio de la Plata
Rosario
Santa Fe
Buenos Aires
La Plata

Tucumán
Córdoba
Mendoza
Aconcagua

Bahía Blanca
Rio Colorado

ARGENTINA

PAMPAS

PATAGONIA

Falkland Islands
(British)

Cape Horn

Strait of Magellan
Tierra del Fuego
Punta Arenas

Atacama Des.
Antofagasta
Coquimbo
Valparaíso
Santiago
Concepción
Puerto Montt

CHILE

Juan Fernández Islands
(Chilean)

PACIFIC OCEAN

West of Greenwich
90°
80°
70°
60°
50°

Longitude
100°
90°
80°
70°
60°
50°

30°
40°
50°

67

MAP CONTINUED O

8

Tropic of Capricorn

25°

I. de San Félix • I. San Ambrosio
(Chile)   (Chile)

9

30°

JUAN FERNÁNDEZ IS.
(Chile)
I. Alejandro,   I. Robinson
Selkirk   Crusoe
I. Santa Clara

10

35°

11

40°

12

ARCHIPIÉLAGO
de los
CHONOS

45°

13

50°

SOUTH AMERICA
SOUTHERN PART
LAMBERT AZIMUTHAL EQUAL-AREA PROJECTION

SCALE OF MILES
0   100   200   300   400   500

SCALE OF KILOMETRES
0   100   200   300   400   500

Capitals of Countries .... ☆
Other Capitals .... △
International Boundaries .... —·—·—
Other Boundaries .... — — —

Copyright by C.S. Hammond & Co., N.Y.

54

55°

15

O   C   E   A   N

P   A   C   I   F   I   C

Mejillones
Antofagasta
Aguas Blancas
Vol. Llullaillaco
22,057
Taltal
Potrerillos
Chañaral
Pueblo Hundido
Caldera
Copiapó
Huasco
Cabo Bascuñán
Vallenar
Cruz Grande
La Serena
Coquimbo
Tongoy
Ovalle
Illapel
Los Vilos
Aconcagua
Viña del Mar
Valparaíso
Santiago
Rancagua
Pichilemu
San Fernando
Curepto
Constitución
Talca
Cauquenes
Linares
Quirihue
Parral
Talcahuano
Concepción
Chillán
Arauco
Lota
Los
Lebu
Cañete
Mulchén
Ángeles
Traiguén
Curacautín
Nueva Imperial
Temuco
Villarrica
Valdivia
Corral
Riñihue
Ranco
La Unión
Osorno
Puerto Varas
G. de Maullín
los Coronados
Ancud
Cast.
Isla de Chiloé
Cabo Quitán
G. Corcovado
Pto. Aisén
Pen. Taitao
C. Tres Montes
G. de Penas
I. Campana
I. Wellington
I. Madre de Dios
I. Hanover
Estrecho Nelson
ARCHIPIÉLAGO
REINA ADELAIDA
Stroit of Magellan
I. Desolación
I. Sta. Inés
I. Clarence
I. Stewart
I. Londonderry
I. Hoste
Puerto Williams
Is. Hermite
Is. Wollston
Cape Horn
Is. Diego Ramírez

Embarcación
Lib. Gen.
San Antonio   Martín
de los Cobres
Jujuy
Orerico
Salta
El
Quebrachal
Rosario
de la Frontera
Antofagasta
de la Sierra
Campo
Gallo
Tucumán
Las
Termas
Santiago
del Estero
Catamarca
Andalgalá
Chilecito
La
Rioja
Dean
Funes
Cristóbal
SAN JUAN
San Juan
Villa Dolores
Córdoba
CÓRDOBA
Alta Gracia
Villa María
Bell Ville
SAN
San Luis
Río Cuarto
Mendoza
Godoy Cruz
Mercedes
Venado Tuerto
Laboulaye
Rufino
LUIS
San Rafael
Ing. Luiggi
Lincoln
MENDOZA
Gen. Pico
Telén
Victorica
Pehuajó
Sta. Rosa
Trenque
Lauquen
LA PAMPA
Cereales
Olavarr
Gen. Acha
Doblas
Bernasconi
Cor. Pringles
NEUQUEN
Colorado
Gen.
Roca
Bahía Blanca
Pt. Huincul
Zapala
Neuquén
Choele
Choel
Picún-Leufú
RÍO NEGRO
El Cuy
los Andes
Sierra
Valcheta
San Carlos de Bariloche
Viedma
Carmen de
Patagones
Nahuel Huapi
San Antonio
Oeste
G. de Maullín
Puerto Montt
Maquinchao
Golfo San Matías
Pen. Valdés
Pta. Norte
Norquincó
Sierra Grande
Pto. Pirámides
Gastre
Telsen
Puerto
Madryn
Pta. Delgada
Esquel
Gaiman
Trelew
Rawson
Las
Plumas
CHUBUT
Camarones
B. Camarones
C. Dos Bahías
Colonia
Sarmiento
Colhue Huapi
Comodoro Rivadavia
Colonia Las Heras
Golfo San Jorge
L. Buenos Aires
Deseado
Cabo Tres Puntas
Puerto Deseado
L. San
Martín
L. Cardiel
San Julián
L. Viedma
Chico
SANTA
CRUZ
Santa Cruz
L. Argentino
Pto.
Coyle
Bahía Grande
Río Gallegos
Pto. Natales
Strait of Magellan
Cerro Manantiales
Punta Arenas
Porvenir
TIERRA DEL FUEGO
ANTÁRTIDA E ISLAS DEL
ATLÁNTICO
SUR
Río
Grande
Ushuaia
Tierra
del Fuego
B. Nassau
Estrecho Le Maire
I. de los Est.
(Staten I.)

FALKLA
Jason Is.
West Falklan
Weddell I.
Falkl

DRAKE PAS

A   95°   B   90°   C   85°   D   80°   E   75°   F   70° Longitude 65° West of

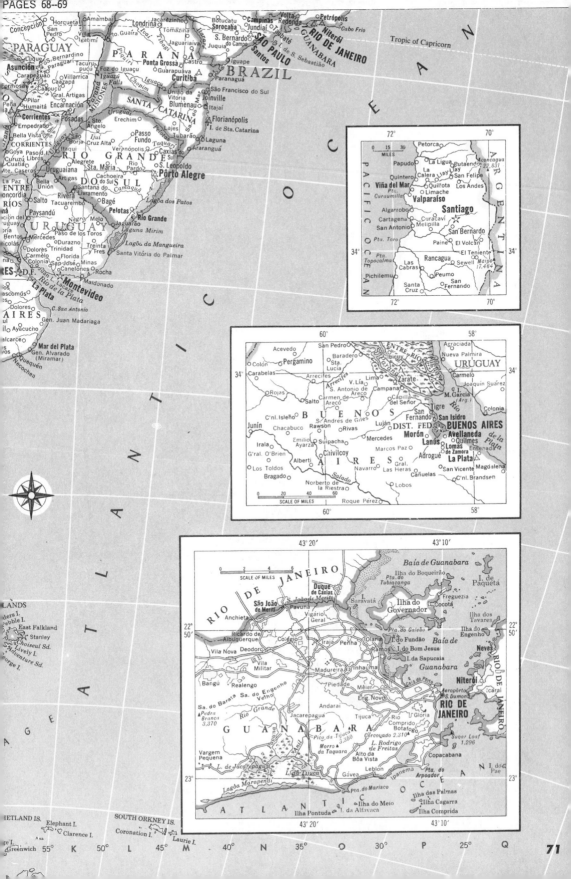

ARCTIC OCEAN

ATLANTIC OCEAN

ICELAND

GREENLAND
(Danish)

Davis Strait

Baffin
Bay

Thule

Baffin Island

Ellesmere Island

North Pole

North
Magnetic
Pole

Victoria
Island

ARCTIC

OCEAN

Great
Bear Lake

Great
Slave Lake

Mackenzie River

Point
Barrow

Bering Strait

ASIA

UNITED STATES

Alaska

Yukon River

Mt.
McKinley

Anchorage

Whitehorse

Juneau

Queen
Charlotte
Islands

Vancouver
Island

Seattle

Portland

CASCADE RANGE

Columbia R.

Vancouver

ROCKY

MOUN

Labrador

Goose
Bay

Newfoundland

St. Pierre &
Miquelon
(French)

Halifax

Nova
Scotia

Boston

New York

Philadelphia

St. Lawrence River

Montreal

Ottawa

Toronto

APPALACHIAN MOUNTAINS

Cleveland

Detroit

Chicago

Great Lakes

Minneapolis

Hudson
Bay

Churchill

Lake
Winnipeg

Winnipeg

CANADA

Edmonton

Calgary

Missouri

Grea

MOUN

Great
Salt Lake

San

PACI

72

VENEZUELA

COLOMBIA

ECUADOR

SOUTH AMERICA

PERU

BRAZIL

BOLIVIA

Bermuda
(British)

BAHAMAS

Cape Canaveral

Miami

Jacksonville

Atlanta

Mt. Mitchell

APPAL

Memphis

New
Orleans

Mississippi River

Dallas

Houston

Rio Grande

P l a i n s

El Paso

Monterrey

Guadalajara

M E X I C O

Mexico City

Veracruz

Yucatán
Peninsula

Gulf of Mexico

Tropic of Cancer

C U B A

Havana

HAITI

DOMINICAN
REPUBLIC

PUERTO
RICO
(to U.S.)

West Indies

JAMAICA

CARIBBEAN SEA

BELIZE

GUATEMALA

HONDURAS

EL SALVADOR

NICARAGUA

COSTA RICA

PANAMA

CENTRAL
AMERICA

CANAL ZONE (to U.S.)

Panama (Canal)

Phoenix

Los Angeles

San Diego

NEVADA

Mt. Whitney

Colo.

Lower California

N S

Galápagos
Islands
(Ecuadoran)

P A C I F I C

O C E A N

Equator

Map of
NORTH AMERICA

SCALE OF MILES

0   200   400   600   800

☆ Capitals of Countries
• Cities
∎∎∎ Boundaries of Countries
▲ Mountain Peaks
╌╌╌ Canals

Water
Lowlands
Depression
Highlands
Mountains

Copyright by C.S. Hammond & Co., N.Y.

73

NORTH AMERICA

LAMBERT AZIMUTHAL EQUAL-AREA PROJECTION

SCALE OF MILES
0 100 200 400 600 800

SCALE OF KILOMETRES
0   200   400   600   800

Capitals of Countries .... ☆
International Boundaries .... _____
Other Boundaries .... _ . _ . _
Canals .... _ _ _ _

© C.S. HAMMOND & Co., N.Y.

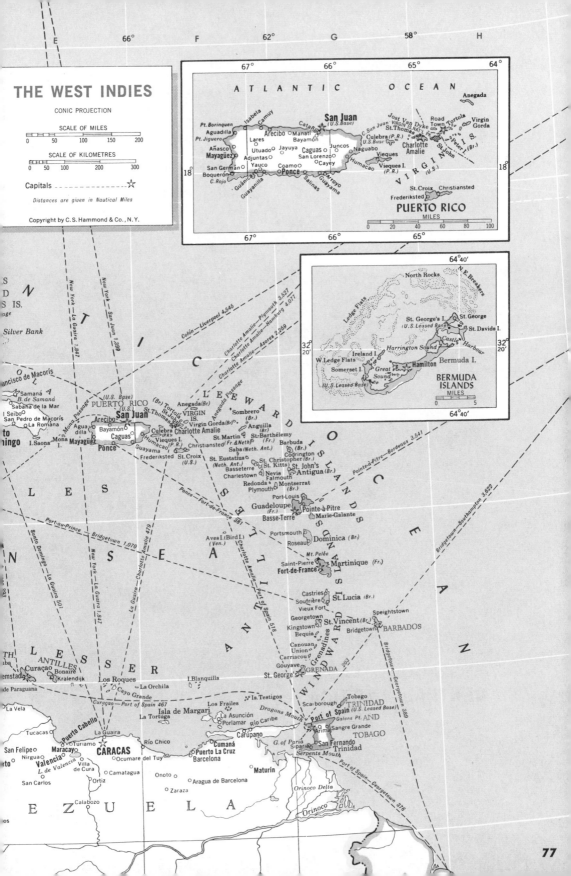

CENTRAL AMERICA

CONIC PROJECTION

SCALE OF MILES

0   25   50   100   150

SCALE OF KILOMETRES

0   25 50   100   150

Capitals of Countries .... ☆

International Boundaries .... ▬ ▬ ▬

Canals .... ╼╼╼╼

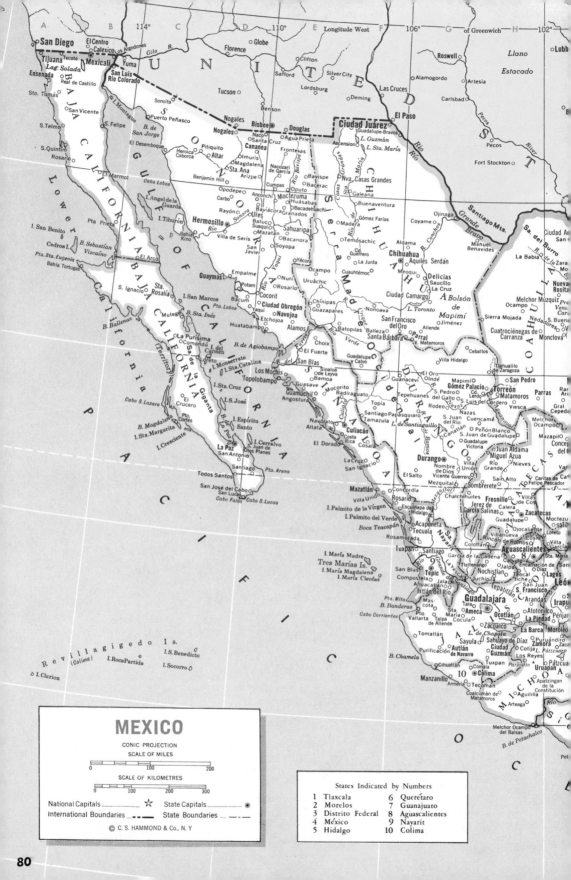

MEXICO

CONIC PROJECTION

SCALE OF MILES

SCALE OF KILOMETRES

National Capitals .... ☆   State Capitals .... ◉
International Boundaries ---·---   State Boundaries ---·---·---

© C. S. HAMMOND & Co., N.Y

States Indicated by Numbers

1	Tlaxcala	6	Querétaro
2	Morelos	7	Guanajuato
3	Distrito Federal	8	Aguascalientes
4	México	9	Nayarit
5	Hidalgo	10	Colima

80

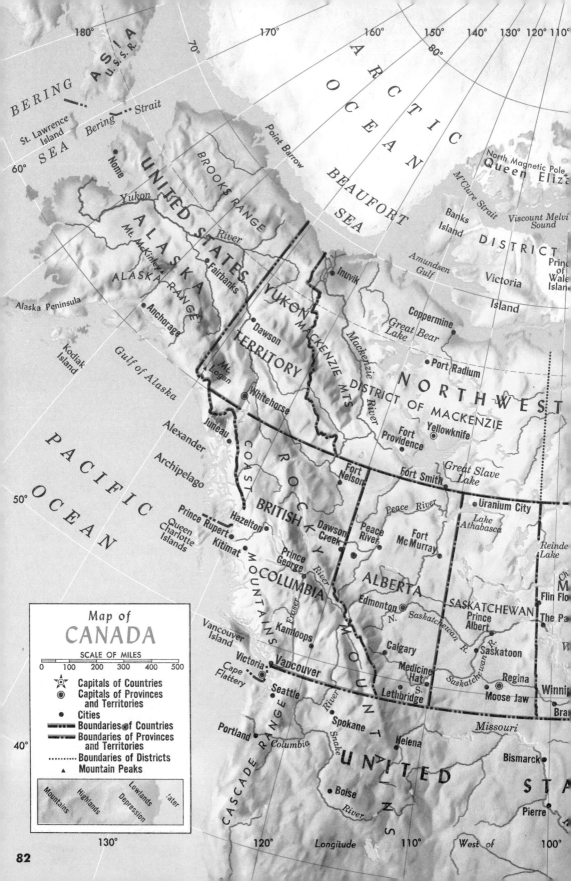

ASIA
BERING
U.S.S.R.

St. Lawrence
Island
SEA
Bering
Strait
60°

Nome

UNITED

Yukon

Point Barrow

ARCTIC

OCEAN

BEAUFORT

SEA

North Magnetic Pole
Queen Eliza

M'Clure Strait

Banks
Island

Viscount Melvi
Sound

DISTRICT

Amundsen
Gulf

Victoria

Prince
of
Wales
Island

70°

180°   170°   160°   150°   140°   130° 120° 110°

STATES

ALASKA

BROOKS RANGE

River

Mt. McKinley

ALASKA RANGE

Fairbanks

Alaska Peninsula

Anchorage

Kodiak
Island

Gulf of Alaska

YUKON

Dawson

MACKENZIE MTS

TERRITORY

Mt.
Logan

Whitehorse

DISTRICT
OF MACKENZIE

Great Bear
Lake

Coppermine

Port Radium

Mackenzie
River

Yellowknife

NORTHWEST

80°

Inuvik

COAST

Alexander

Archipelago

Juneau

PACIFIC

50°

OCEAN

Fort
Providence

Fort
Nelson

Fort Smith

Great Slave
Lake

Uranium City

Prince Rupert

Hazelton

BRITISH

ROCK

Dawson
Creek

Peace River

Lake
Athabasca

Reinde
Lake

Kitimat

Queen
Charlotte
Islands

COLUMBIA

Prince
George

Peace
River

Fort
McMurray

Fraser

River

ALBERTA

SASKATCHEWAN

Ch

M
Flin Flo

The Pa

Vancouver
Island

MOUNTAINS

Kamloops

Edmonton

N.

Saskatchewan

Prince
Albert

Saskatoon

R.

Map of
CANADA

SCALE OF MILES

0   100   200   300   400   500

Capitals of Countries
Capitals of Provinces
and Territories
Cities
Boundaries of Countries
Boundaries of Provinces
and Territories
Boundaries of Districts
Mountain Peaks

Mountains   Highlands   Lowlands   Depression   ater

Victoria
Cape
Flattery

Vancouver

Seattle

Spokane

Portland

CASCADE RANGE

Columbia

Boise

River

Snake

River

Calgary

Medicine
Hat

Saskatchewan

S.

Lethbridge

MOUNT

River

UNITED

Helena

Regina

Moose Jaw

Winnip

Bra

Missouri

STA

Bismarck

Pierre

40°

130°   120°   Longitude   110°   West of   100°

82

90° 80° 70° 60° 50° 40° 30° 20°

G R E E N L A N D
(Danish)

ICELAND

⊛ Reykjavik

80°

70°

60°

h Islands

Devon Island

• Thule

B A F F I N

B A Y

Arctic Circle

Lancaster Sound

F R A N K L I N

B a f f i n

Gulf of Boothia

Davis Strait

⊛ Godthåb

Cape
Farewell

A T L A N T I C

O C E A N

50°

Foxe

Basin

B a f f i n   I s l a n d

• Frobisher Bay

TRICT

OF T E R R I T O R I E S

WATIN

Southampton
Island

Hudson Strait

• Chesterfield
Inlet

H U D S O N

Ungava
Peninsula

• Fort-
Chimo

• Nain

Battle
Harbour

50°

B A Y

• Inoucdjouac

Scheffervile

Goose Bay

N e w f o u n d l a n d

• Churchill

Belcher
Islands

River

• Port
Nelson

TOBA

Severn   River

Fort-George

James

Bay

Sept-Îles

Anticosti
Island

Grand
Falls

Gander

Corner
Brook

Newfoundland

St.
John's ⊛

Q U É B E C

Lake
Mistassini

Gulf of
St. Lawrence

St. Pierre &
Miquelon
(French)

eg

Severn River

Moosonee

O N T A R I O

Lake Nipigon

Kenora

*Lake of
the Woods*

Thunder
Bay

Kapuskasing

Timmins

• Rouyn

Chicoutimi

Québec

Trois
Rivières

Gaspé
Peninsula

St. Lawrence River

**NEW
BRUNSWICK**

**PRINCE
EDWARD
ISLAND**

Charlottetown

Sydney

Cape Breton
Island

Sable Island

Moncton

N O V A   S C O T I A

Fredericton

Saint
John

Sherbrooke

Halifax

Sault-
Ste-Marie

Sudbury

North
Bay

Montréal

Cornwall

Cape Sable

Yarmouth

Duluth

Lake Superior

Lake Huron

Ottawa

A P P A L A C H I A N   M T S.

ES

St. Paul

Mississippi R.

Minneapolis

Milwaukee

Lake Michigan

Toronto ⊛

Lake
Ontario

Boston

Detroit

Windsor

Lake Erie

Buffalo

New York

Greenwich

90°

80°

70°

Copyright by C. S. HAMMOND & Co. N. Y.

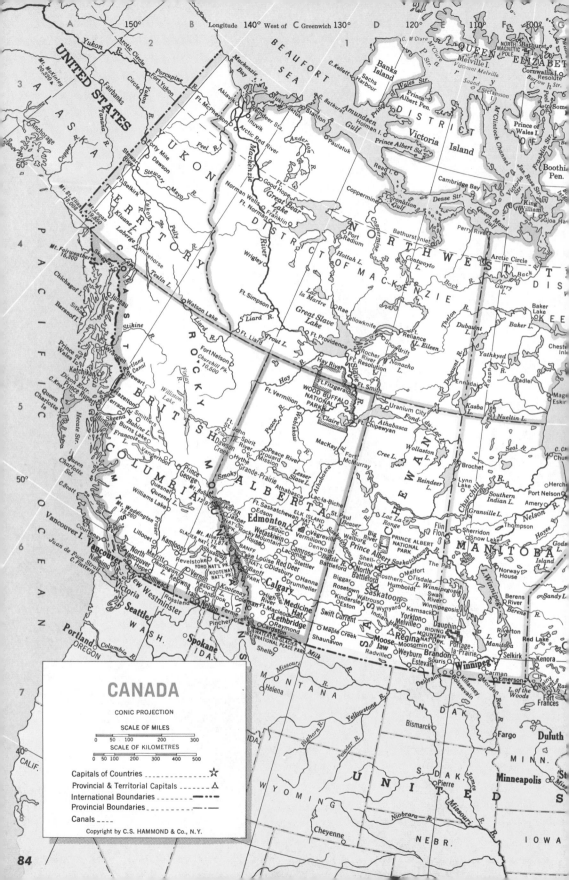

CANADA

CONIC PROJECTION

SCALE OF MILES

0 50 100   200   300

SCALE OF KILOMETRES

0 100 200   300   400   500

Capitals of Countries .... ☆
Provincial & Territorial Capitals ...... △
International Boundaries .... —·—·—
Provincial Boundaries .... —··—··—
Canals ....

MARITIME PROVINCES

SCALE OF MILES

0 10 20 30 40 50

Provincial Capitals _____ ⊛ Provincial Boundaries _ _ _ _
County Seats _____ • County Boundaries _ _ . _ _
International Boundaries _ . _ . _

Copyright by C. S. HAMMOND & CO., N.Y.

GASPÉ PENINSULA

QUEBEC
SOUTHERN PART

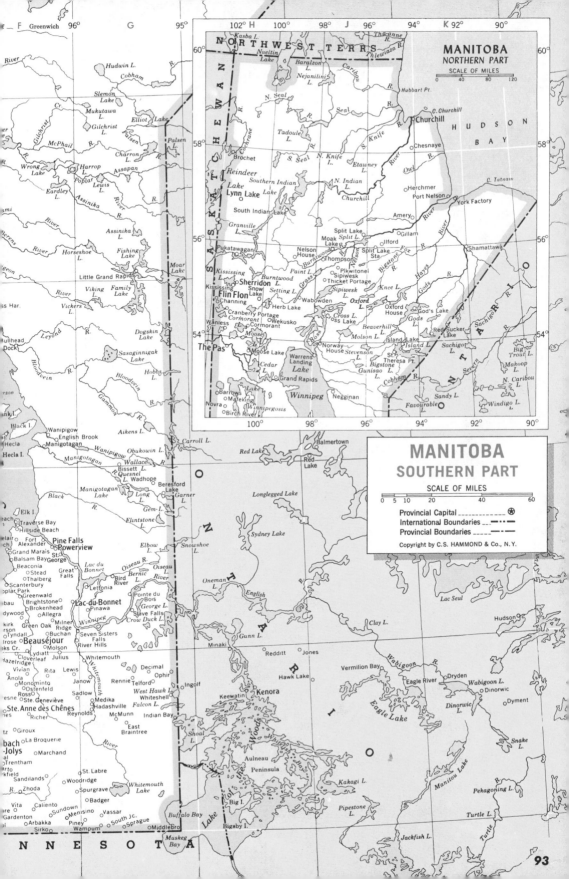

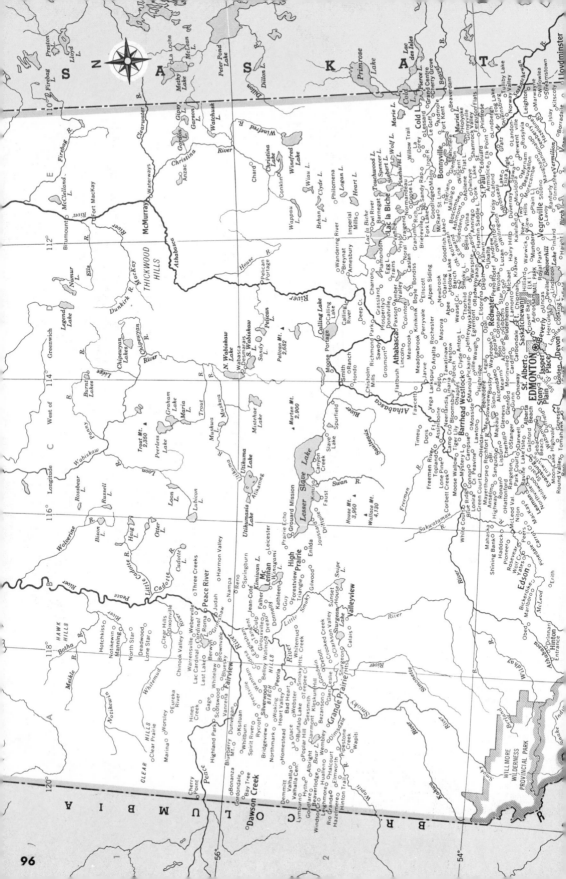

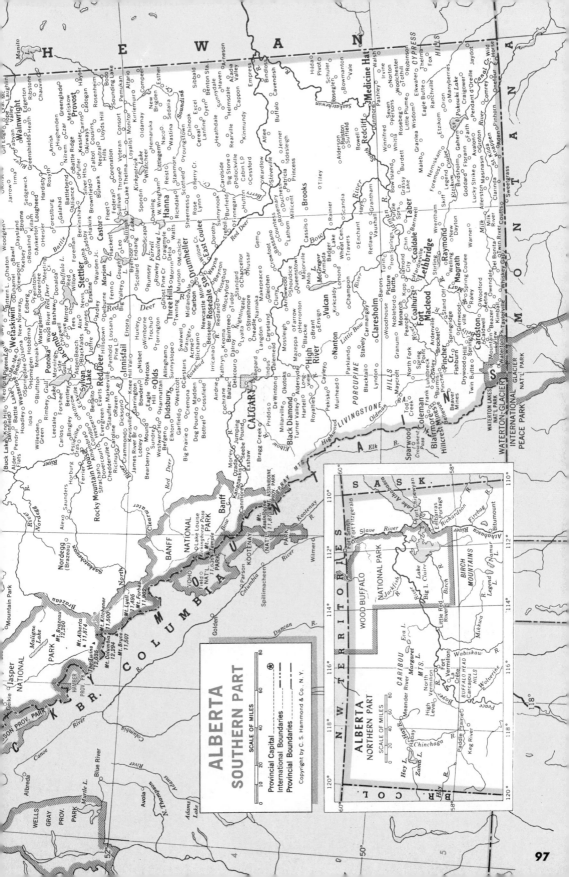

BRITISH
COLUMBIA
SOUTHERN PART

SCALE OF MILES

0   15   30   60   90   120

Provincial Capital ⊛
State Capital ⊙
International Boundaries
Provincial Boundaries

Copyright by C. S. HAMMOND & CO., N.Y.

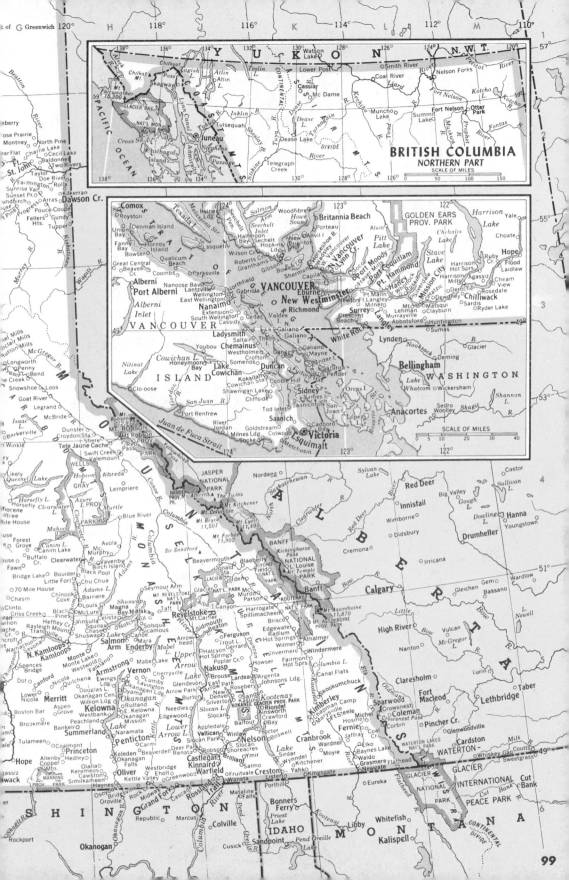

BRITISH COLUMBIA
NORTHERN PART
SCALE OF MILES
0   50   100   150

SCALE OF MILES
0   10   20   30   40

99

Map of
UNITED STATES
LAMBERT CONFORMAL CONIC PROJECTION
Copyright by C. S. HAMMOND & Co., N.Y.

SCALE OF MILES

0   50   100   200   300

Capitals of Countries
State and Provincial Capitals
International Boundaries
State Boundaries
Provincial Boundaries

Copyright by C. S. HAMMOND & Co., N.Y.

APPROXIMATE ELEVATIONS

10,000 ft.
5,000 ft.
2,000 ft.
1,000 ft.
500 ft.
Sea level
Depression

Longitude 90° West of Greenwich

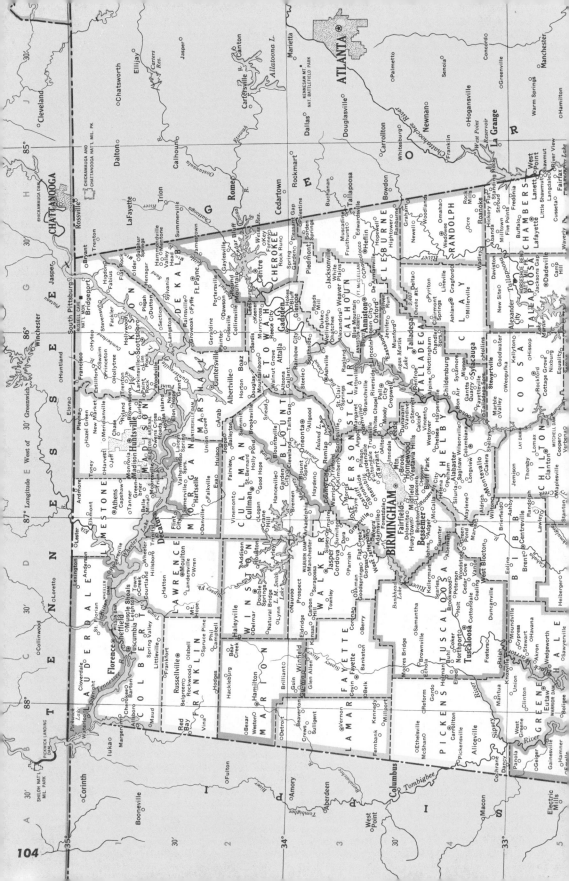

ALABAMA

SCALE

State Capitals.............⊛
County Seats.............◉
© C.S. HAMMOND & Co., N.Y.

105

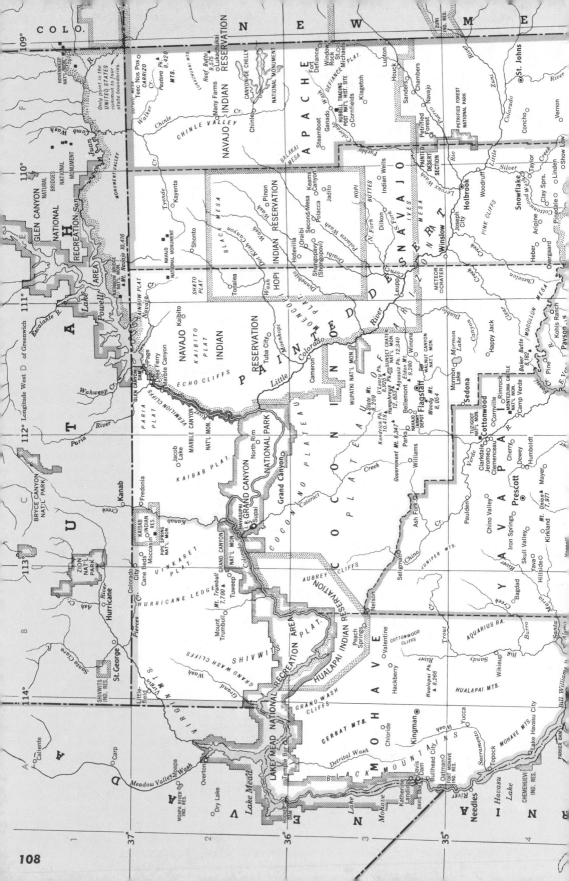

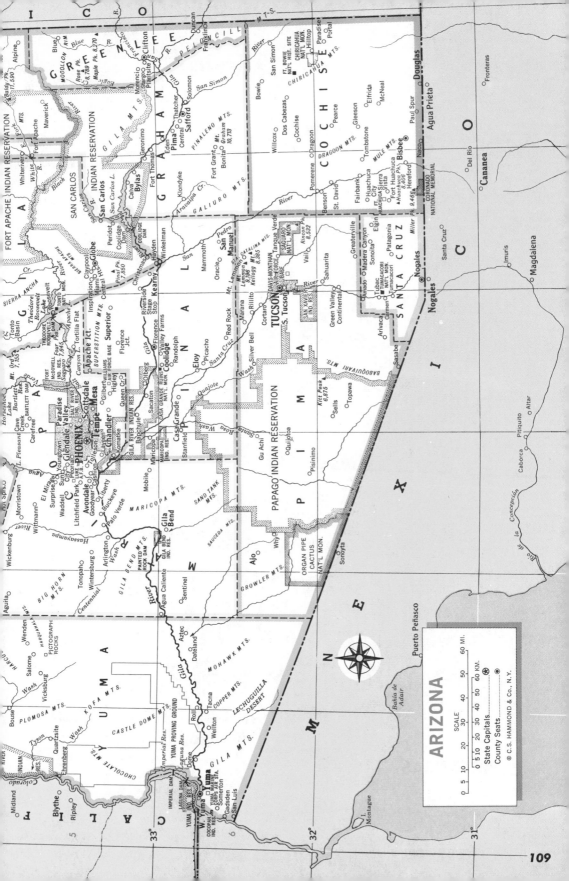

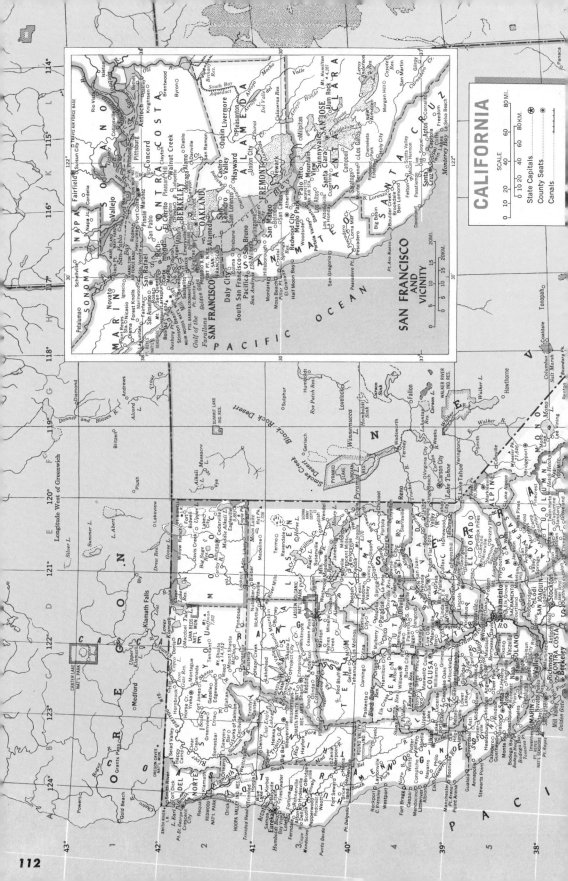

Copyright by C. S. Hammond & Co., N. Y.

SACRAMENTO
AND
VICINITY

0 5 10 15 20KM.

LOS ANGELES
AND VICINITY

113

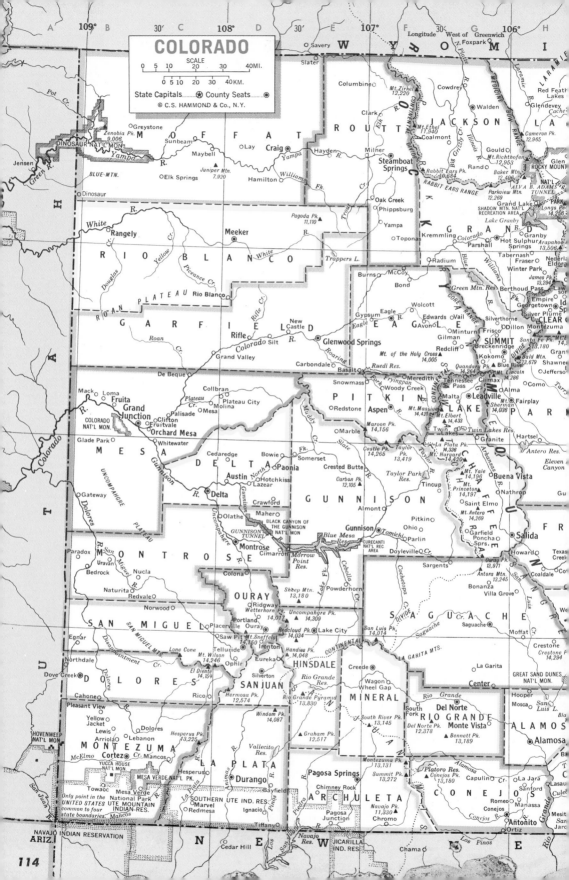

COLORADO map (C.S. Hammond & Co., N.Y.)

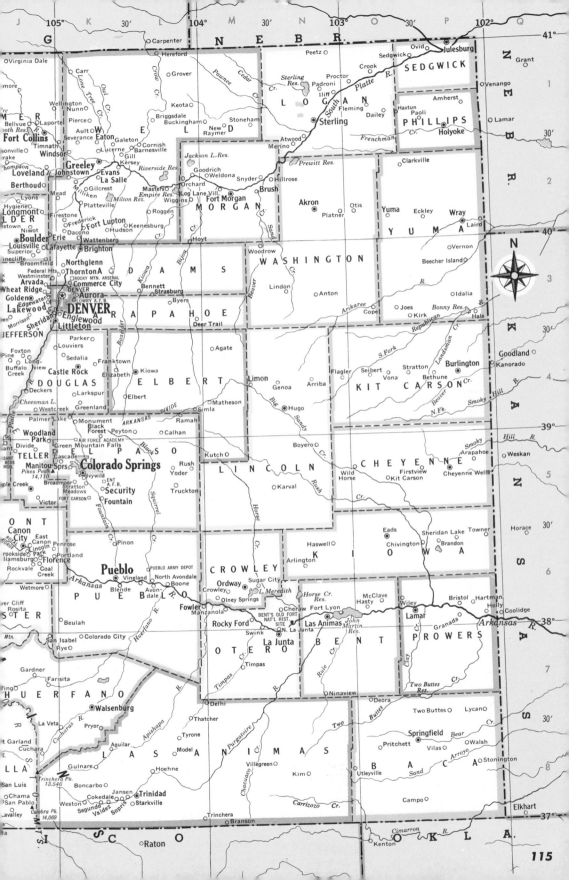

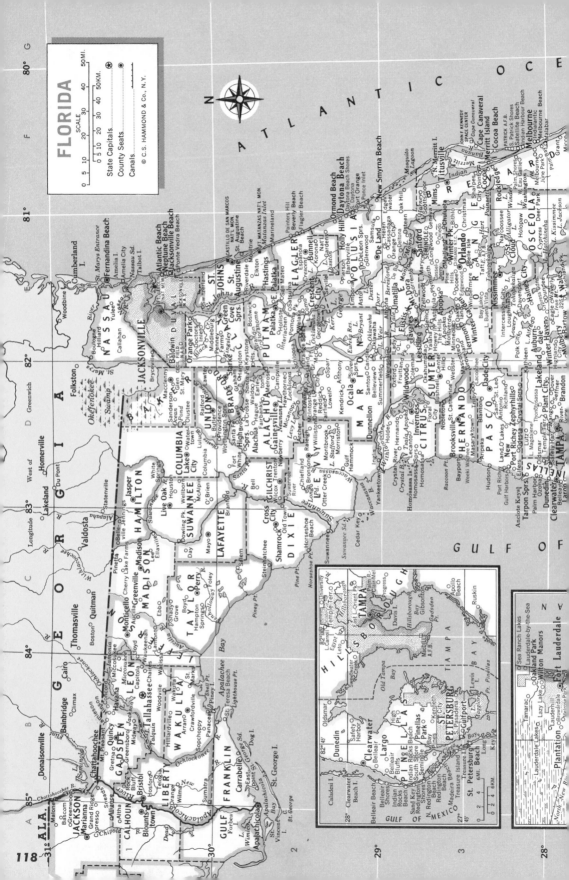

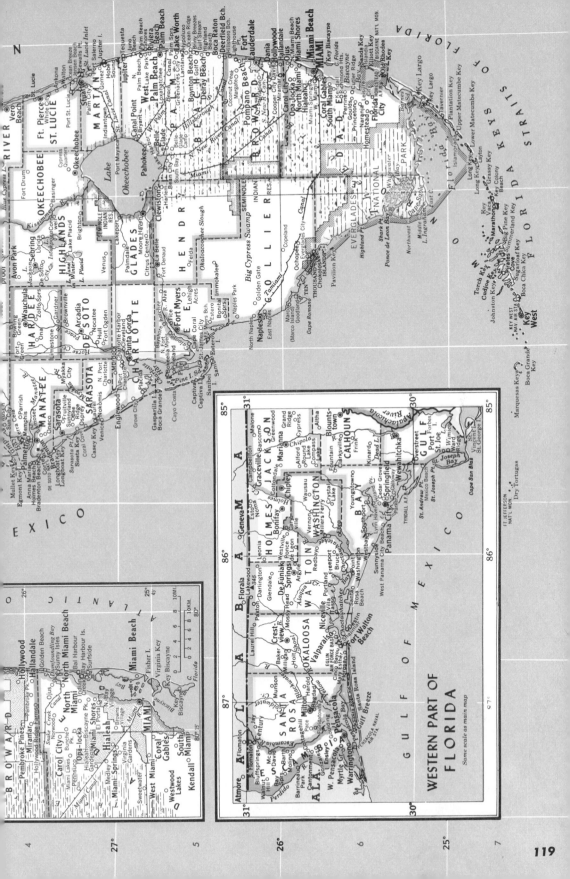

WESTERN PART OF FLORIDA

Same scale as main map

119

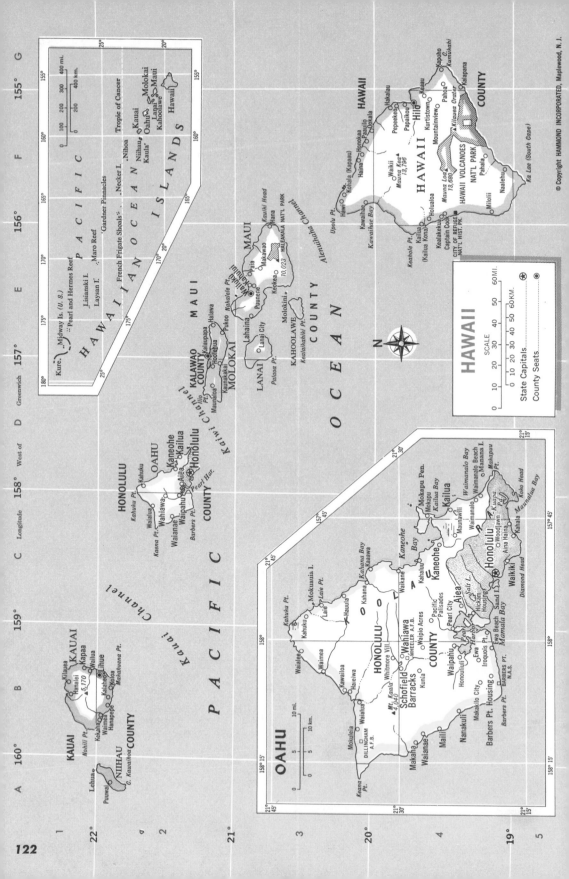

HAWAIIAN OCEAN ISLANDS

PACIFIC OCEAN

Kure

Midway Is. (U.S.)

Pearl and Hermes Reef

French Frigate Shoals

Maro Reef

Gardner Pinnacles

Lisianski I.

Laysan I.

Necker I.

Nihoa

Niihau

Kaula

Tropic of Cancer

Kauai
Oahu
Lanai
Kahoolawe
Molokai
Maui
Hawaii

400 mi.
400 km.

HAWAII

KAUAI

Lehua
Puuwai
NIIHAU

Kilauea
Hanalei
Kapaa
Wailua
Kalaheo
Lihue
Kekaha
Waimea
Hanapepe

Nohili Pt.
5,170
Makahuena Pt.
C. Kawaihoa

KAUAI COUNTY

Kauai Channel

OAHU

HONOLULU

Kahuku Pt.

Waialua
Kahuku
Wahiawa
Kaneohe
Kailua
Honolulu
Aiea
Waipahu
Waianae
Pearl Har.

Kaena Pt.
Barbers Pt.

HONOLULU COUNTY

Kaiwi Channel

MOLOKAI

KALAWAO COUNTY

Kalaupapa
Hoolehua
Kaunakakai
Maunaloa
Kualapuu
Pukoo
Halawa

Ilio Pt.
Nakalele Pt.

MAUI

LANAI

Lanai City

Kaumalapau
Palaoa Pt.

KAHOOLAWE

Kealaikahiki Pt.

MAUI

Kapalua
Wailuku
Kahului
Paia
Makawao
Keokea
Lahaina
Puunene

Kauiki Head
Hana

Kawaihae Head

HALEAKALA NAT'L PARK
10,023

Molokini

MAUI COUNTY

Alenuihaha Channel

HAWAII

HAWAII COUNTY

Hilo

Upolu Pt.

Hawi
Kapaau (Halawa)
Kohala (Kapaau)
Waikii
Honokaa
Paauilo
Laupahoehoe
Pepeekeo
Papaikou
Mountainview
Kurtistown
Pahoa
Apoho
Keaau
Kumukahi
Kalapana

Kawaihae
Kawaihae Bay
Waimea
Holualoa
Kailua
Kailua (Kona)
Keauhou
Kealakekua
Captain Cook
Keaholo Pt.
CITY OF REFUGE NAT'L HIST. PK.

Mauna Kea
13,796
Mauna Loa
13,680
HAWAII VOLCANOES NAT'L PARK
Kilauea Crater

Pahala
Naalehu
Pahoa
Milolii

Ka Lae (South Cape)

HAWAII
SCALE
0 10 20 30 40 50 60 MI.
0 10 20 30 40 50 60 KM.
⊕ State Capitals
◎ County Seats

N

OAHU

Keana Pt.

Mokuleia

Kahuku
Kahuku Pt.
Waialee
Waimea
Kawailoa
Haleiwa
Laie
Hauula
Kahana
Waikane
Kaaawa
Kahaluu
Kaneohe
Kailua
Waimanalo
Waimanalo Beach
Kahalii

Mokuauia I.
Laie Pt.
Kahana Bay
Mokapu Pen.
Mokapu Pt.
Mokapu
Manana I.

Mt. Kaala
4,040
Schofield Barracks
WHEELER A.F.B.
Whitmore Vill.
Wahiawa
Waipio Acres
Pearl City
Pacific Palisades
Aiea
Woodlawn
Aina Haina

Kunia
Waipahu
Honouliuli
Ewa
Iroquois Pt.
Makakilo City
Pearl Harbor
Hickam A.F.B.
Salt L.
Sand I.
Honolulu
Waikiki
Kahala
Diamond Head
Koko Head
Mamala Bay
Maunalua Bay

DILLINGHAM A.F.B.
Waialua
Makaha
Waianae
Maili
Nanakuli
Barbers Pt. Housing
BARBERS PT. N.A.S.
Barbers Pt.

HONOLULU COUNTY

Waianae Range

Koolau Range

Kaneohe Bay
Kailua Bay
Waimanalo Bay

Kailua

Kaupo Pd.

10 mi.
10 km.

A 160° B 159° C Longitude 158° West of D Greenwich 157° E 156° F 155° G

1 22° σ 2 21° 3 20° 4 19° 5

PACIFIC OCEAN

IDAHO

SCALE

0   20   40   60   80 MI.

0   20   40   60   80 KM.

State Capitals .... ✪
County Seats .... ◉

© C.S. HAMMOND & Co., N.Y.

Map labels (geographic features and place names):

A 116° Longitude B West 114° C Greenwich 112° D

BRITISH COLUMBIA   WATERTON-GLACIER   ALBERTA

INT'L PEACE PK.

WATERTON LAKES NAT'L PARK

BOUNDARY
Metaline Falls
Priest L.
Bonners Ferry
Pend Oreille R.
KALISPEL IND. RES.
Sandpoint
Priest River
BONNER
Libby
Kootenai R.
Clark Fork
GLACIER NATIONAL PARK
BLACKFEET INDIAN RESERVATION
Kalispell
Hungry Horse Res.
South Fork
Missouri R.
48°

Spirit Lake
Rathdrum
Hayden
KOOTENAI
Coeur d'Alene
Post Falls
Spokane
Lake Pend Oreille
CABINET MTS.
Clark Fork
Flathead L.
FLATHEAD INDIAN RESERVATION
Great Falls

Smelterville
Osburn
Wallace
Mullan
SHOSHONE
Kellogg
Coeur d'Alene L.
St. Maries
BENEWAH
St. Joe R.
Avery
E. Sister Pk. 6,866
Blackfoot R.
Helena ☉

Colfax
Pullman
Potlatch
LATAH
Moscow
Troy
Genesee
Clearwater
Lapwai
Lewiston
NEZ PERCE NAT'L HIST PARK
Spokane R.
WASHINGTON
Elk River
CLEARWATER
Headquarters
Pierce
Lolo Pass 5,187
Lochsa R.
Missoula
Butte
CONTINENTAL DIVIDE
46°

Enterprise
Lewiston Orchards
Craigmont
Nezperce
Cottonwood
Kooskia
Weippe
Kamiah
Selway R.
IDAHO
MOUNTAINS
Elk City
White Bird
Grangeville
High Mtn. Sheep Res.
Waugh Mtn. 8,882
Lost Trail Pass 6,990
Salmon
Baker
Cobalt
Big Hole R.
Bitterroot R.
Clark Fork R.
Dillon
Bozeman

Riggins
He-Devil Mtn. 9,387
Salmon River
Mormon Mtn. 9,545
LEMHI
Leadore
BEAVERHEAD MTS.
Hebgen L.
YELLOWSTONE NATIONAL PARK

ADAMS
New Meadows
McCall
Warm Lake
SALMON
South Fork
VALLEY
Twin Pks. 10,328
Challis
Salmon R.
LEMHI RANGE
MONTANA
CENTENNIAL MTS.
Island Park Res.
Shoshone L.

OXBOW DAM
Council
BROWNLEE DAM
Cambridge
Cascade Res.
Cascade
Cape Horn Mtn. 9,600
SALMON RIVER MTS.
Clayton
CUSTER
Castle Pk. 11,820
Borah Pk. 12,662
LOST RIVER RA.
CLARK
Dubois
FREMONT
Ashton
St. Anthony
Jackson L.
GRAND TETON NAT'L PARK
44°

WASHINGTON
Weiser
Payette
Vale
PAYETTE
Fruitland
New Plymouth
Parma
GEM
Payette R.
Emmett
Garden Valley
BOISE
Idaho City
Garden City
Atlanta
SAWTOOTH RA.
Mackay
Moore
Arco
NAT'L REACTOR TESTING STA.
U.S.A.E.C.
Mud L.
JEFFERSON
Rexburg
MADISON
Rigby
St. Anthony
Driggs
TETON
Jackson

Caldwell
Boise ✪
Meridian
CANYON
Arrowrock Res.
Anderson Ranch Res.
CAMAS
Ketchum
Sun Valley
Hailey
BLAINE
Bellevue
BUTTE
Atomic City
7,559
Idaho Falls
Iona
Ammon
Shelley
BONNEVILLE
Palisades Res.
Jackson
Grays R.

Homedale
Owyhee R.
Murphy
ADA
ELMORE
Mountain Home
MOUNTAIN HOME A.F.B.
Fairfield
Carey
CRATERS OF THE MOON NAT'L MON.
BINGHAM
Springfield
Blackfoot
FORT HALL IND. RES.
Chubbuck
Blackfoot River Res.
CARIBOU

OREGON
Snake R.
Hammett
GOODING
Bliss
Glenns Ferry
LINCOLN
Richfield
Shoshone
MINIDOKA
Aberdeen
American Falls Res.
Pocatello
Inkom
Lava Hot Sprs.
Soda Sprs.
4

C.J. Strike Res.
Bruneau R.
SNAKE
Wendell
Gooding
Shoshone
JEROME
Jerome
Paul
Rupert
Walcott Res.
American Falls
McCammon
POWER
BANNOCK
Grace
Georgetown

Triangle
OWYHEE
Buhl
Filer
Shoshone Falls
Kimberly
Burley
Heyburn
Snake R.
Downey
Montpelier
BEAR LAKE

Riddle
Salmon Cr. Res.
TWIN FALLS
Twin Falls
Albion
CASSIA
Cache Pk. 10,340
Oakley
ONEIDA
Malad City
FRANKLIN
Preston
Franklin
Paris
Bear L.

Three Creek
WESTERN SHOSHONE IND. RES.
NEVADA
Almo
UTAH
42°

N

© C.S. HAMMOND & Co., Maplewood, N.J.

123

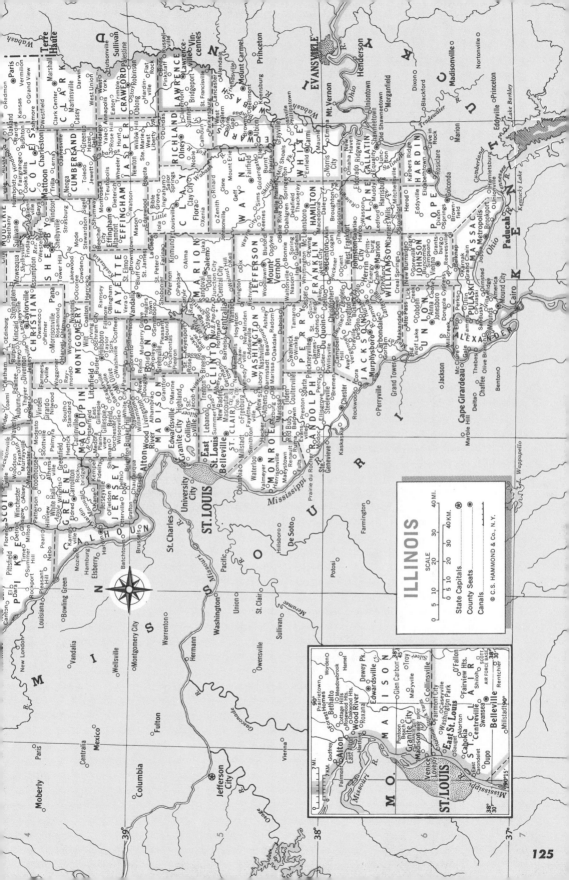

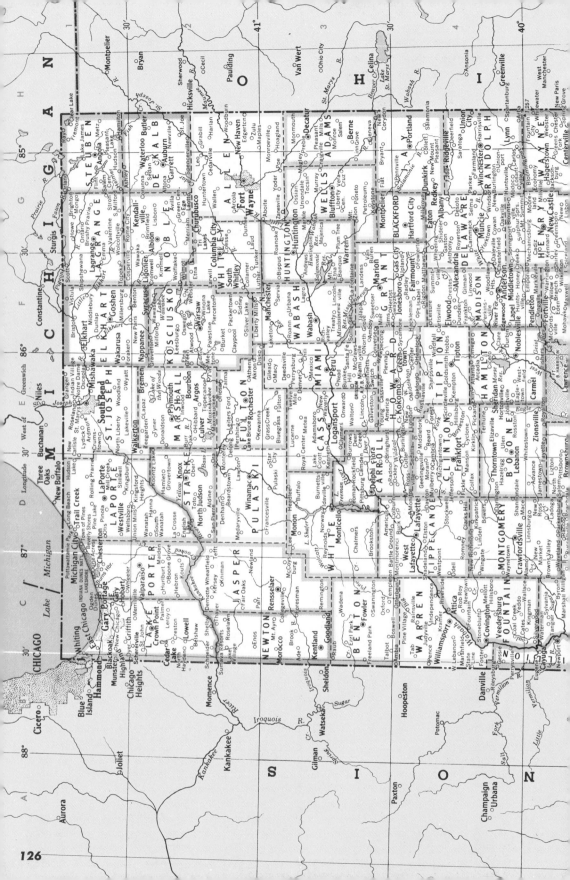

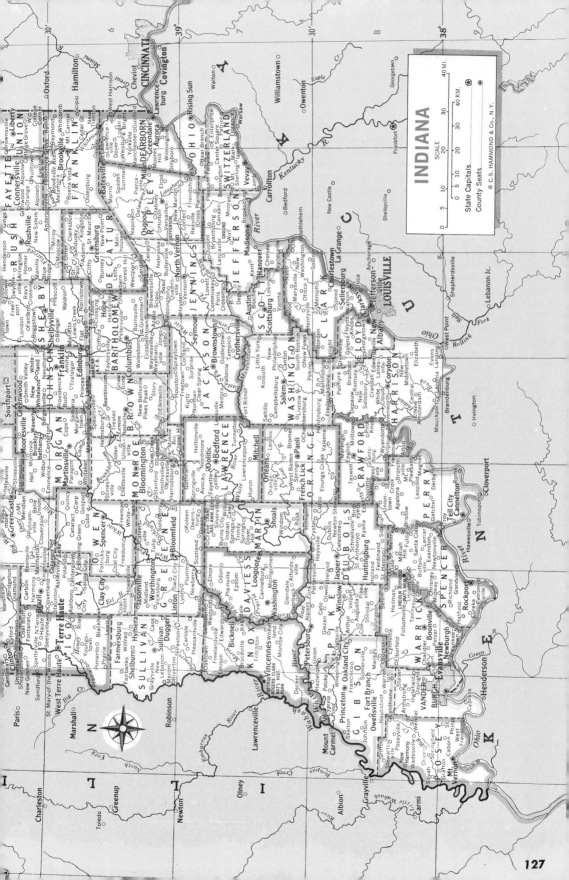

INDIANA

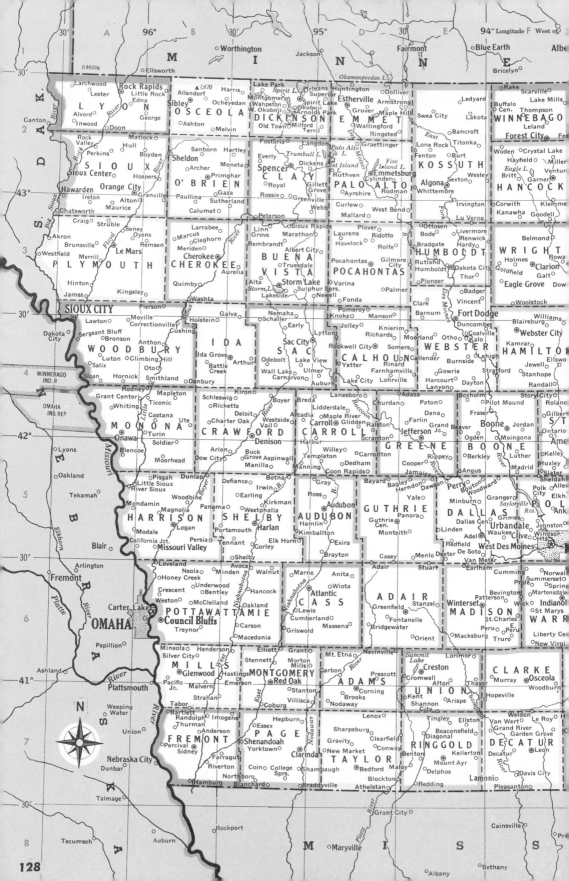

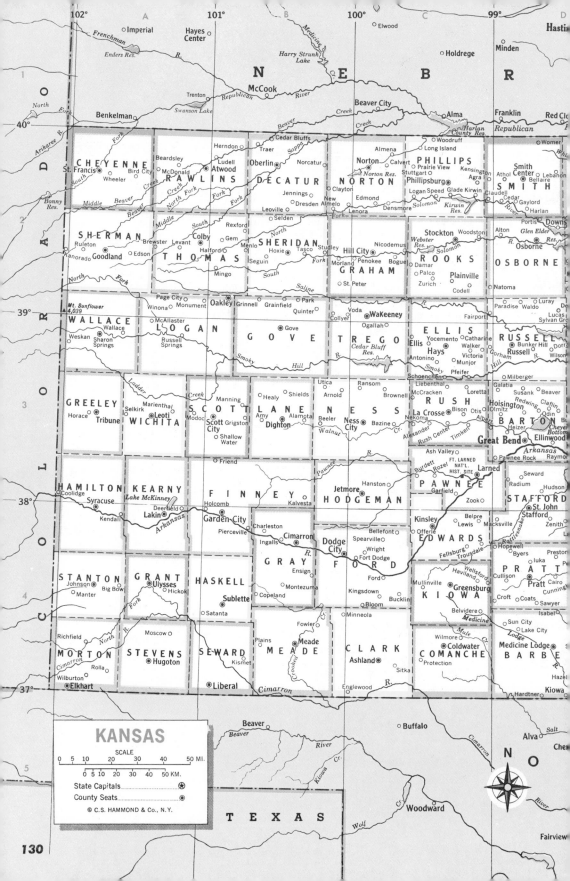

KANSAS

SCALE
0 5 10 20 30 40 50 MI.
0 5 10 20 30 40 50 KM.
State Capitals............⊛
County Seats.............◉
© C.S. HAMMOND & Co., N.Y.

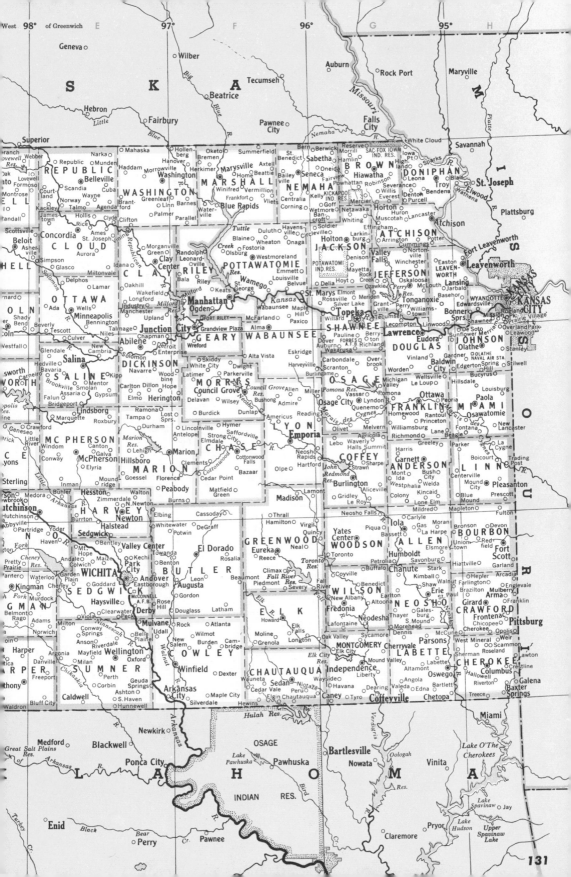

WESTERN PART OF KENTUCKY
Same scale as main map.

LOUISIANA

SCALE

0 5 10   20   30   40 MI.

0 5 10 20   30   40 KM.

State Capitals.................................⊛

Parish Seats.................................◉

Canals.................................

© C.S. HAMMOND & Co., N.Y.

134

NEW ORLEANS, BATON ROUGE AND VICINITY

0 5 10 15 20 MI.

0 5 10 15 20 KM.

Longitude 91° West of Greenwich

135

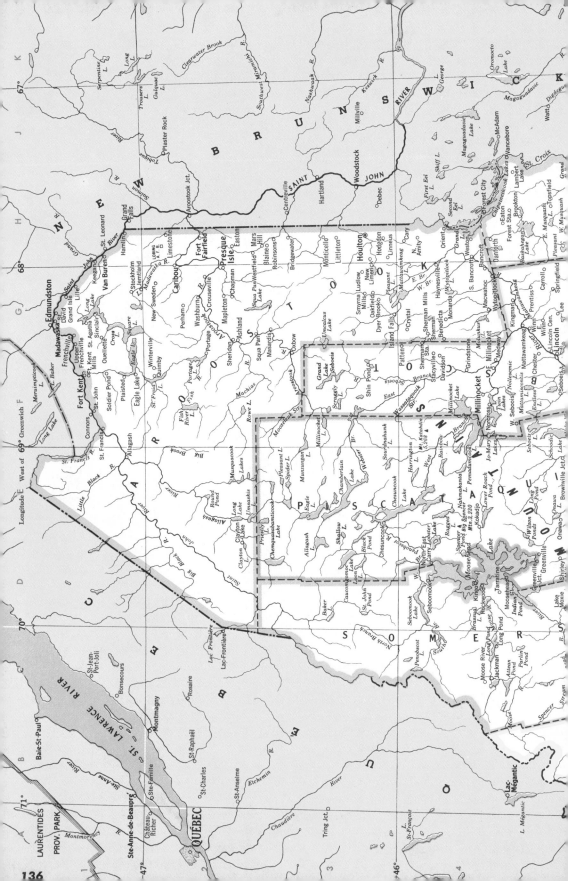

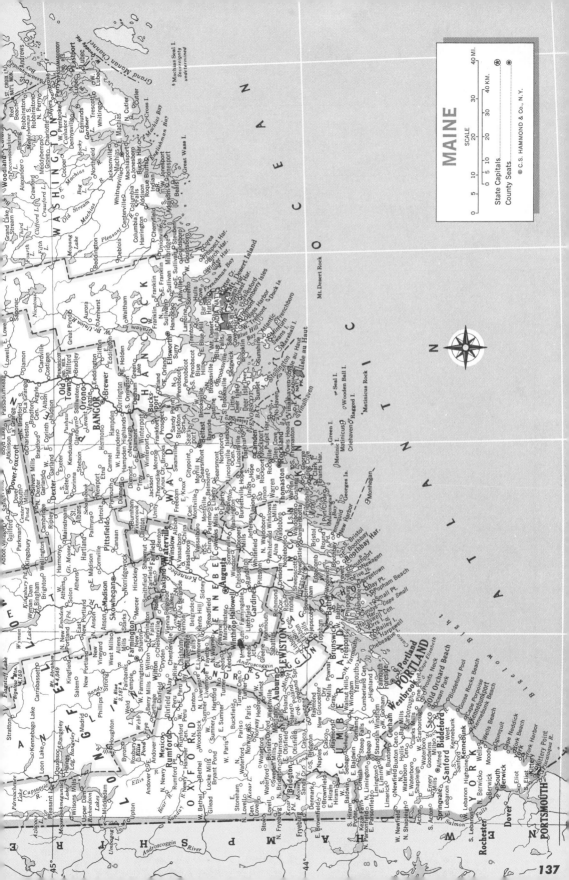

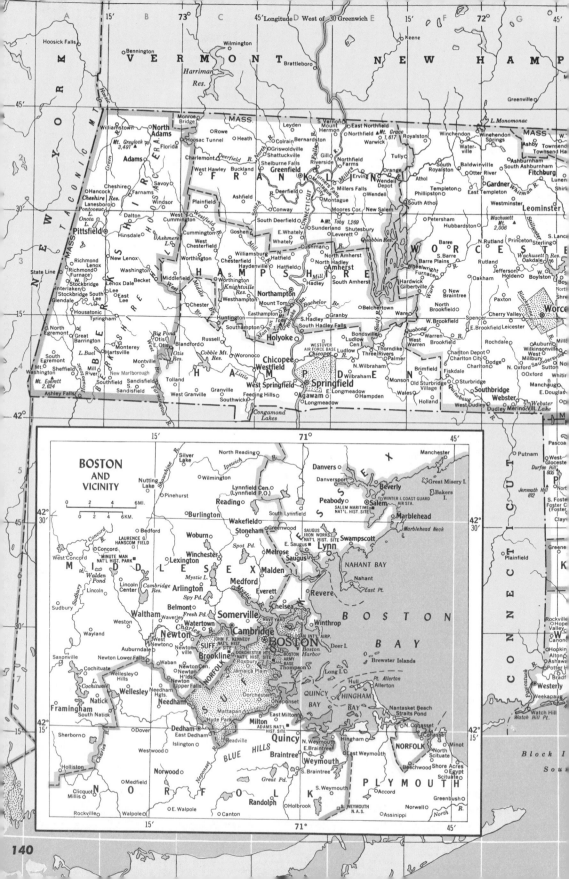

NORTHEASTERN PART OF MINNESOTA

Same scale as main map

MINNESOTA

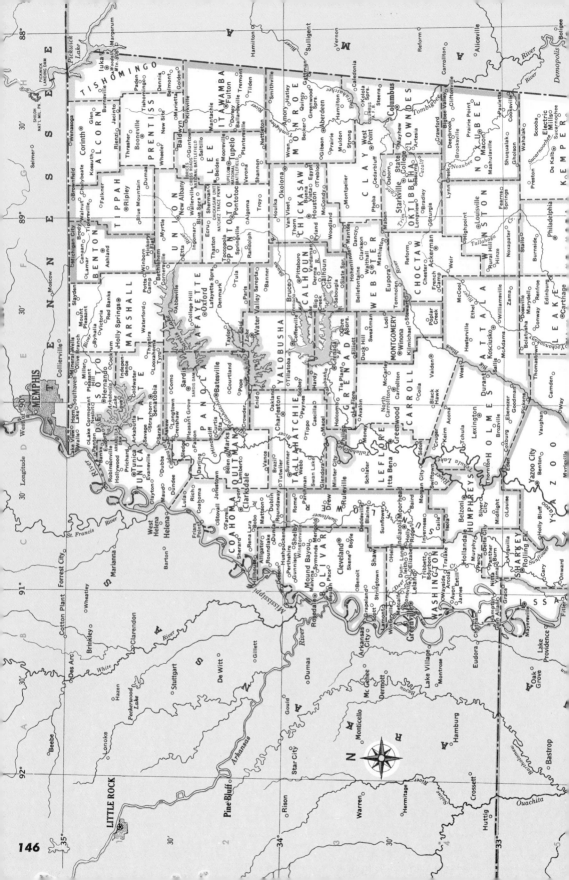

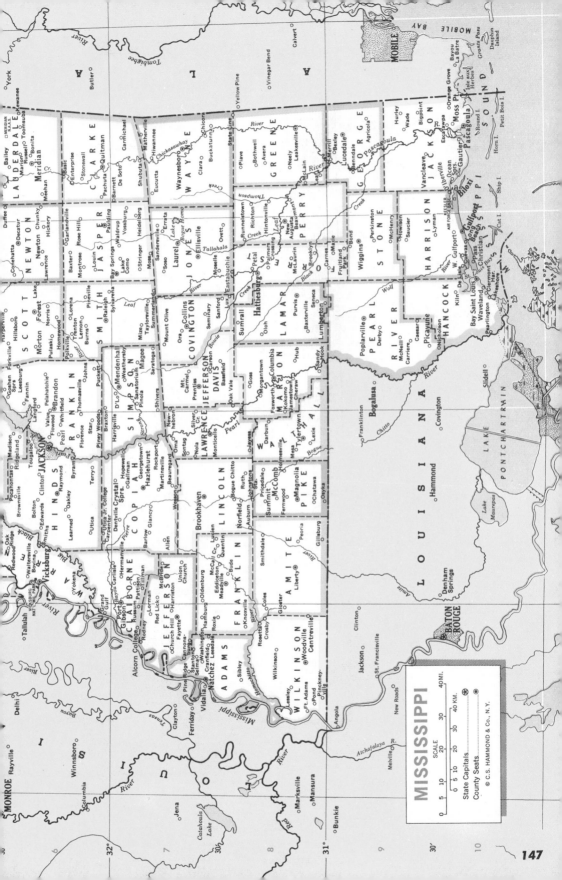

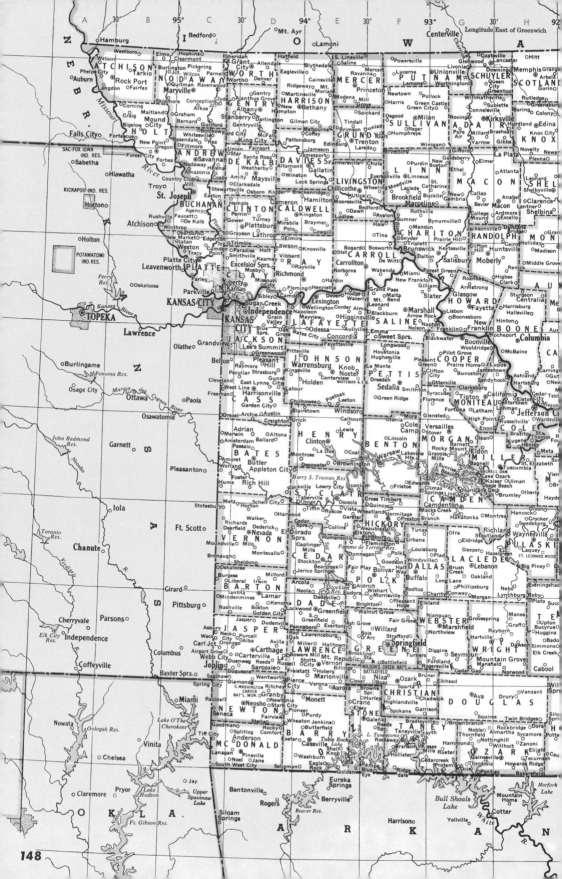

MISSOURI

SCALE

0 5 10   20   30   40   50 MI.

0 5 10 20   30   40 50 KM.

State Capitals .... ⊛

County Seats .... ○

© C.S. HAMMOND & Co., N.Y.

149

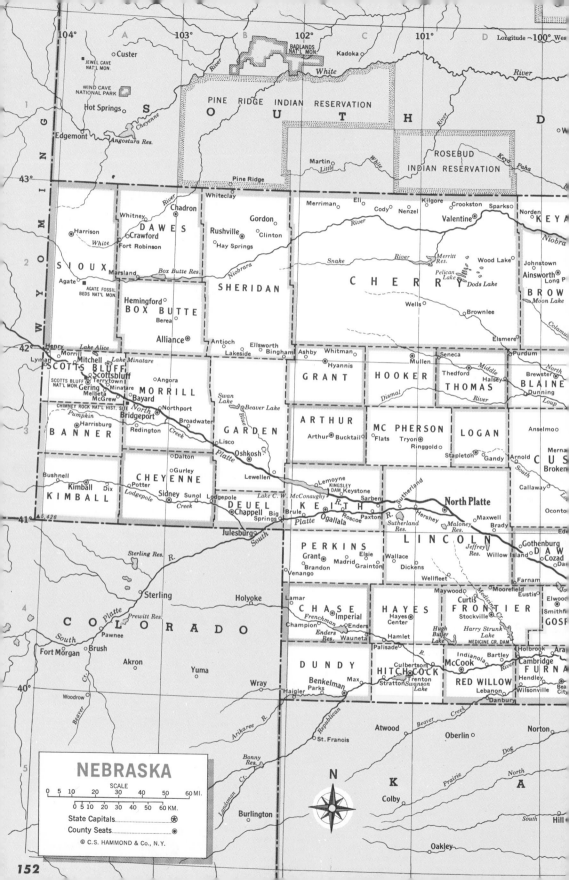

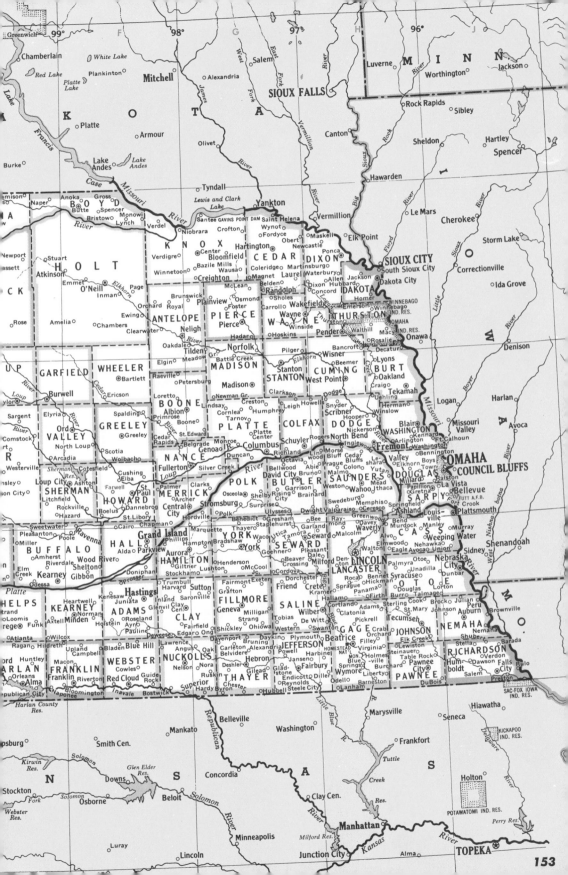

153

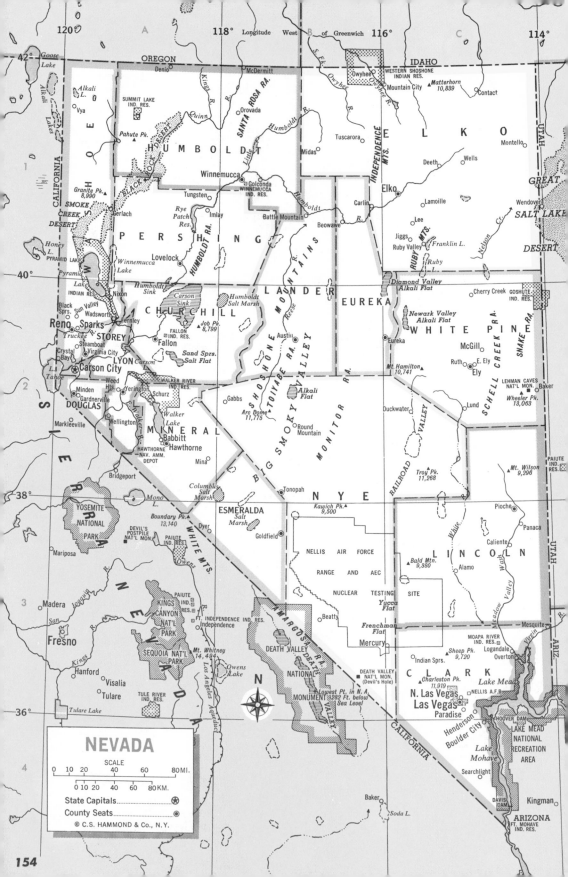

NEVADA

SCALE
0 10 20 40 60 80 MI.
0 10 20 40 60 80 KM.

State Capitals..............⊛
County Seats..............◉

© C.S. HAMMOND & Co., N.Y.

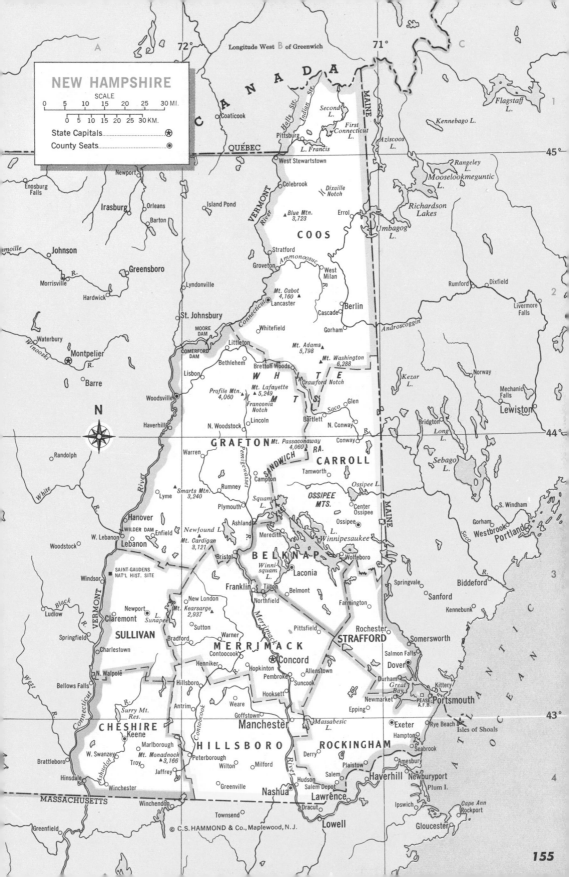

NEW HAMPSHIRE

SCALE

0 5 10 15 20 25 30 MI.

0 5 10 15 20 25 30 KM.

State Capitals..................⯨

County Seats....................◉

CANADA

Longitude West B of Greenwich

QUÉBEC

VERMONT

MAINE

MASSACHUSETTS

COOS

GRAFTON

CARROLL

BELKNAP

SULLIVAN

MERRIMACK

STRAFFORD

CHESHIRE

HILLSBORO

ROCKINGHAM

WHITE MTS.

OSSIPEE MTS.

SANDWICH RA.

Coaticook
Second L.
First Connecticut L.
Halls Str.
Indian Str.
Flagstaff L.
Kennebago L.
Pittsburg
L. Francis
West Stewartstown
Aziscoos L.
Rangeley L.
Mooselookmeguntic L.
Newport
Island Pond
Colebrook
Dixville Notch
Errol
Richardson Lakes
Enosburg Falls
Irasburg
Orleans
Barton
Blue Mtn. 3,723
Umbagog L.
Johnson
Greensboro
Lyndonville
Stratford
Umbagog L.
Rumford
Dixfield
Morrisville
Hardwick
Groveton
Ammonoosuc
West Milan
Berlin
Mt. Cabot 4,160
Lancaster
Waterbury
St. Johnsbury
Whitefield
Cascade
Gorham
Androscoggin
Livermore Falls
Norway
Kezar L.
Montpelier
Barre
MOORE DAM
Littleton
Bethlehem
Bretton Woods
Mt. Adams 5,798
Mt. Washington 6,288
COMERFORD DAM
Lisbon
Profile Mtn. 4,060
Mt. Lafayette 5,249
Crawford Notch
Mechanic Falls
Woodsville
Franconia Notch
Glen
Lewiston
Haverhill
N. Woodstock
Lincoln
Saco
Bartlett
N. Conway
Bridgton
Long L.
Randolph
Warren
Mt. Passaconaway 4,060
Conway
Sebago L.
Rumney
Tamworth
Smarts Mtn. 3,240
Campton
Lyme
Plymouth
Ossipee L.
Squam L.
Ashland
Center Ossipee
Hanover
WILDER DAM
Enfield
Newfound L.
Meredith
Ossipee
S. Windham
W. Lebanon
Mt. Cardigan 3,121
Bristol
L. Winnipesaukee
Gorham
Westbrook
Woodstock
Lebanon
Wolfeboro
Portland
SAINT-GAUDENS NAT'L HIST. SITE
Winnisquam L.
Windsor
Franklin
Laconia
Springvale
Biddeford
Ludlow
Newport
L. Sunapee
Mt. Kearsarge 2,937
Tilton
Belmont
Kennebunk
Claremont
New London
Northfield
Farmington
Springfield
Charlestown
Sutton
Warner
Pittsfield
Rochester
Somersworth
N. Walpole
Bradford
Hillsboro
Contoocook
Henniker
Hopkinton
Allenstown
Dover
Bellows Falls
Antrim
Weare
Pembroke
Suncook
Durham
Great Bay
Kittery
Surry Mt. Res.
Goffstown
Hooksett
Newmarket
PEASE A.F.B.
Portsmouth
KEENE
Marlborough
Manchester
Massabesic L.
Epping
Exeter
Rye Beach
Isles of Shoals
Brattleboro
W. Swanzey
Peterborough
Derry
Hampton
Troy
Mt. Monadnock 3,166
Wilton
Milford
Seabrook
Amesbury
Hinsdale
Jaffrey
Greenville
Plaistow
Salem
Haverhill
Newburyport
Winchester
Winchendon
Nashua
Hudson
Salem Depot
Plum I.
Townsend
Dracut
Lawrence
Ipswich
Cape Ann
Rockport
Greenfield
Lowell
Gloucester

Connecticut River
Pemigewasset
Merrimack River
Contoocook R.
Ashuelot R.
Black R.
White R.
Winooski R.
Lamoille R.
West R.

ATLANTIC OCEAN

N

© C.S. HAMMOND & Co., Maplewood, N.J.

155

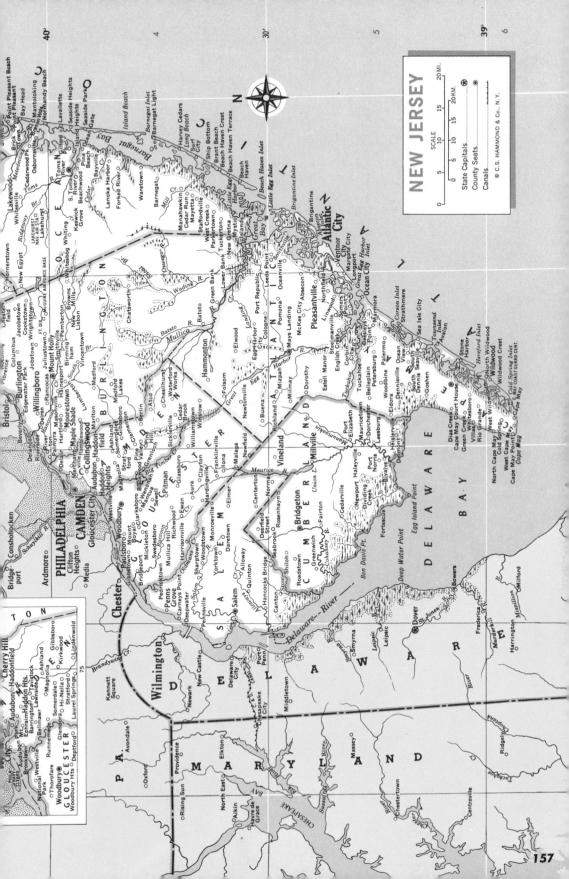

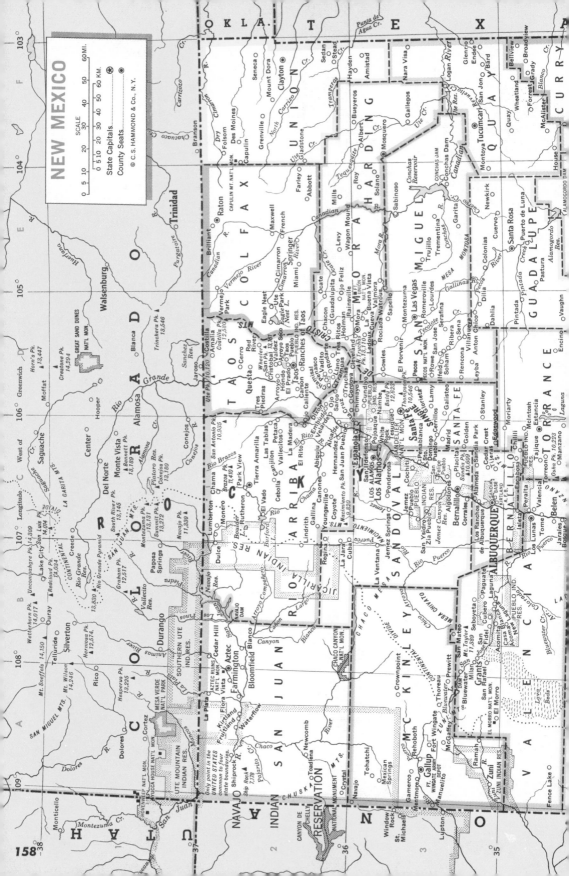

NEW MEXICO

SCALE
0 5 10 20 30 40 50 60 KM.
0 10 20 30 40 50 60 MI.

State Capitals.................⊛
County Seats..................⊙

158
-38

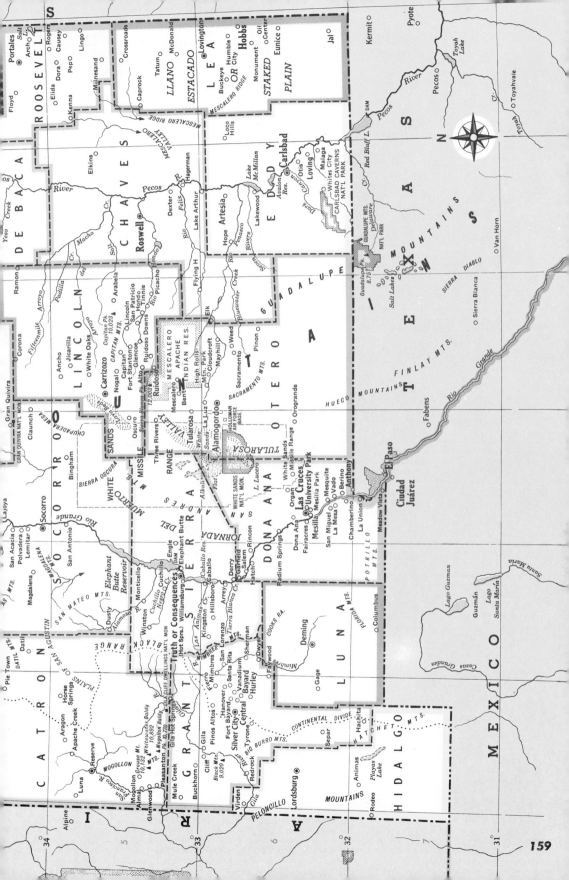

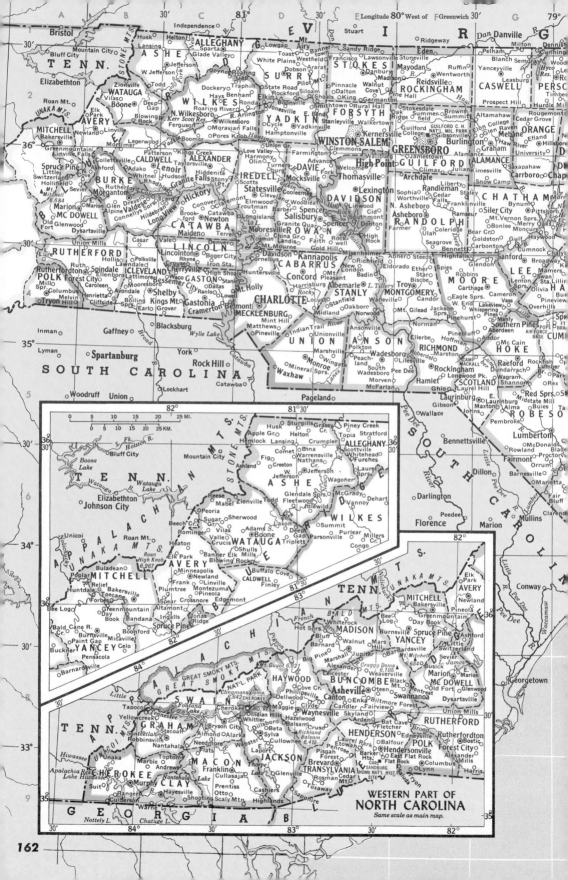

WESTERN PART OF
NORTH CAROLINA
Same scale as main map.

162

163

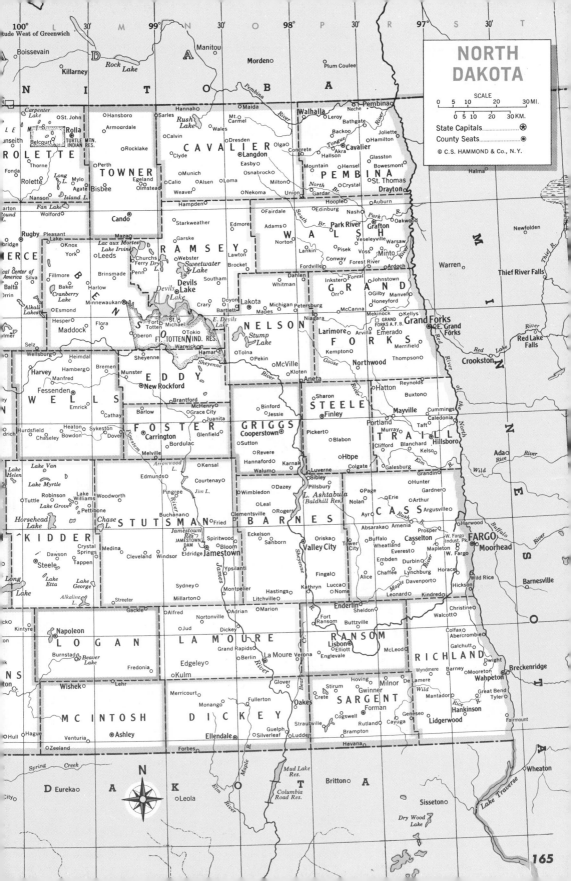

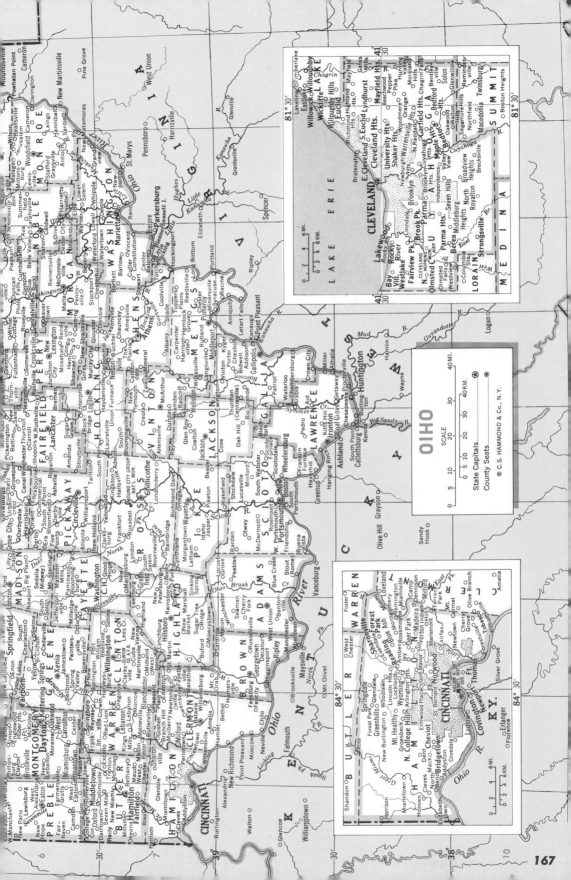

OKLAHOMA

SCALE

0 5 10   20   30   40 MI.

0 5 10   20   30   40 KM.

State Capitals .... ✹

County Seats .... ⊙

Ⓒ C.S. HAMMOND & CO., N.Y.

169

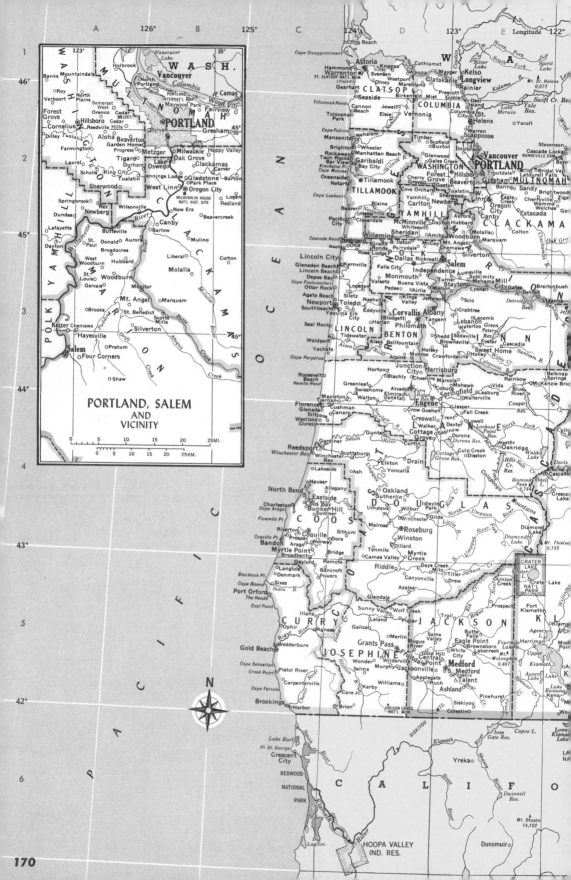

PORTLAND, SALEM
AND
VICINITY

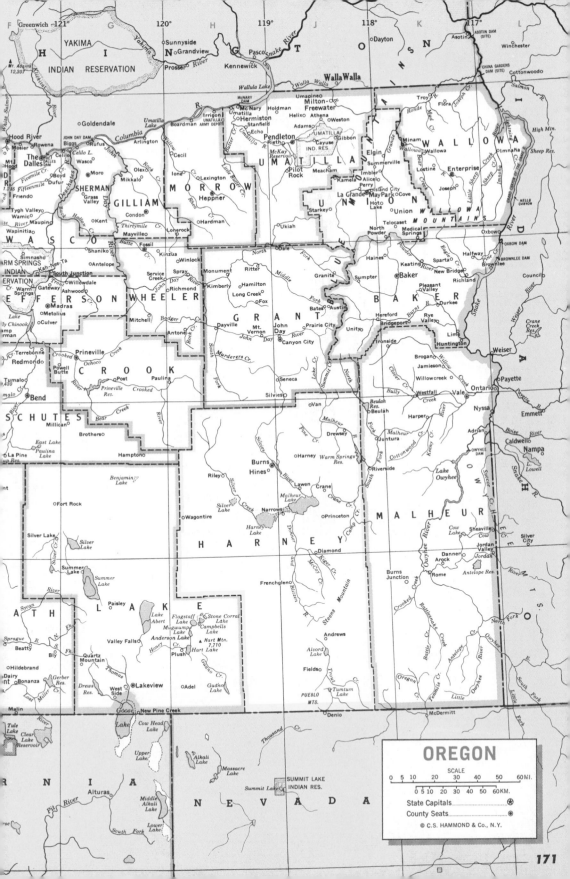

OREGON

SCALE

0 5 10 20 30 40 50 60 MI.

0 5 10 20 30 40 50 60 KM.

State Capitals .... ⊛

County Seats .... ◉

© C.S. HAMMOND & CO., N.Y.

171

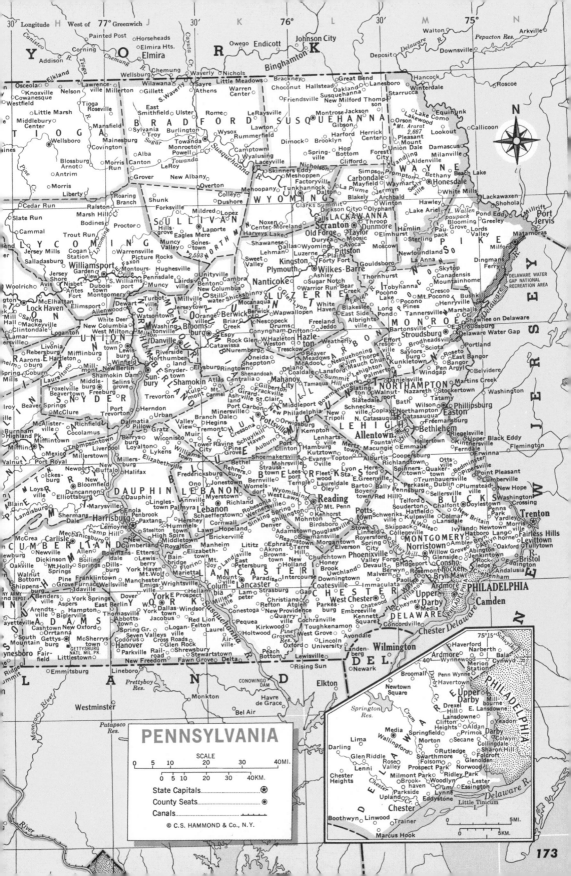

PENNSYLVANIA

SCALE
0 5 10 20 30 40MI.
0 5 10 20 30 40KM.

State Capitals .... ⊛
County Seats .... ◉
Canals

© C.S. HAMMOND & Co., N.Y.

173

SOUTH CAROLINA

SCALE

0 5 10   20   30   40MI.

0 5 10   20   30   40 KM.

State Capitals.............................⊛

County Seats................................◉

Canals...

© C.S. HAMMOND & Co., N.Y.

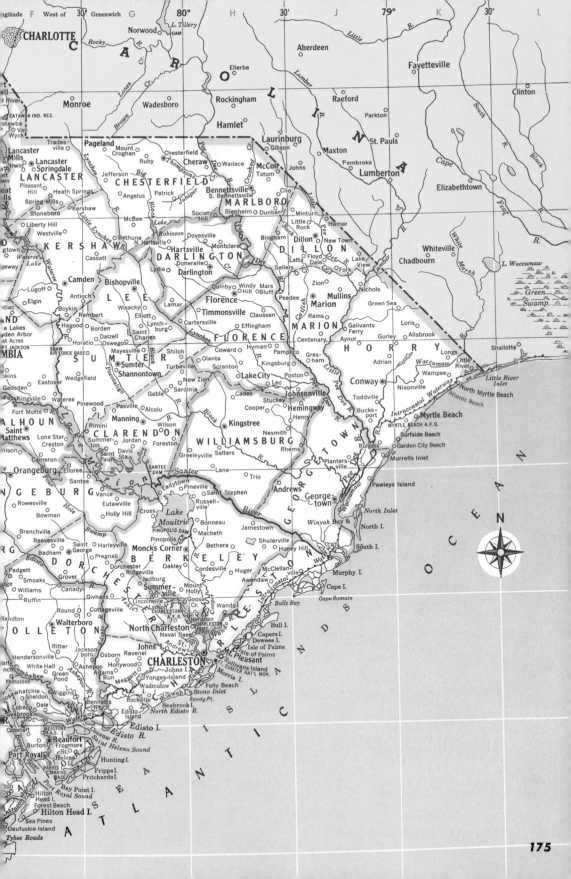

SOUTH DAKOTA

SCALE

0 5 10 20 40 60MI.

0 5 10 20 40 60KM.

State Capitals ⊛

County Seats ◉

© C.S. HAMMOND & Co., N.Y.

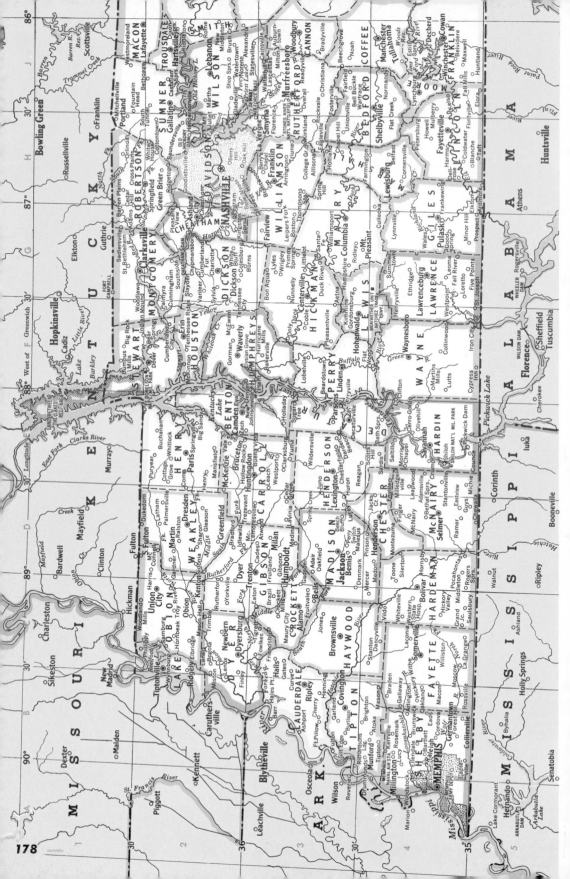

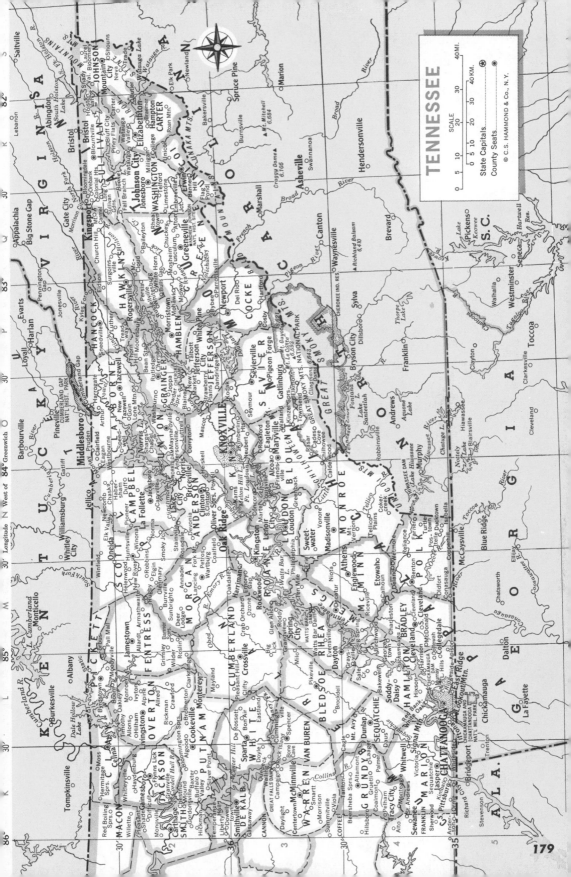

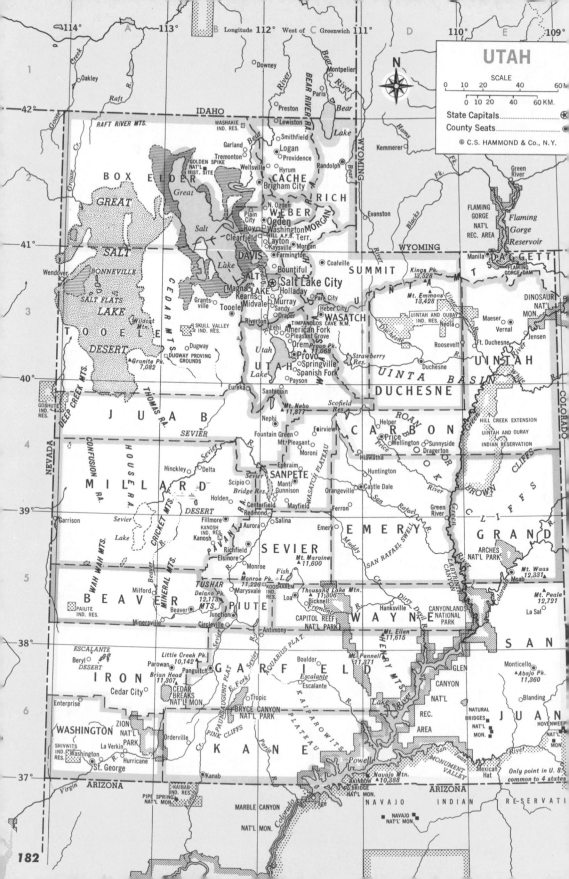

UTAH

SCALE

0 10 20   40   60 M.

0 10 20   40   60 KM.

State Capitals .... ⊛
County Seats .... ○

© C.S. HAMMOND & Co., N.Y.

114°   A   113°   B   Longitude 112°   West of C   Greenwich 111°   D   110°   E   109°

N

1

Oakley
Downey
Montpelier
Paris
Bear

IDAHO

2

Raft Creek R.
RAFT RIVER MTS.
Goose Creek Ct.
42°

Smithfield
Garland
Logan
Tremonton
Providence
Wellsville
Hyrum
Randolph
CACHE
Brigham City
RICH
Bear Lake
Preston
Lewiston

WYOMING

Kemmerer

BOX ELDER

GREAT

Great

Salt

N. Ogden
Plain City
Roy
Ogden
Washington
WEBER
MORGAN
Evanston
Clearfield
HILL A.F.B. Terr.
Layton
Kaysville
Morgan
Farmington
DAVIS
Coalville
SUMMIT
FLAMING
GORGE
NAT'L
REC. AREA

Flaming
Gorge
Reservoir

Manila
DAGGETT
FLAMING
GORGE DAM

3

41°
BONNEVILLE
Wendover
SALT
Lake
SALT
LAKE
Magna
Grants-
ville
Salt Lake City
Holladay
Park City
Midvale
Murray
Sandy
Draper
Heber City
WASATCH
Kings Pk.
13,528
Mt. Emmons
13,428
UINTAH AND OURAY
IND. RES.
Neola
Maeser
Vernal
Jensen
Ft. Duchesne
Roosevelt
Duchesne
DINOSAUR
NAT'L
MON.

LAKE
Tooele
SALT FLATS
SKULL VALLEY
IND. RES.
Wildcat
Mtn.
Riverton
Lehi
TIMPANOGOS CAVE N.M.
American Fork
Pleasant Grove
Orem
Provo Pk.
7,068
UINTAH
COLORADO

4

40°
TOOELE
DESERT
Dugway
DUGWAY PROVING
GROUNDS
Granite Pk.
7,082
Eureka
Santaquin
Provo
Springville
Spanish Fork
Payson
UTAH
Utah
Lake
Strawberry
Res.
UINTA
BASIN
HILL CREEK EXTENSION
UINTAH AND OURAY
INDIAN RESERVATION
GOSHUTE
IND.
RES.
DEEP CREEK MTS.
THOMAS RA.
CEDAR MTS.

NEVADA

DUCHESNE
Mt. Nebo
11,877
Scofield
Res.
Nephi
Fountain Green
Fairview
Helper
Price
Wellington
Sunnyside
Dragerton
CARBON
ROAN
BROWN
CLIFFS

5

39°
JUAB
SEVIER
Hinckley
Delta
CONFUSION RA.
HOUSE RA.
Sevier
Scipio
Ephraim
Manti
SANPETE
Mt. Pleasant
Moroni
Hiawatha
Huntington
Castle Dale
Orangeville
Ferron
Green
River
EMERY
GRAND
ARCHES
NAT'L PARK
Mt. Waas
12,331
Moab
WASATCH PLATEAU

MILLARD
Garrison
Holden
Centerfield
Gunnison
Mayfield
Emery
SAN RAFAEL SWELL
LABYRINTH CANYON
Mt. Peale
12,721
La Sal
Sevier
Lake
Fillmore
KANOSH
IND. RES.
Kanosh
Redmond
Salina
Aurora
Richfield
Elsinore
SEVIER
Mt. Marvine
11,600
Fish L.
Monroe
Thousand Lake Mtn.
11,306
Bicknell
Fremont
Loa
Hanksville
CANYONLANDS
NATIONAL
PARK
Colorado R.
DIRTY DEVIL
CRICKET MTS.
PAVANT RA.
DESERT
Bridge Res.

6

38°
BEAVER
PAIUTE
IND. RES.
Milford
Beaver
Junction
TUSHAR
MTS.
Delano Pk.
12,173
Monroe Pk.
11,226
Marysvale
KOOSHAREM
IND. RES.
PIUTE
Antimony
CAPITOL REEF
NAT'L PARK
Mt. Ellen
11,615
WAYNE
HENRY MTS.
GLEN
CANYON
NAT'L
REC.
AREA
NATURAL
BRIDGES
NAT'L
MON.
Monticello
Abajo Pk.
11,360
Blanding
JUAN
SAN
Minersville
Circleville
WAH WAH MTS.
MINERAL MTS.
Sevier R.

37°
ESCALANTE
DESERT
Beryl
Parowan
Little Creek Pk.
10,142
Brian Head
11,307
Panguitch
Tropic
GARFIELD
Boulder
Escalante
Mt. Pennell
11,371
AQUARIUS PLAT.
IRON
Enterprise
Cedar City
CEDAR
BREAKS
NAT'L MON.
BRYCE CANYON
NAT'L PARK
PAUNSAUGUNT FLAT
KAIPAROWITS PLATEAU
Lake
Powell
Mexican
Hat
HOVENWEEP
NAT'L
MON.
San Juan River
MONUMENT
VALLEY
Only point in U.S.
common to 4 states

WASHINGTON
ZION
NAT'L
PARK
SHIVWITS
IND. RES.
La Verkin
Washington
Hurricane
St. George
Orderville
PINK CLIFFS
Virgin R.
KANE
Kanab
Navajo Mtn.
10,388
RAINBOW
BRIDGE
NAT'L MON.
Page
Colorado R.
NAVAJO
INDIAN
RESERVATI

ARIZONA

KAIBAB
IND. RES.
PIPE SPRING
NAT'L MON.
MARBLE CANYON
NAT'L MON.
NAVAJO
NAT'L MON.

VERMONT

SCALE

0 5 10 15 20 25 MI.

0 5 10 15 20 25 KM.

State Capitals .... ⊛
County Seats .... ◉
Canals ....-.-.-.

© C.S. HAMMOND & Co., N.Y.

183

WESTERN PART OF VIRGINIA

Same scale as main map.

VIRGINIA

SCALE

0 5 10 20 30 40 MI.

0 5 10 20 30 40 KM.

National Capital..............................★

State Capitals..................................⊛

County Seats...................................◉

Canals..

© C.S. HAMMOND & Co., N.Y.

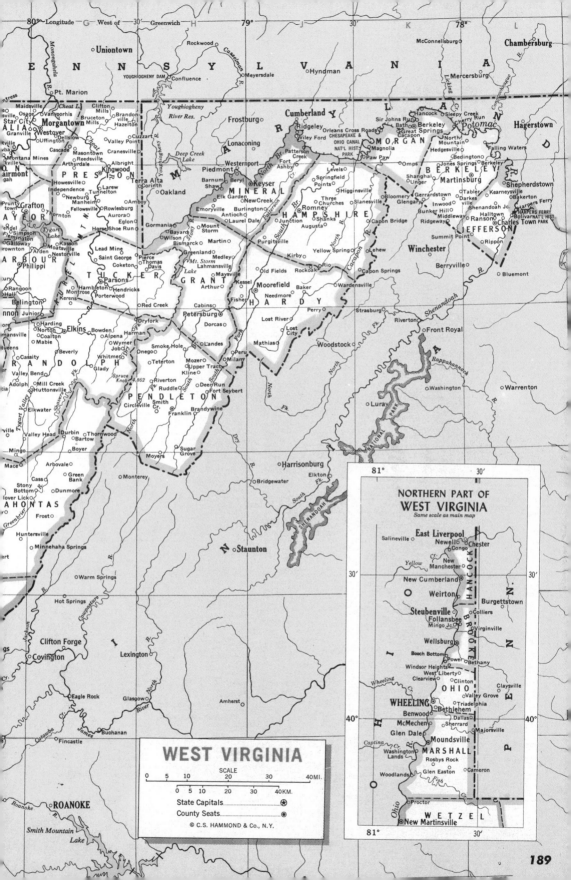

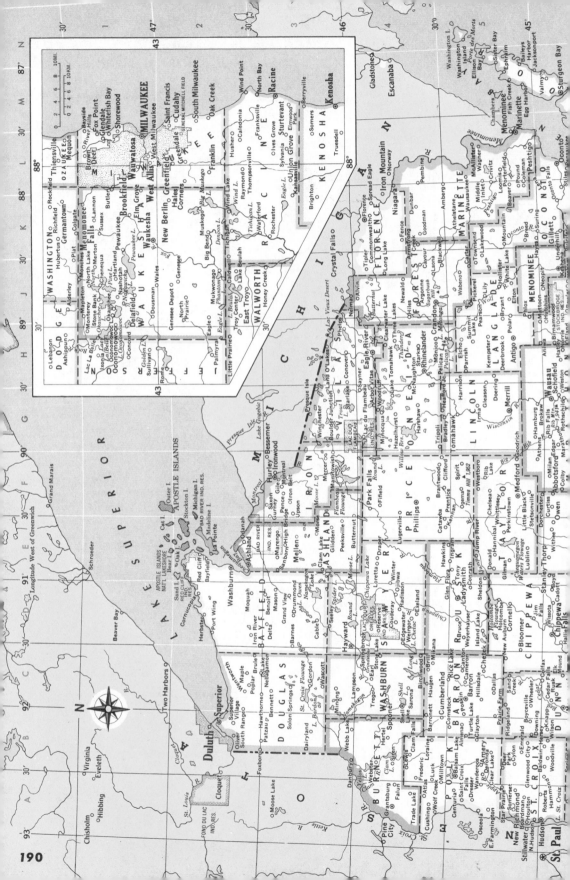

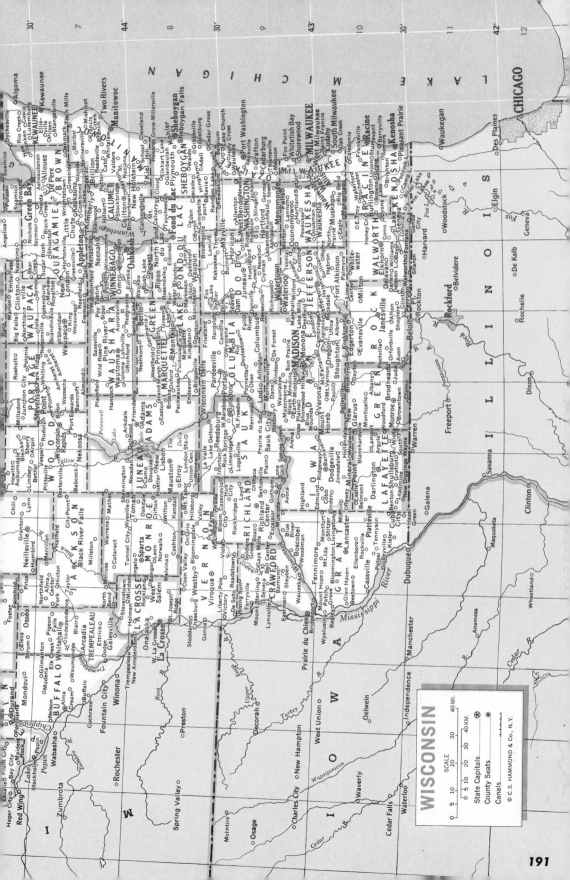

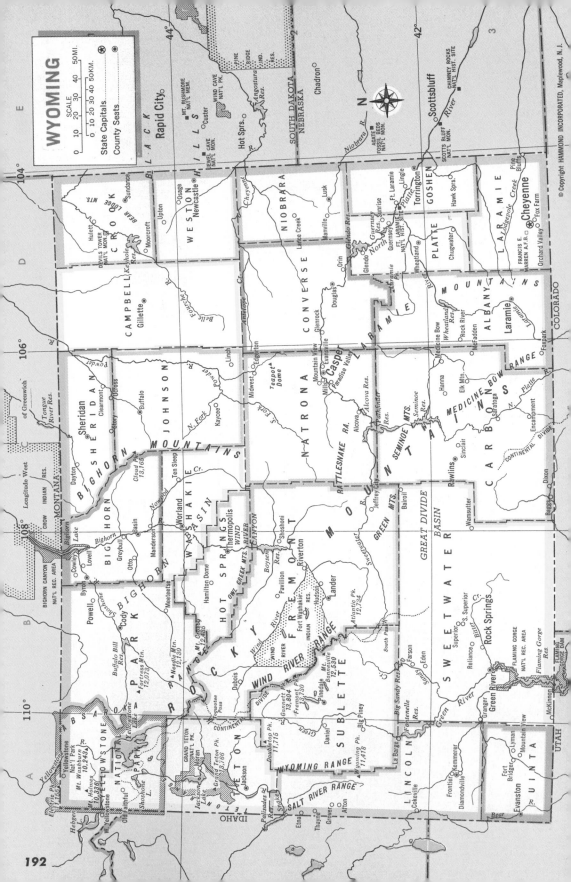

WYOMING

SCALE

10 20 30 40 50 MI.

0 10 20 30 40 50 KM.

State Capitals.......... ⊛ ◉

County Seats.......... ◉

GLOSSARY OF GEOGRAPHICAL TERMS

A. = Arabic Camb. = Cambodian Ch. = Chinese Dan. = Danish Du. = Dutch
Finn. = Finnish Fr. = French Ger. = German Ice. = Icelandic It. = Italian
Jap. = Japanese Mong. = Mongol Nor. = Norwegian Per. = Persian
Port.=Portuguese Russ.=Russian Sp.=Spanish Sw.=Swedish Turk. =Turkish

Å	Nor., Sw.	Stream
Abajo	Sp.	Lower
Ada, Adasi	Turk.	Island
Altiplano	Sp.	Plateau
Älv, Alf, Elf	Sw.	River
Arrecife	Sp.	Reef
Baai	Du.	Bay
Bahía	Sp.	Bay
Bahr	Arabic	Marsh, Lake, Sea, River
Baia	Port.	Bay
Baie	Fr.	Bay, Gulf
Bañados	Sp.	Marshes
Barra	Sp.	Reef
Belt	Ger.	Strait
Ben	Gaelic	Mountain
Berg	Ger., Du.	Mountain
Bir	Arabic	Well
Boca	Sp.	Gulf, Inlet
Bolshoi, Bolshaya	Russ.	Big
Bolsón	Sp.	Depression
Bong	Korean	Mountain
Bucht	Ger.	Bay
Bugt	Dan.	Bay
Bukhta	Russ.	Bay
Burnu, Burun	Turk.	Cape, Point
By	Dan., Nor., Sw.	Town
Cabo	Port., Sp.	Cape
Campos	Port.	Plains
Canal	Port., Sp.	Channel
Cap, Capo	Fr., It.	Cape
Catarátas	Sp.	Falls
Central, Centrale	Fr., It.	Middle
Cerrito, Cerro	Sp.	Hill
Ciénaga	Sp.	Swamp
Ciudad	Sp.	City
Col	Fr.	Pass
Cordillera	Sp.	Mt. Range
Côte	Fr.	Coast
Cuchilla	Sp.	Mt. Range
Dağ, Dagh	Turk.	Mountain
Dağlari	Turk.	Mt. Range
Dal	Nor., Sw.	Valley
Darya	Per.	Salt Lake
Dasht	Per.	Desert, Plain
Deniz, Denizi	Turk.	Sea, Lake
Desierto	Sp.	Desert
Eiland	Du.	Island
Elv	Dan., Nor.	River
Emi	Berber	Mountain
Erg	Arabic	Dune, Desert
Est, Este	Fr., Port., Sp.	East
Estrecho, Estreito	Sp., Port.	Strait
Étang	Fr.	Pond, Lagoon, Lake
Fjørd	Dan., Nor.	Fiord
Fleuve	Fr.	River
Gebel	Arabic	Mountain
Gebirge	Ger.	Mt. Range
Gobi	Mongol	Desert
Gol	Mongol, Turk.	Lake, Stream
Golf	Ger., Du.	Gulf
Golfe	Fr.	Gulf
Golfo	Sp., It., Port.	Gulf
Gölü	Turk.	Lake
Gora	Russ.	Mountain
Grand, Grande	Fr., Sp.	Big
Groot	Du.	Big
Gross	Ger.	Big
Grosso	It., Port.	Big
Guba	Russ.	Bay, Gulf
Gunto	Jap.	Archipelago
Gunung	Malay	Mountain
Higashi, Higasi	Jap.	East
Ho	Ch.	River
Hoek	Du.	Cape
Holm	Dan., Nor., Sw.	Island
Hu	Ch.	Lake
Hwang	Ch.	Yellow
Île	Fr.	Island
Insel	Ger.	Island
Irmak	Turk.	River
Isla	Sp.	Island
Isola	Sp.	Island
Jabal, Jebel	Arabic	Mountains
Järvi	Finn.	Lake
Jaure	Sw.	Lake
Jezira	Arabic	Island
Jima	Jap.	Island
Joki	Finn.	River
Kaap	Du.	Cape
Kabir, Kebir	Arabic	Big
Kanal	Russ., Ger.	Canal, Channel
Kap, Kapp	Nor., Sw., Ice.	Cape
Kawa	Jap.	River
Khrebet	Russ.	Mt. Range
Kiang	Ch.	River
Kita	Jap.	North
Klein	Du., Ger.	Small
Kô	Jap.	Lake
Ko	Thai.	Island
Koh	Camb., Khmer	Island
Köping	Sw.	Borough
Körfez, Körfezi	Turk.	Gulf
Kuh	Per.	Mountain

Kul..................... Sinkiang Turki...Lake
Kum..................... Turk. ....Desert
Lac..................... Fr. ....Lake
Lago.................... Port., Sp., It. ..Lake
Lagôa................... Port. ....Lagoon
Laguna.................. Sp. ....Lagoon
Lagune..................Fr. ....Lagoon
Llanos..................Sp. ....Plains
Mar..................... Sp., Port. ....Sea
Mare..................... It. ....Sea
Meer.................... Du. ....Lake
Meer.................... Ger. ....Sea
Mer..................... Fr. ....Sea
Meseta................. Sp. ....Plateau
Minami................. Jap. ....Southern
Misaki..................Jap. ....Cape
Mittel.................. Ger. ....Middle
Mont.................... Fr. ....Mountain
Montagne............ Fr. ....Mountain
Montaña............... Sp. ....Mountains
Monte................. Sp., It., Port.
                     Mountain
More.................... Russ. ....Sea
Muong................. Siamese ....Town
Mys..................... Russ. ....Cape
Nam.................... Burm., Lao......River
Nevado.............. Sp. .....Snow covered
                     peak
Nieder................. Ger. ....Lower
Nishi, Nisi..........Jap. ....West
Nizhni,
   Nizhnyaya....... Russ. ....Lower
Nor..................... Mong. ....Lake
Nord.................... Fr., Ger. ....North
Norte.................. Sp., It., Port. North
Nos..................... Russ. ....Cape
Novi, Novaya....... Russ. ....New
Nusa................... Malay ....Island
O....................... Jap. ....Big
Ö....................... Nor., Sw ....Island
Ober................... Ger. ....Upper
Occidental,
   Occidentale......Sp., It. ....Western
Oeste.................. Port. ....West
Oriental.............. Sp., Fr. ....Eastern
Orientale............It. ....Eastern
Ost..................... Ger. ....East
Ostrov................. Russ. ....Island
Ouest.................. Fr. ....West
öy...................... Nor. ....Island
Ozero................. Russ. ....Lake
Pampa................. Sp. ....Plain
Paso................... Sp. ....Pass
Passo................. It., Port. ....Pass
Pequeño..............Sp. ....Small
Peski..................Russ. ....Desert
Petit................... Fr. ....Small
Pic..................... Fr. ....Mountain
Pico................... Port.,Sp. ..Mountain,
                     Peak
Pik......................Russ. ....Peak
Pointe.................Fr. ....Point
Poluostrov...........Russ. ....Peninsula

Ponta................... Port. ....Point
Presa.................. Sp. ....Reservoir
Proliv.................. Russ. ....Strait
Pulou, Pulo......... Malay ....Island
Punta.................. Sp., It., Port.
                     Point
Ras..................... Arabic ....Cape
Ría..................... Sp. ....Estuary
Río..................... Sp. ....River
Rivier, Rivière..... Du., Fr. ....River
Rud.................... Per. ....River
Saki.................... Jap. ....Cape
Salto.................. Sp., Port. ....Falls
San..................... Ch., Jap., Korean
                     Hill
See..................... Ger. ....Sea, Lake
Selvas................. Sp., Port. ......Forest
Serra.................. Port. ....Mts.
Serranía.............. Sp. ....Mts.
Severni,
   Servernaya....... Russ. ....North
Shan.................. Ch., Jap. ....Hill, Mts.
Shima................. Jap. ....Island
Shoto................. Jap. ....Islands
Sierra................. Sp. ....Mountains
Sjö..................... Nor., Sw. Lake, Sea
Spitze................. Ger. ....Mt. Peak
Sredni,
   Srednyaya........ Russ. ....Middle
Stad.................... Dan., Nor., Sw.
                     City
Stari, Staraya..... Russ. ....Old
Su...................... Turk. ....River
Sud, Süd.............. Sp., Fr., Ger. ..South
Sul..................... Port. ....South
Sungei................ Malay ....River
Sur..................... Sp. ....South
Tagh.................. Turk. ....Mt. Range
Tal..................... Ger. ....Valley
Tandjong,
   Tanjung........... Malay.....Cape, Point
Tso..................... Tibetan ....Lake
Val..................... Fr. ....Valley
Velho.................. Port. ....Old
Verkhni.............. Russ. ....Upper
Vesi................... Finn. ....Lake
Vishni,
   Vishnyaya........ Russ. ....High
Vostochni,
   Vostochnaya... Russ. ..East, Eastern
Wadi................... Arabic........Dry River
Wald.................. Ger. ....Forest
Wan................... Jap. ....Bay
Yama.................. Jap. ....Mountain
Yug, Yuzhni,
   Yuzhnaya........ Russ.
                South, Southern
Zaliv.................. Russ. ....Bay, Gulf
Zapadni,
   Zapadnaya....... Russ. ....Western
Zee..................... Du. ....Sea
Zemlya................Russ. ....Land
Zuid................... Du. ....South

WORLD
STATISTICAL TABLES
and
DISTRIBUTION MAPS

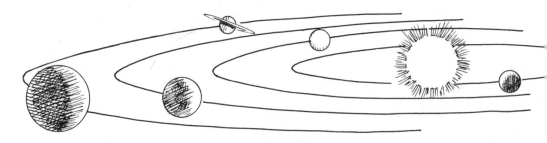

Elements of the Solar System

PLANETS	DISTANCE FROM SUN IN MILES		PERIOD OF REVOLUTION AROUND SUN IN DAYS	EQUATORIAL DIAMETER IN MILES	DENSITY (EARTH=1)
	MAXIMUM	MINIMUM			
Sun . .	......	......	......	864,000	0.26
Mercury .	43,404,000	28,599,000	87.97	3,100	0.68
Venus . .	67,730,000	66,814,000	224.70	7,600	0.94
Earth . .	94,560,000	91,446,000	365.26	7,927	1.00
Mars . .	154,936,000	128,476,000	687	4,200	0.71
Jupiter .	507,289,000	460,465,000	4,332.59	88,698	0.24
Saturn .	936,637,000	837,655,000	10,759.20	75,060	0.12
Uranus .	1,868,930,000	1,700,745,000	30,685.93	29,200	0.25
Neptune .	2,820,610,000	2,773,510,000	60,187.64	27,700	0.41
Pluto . .	4,585,000,000	2,753,000,000	90,470.23	3,725	approx. 0.7

Dimensions of the Earth

Superficial area	192,426,000	sq. miles
Land surface	52,426,000	" "
North America	9,363,000	" "
South America	6,886,000	" "
Europe	4,056,000	" "
Asia	17,129,000	" "
Africa	11,707,000	" "
Australia	2,942,000	" "
Water surface	140,000,000	" "
Atlantic Ocean	31,862,000	" "
Pacific Ocean	64,186,000	" "
Indian Ocean	28,350,000	" "
Arctic Ocean	5,427,000	" "
Equatorial circumference	24,894	miles
Meridional circumference	24,811	"
Equatorial diameter	7,926.677	"
Polar diameter	7,899.988	"
Equatorial radius	3,963.34	"
Polar radius	3,949.99	"
Volume of the Earth	260,000,000,000	cubic miles
Mass, or weight	5,890,000,000,000,000,000,000	tons
Mean distance from the Sun	93,003,000	miles

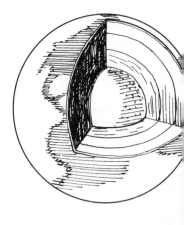

The Moon, the only satellite of the Earth, from which her mean distance is 238,857 miles, occupies an average period, in her revolution round the earth, of 29 days, 12 hours, 44 minutes, 3 seconds; her diameter is 2,160 miles, and her mean density 0.60.

Principal Lakes and Inland Seas

	AREA IN SQUARE MILES		AREA IN SQUARE MILES
Caspian Sea	143,550	Lake Bangweulu Approx.	1,000
Lake Superior	31,800	Vattern	733
Lake Victoria	26,828	Dead Sea	405
Aral Sea	25,300	Lake Balaton	266
Lake Huron	23,000	Lake Geneva	225
Lake Michigan	22,400	Lake of Constance	208
Lake Tanganyika	12,700	Lough Neagh	153
Great Bear Lake	12,275	Lake Garda	143
Lake Baykal	11,780	Lake Neuchatel	83
Lake Nyasa	11,430	Lake Maggiore	82
Great Slave Lake	10,980	Lough Corrib	71
Lake Erie	9,910	Lake Como	56
Lake Winnipeg	9,464	Lake of Lucerne	44.5
Lake Ontario	7,600	Lake of Zurich	34
Lake Ladoga	6,835		
Lake Balkhash	6,720		
Lake Chad	5,300		
Lake Onega	3,710		
Lake Titicaca	3,200		
Lake Athabasca	3,120		
Lake Nicaragua	3,100		
Reindeer Lake	2,467		
Issyk-Kul	2,358		
Vanern	2,156		
Lake Albert	2,075		
Lake Urmia	1,815		
Great Salt Lake	1,500		
Lake Van	1,453		
Lake Peipus	1,400		
Lake Tana	1,219		

Oceans and Seas of the World

	AREA IN SQ. MILES	GREATEST DEPTH IN FEET	VOLUME IN CUBIC MILES
Pacific Ocean	64,186,000	36,198	167,025,000
Atlantic Ocean	31,862,000	28,374	77,580,000
Indian Ocean	28,350,000	25,344	68,213,000
Arctic Ocean	5,427,000	17,880	3,026,000
Caribbean Sea	970,000	24,720	2,298,400
Mediterranean Sea	969,000	16,896	1,019,400
South China Sea	895,000	15,000	......
Bering Sea	875,000	15,800	788,500
Sea of Okhotsk	590,000	11,070	454,700
East China Sea	482,000	9,500	52,700
Sea of Japan	389,000	12,280	383,200
Hudson Bay	317,500	846	37,590
North Sea	222,000	2,200	12,890
Black Sea	185,000	7,365	......
Red Sea	169,000	7,200	53,700
Baltic Sea	163,000	1,506	5,360

Longest Rivers of the World

	LENGTH IN MILES		LENGTH IN MILES		LENGTH IN MILES
Nile, Africa	4,145	Amur, Asia	2,900	Indus, Asia	1,800
Amazon, S.A.	3,900	Lena, U.S.S.R.	2,650	Brahmaputra, Asia	1,800
Mississippi-Missouri, U.S.A.	3,741	Mackenzie, Canada	2,635	Salween, Asia	1,770
Yangtze, China	3,430	Mekong, Asia	2,600	Danube, Europe	1,760
Ob-Irtysh, U.S.S.R.	3,362	Niger, Africa	2,600	Euphrates, Asia	1,700
Yenisey-Angara, U.S.S.R.	3,100	Parana, S.A.	2,450	Orinoco, S.A.	1,700
Hwang (Yellow), China	2,903	Murray-Darling, Australia	2,371	Zambezi, Africa	1,700
Congo, Africa	2,900	Volga, U.S.S.R.	2,292	Syr-Dar'ya, U.S.S.R.	1,660
		St. Lawrence, Canada-U.S.A.	2,100	Saskatchewan, Canada	1,660
		Madeira, S.A.	2,013	Paraguay, S.A.	1,584
		Purus, S.A.	1,995	Ural, U.S.S.R.	1,575
		Yukon, Alaska-Canada	1,979	Ganges, India	1,540
		Rio Grande, U.S.A.-Mexico	1,885	Amu-Dar'ya, U.S.S.R.	1,500
		São Francisco, S.A.	1,811	Arkansas, U.S.A.	1,450
				Colorado, U.S.A.-Mexico	1,450
				Irrawaddy, Burma	1,425
				Dnieper, U.S.S.R.	1,420
				Rio Negro, S.A.	1,400
				Ohio, U.S.A.	1,306
				Orange, Africa	1,300
				Red, Texas, U.S.A.	1,222
				Don, U.S.S.R.	1,222
				Columbia, U.S.A.-Canada	1,214
				Tigris, Asia	1,181
				Snake, U.S.A.	1,038
				Uruguay, S.A.	1,000
				Magdalena, Colombia	1,000
				Platte-N. Platte, U.S.A.	990
				Canadian, U.S.A.	906
				Colorado, Texas, U.S.A.	894
				Tennessee, U.S.A.	869
				Dniester, U.S.S.R.	852

Great Ship Canals

	LENGTH IN MILES	DEPTH IN FEET
Baltic-White Sea, U.S.S.R.	141	....
Suez, Egypt	100.76	34
Albert, Belgium	81	16.5
Moscow-Volga, U.S.S.R.	80	18
Kiel, Germany	61	37
Göta, Sweden	54	10
Panama, Canal Zone, U.S.A.	50.72	41
Houston Ship, U.S.A.	50	36
Amsterdam-Rhine, Netherlands	45	41
Beaumont-Port Arthur, U.S.A.	40	32
Manchester Ship, England	35.5	28
Chicago Sanitary and Ship, U.S.A.	30	22
Welland, Canada	27.6	30
Juliana, Netherlands	21	11.8
Chesapeake and Delaware, U.S.A.	19	27
Cape Cod, U.S.A.	13	25
Lake Washington, U.S.A.	8	30
Corinth, Greece	4	26.25
Sault Ste. Marie, U.S.A.	1.6	24.5
Sault Ste. Marie, Canada	1.4	18.25

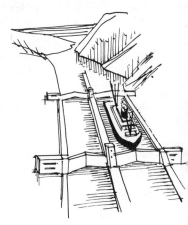

	FEET		FEET
Mt. Everest, Nepal-Tibet	29,028	Mt. Ararat, Turkey	16,946
Mt. Godwin Austen (K2), India	28,250	Vinson Massif, Antarctica	16,864
Kanchenjunga, Nepal-India	28,208	Margherita (Ruwenzori),	
Dhaulagiri, Nepal	26,810	Africa	16,795
Nanga Parbat, India	26,660	Kazbek, U.S.S.R.	16,512
Annapurna, Nepal	26,504	Djaja, Indonesia	16,503
Nanda Devi, India	25,645	Mont Blanc, France	15,771
Mt. Kamet, India	25,447	Klyuchevskaya Sopka, U.S.S.R.	15,584
Gurla Mandhata, Tibet	25,355	Monte Rosa, Italy-Switzerland	15,203
Tirich Mir, Pakistan	25,230	Ras Dashan, Ethiopia	15,157
Minya Konka, China	24,902	Matterhorn, Switzerland	14,688
Muztagh Ata, China	24,757	Mt. Whitney, California	14,494
Mt. Communism, U.S.S.R.	24,599	Mt. Elbert, Colorado	14,433
Pobeda Peak, U.S.S.R.	24,406	Mt. Rainier, Washington	14,410
Chomo Lhari, India-Tibet	23,997	Mt. Shasta, California	14,162
Muztagh, China	23,891	Pikes Peak, Colorado	14,110
Aconcagua, Argentina	22,831	Finsteraarhorn, Switzerland	14,022
Ojos del Salado, Argentina-		Mauna Kea, Hawaii	13,796
Chile	22,572	Mauna Loa, Hawaii	13,680
Tupungato, Chile-Argentina	22,310	Jungfrau, Switzerland	13,642
Cerro Mercedario, Argentina	22,211	Cameroon, Cameroon	13,350
Huascarán, Peru	22,205	Gran Paradiso, Italy	13,323
Llullaillaco Volcano, Chile	22,057	Mt. Robson, British Columbia	12,972
Ancohuma, Bolivia	21,489	Grossglockner, Austria	12,461
Illampu, Bolivia	21,276	Fuji, Japan	12,389
Chimborazo, Ecuador	20,561	Mt. Cook, New Zealand	12,349
Mt. McKinley, Alaska	20,320	Semeru, Indonesia	12,060
Mt. Logan, Yukon	19,850	Mulhacén, Spain	11,411
Cotopaxi, Ecuador	19,347	Mt. Etna, Italy	11,053
Kilimanjaro, Tanzania	19,340	Lassen Peak, California	10,457
El Misti, Peru	19,101	Mt. Kosciusko, Australia	7,316
Citlaltépetl, Mexico	18,855	Mt. Mitchell, No. Carolina	6,684
Mt. Elbrus, U.S.S.R.	18,510		
Mt. Demavend, Iran	18,376		
Mt. St. Elias, Alaska-Yukon	18,008		
Vilcanota, Peru	17,999		
Popocatépetl, Mexico	17,887		
Dikh-Tau, U.S.S.R.	17,070		
Mt. Kenya, Kenya	17,058		

Principal Islands of the World

	AREA IN SQUARE MILES		AREA IN SQUARE MILES		AREA IN SQUARE MILES
Greenland	840,000	Vancouver	12,408	Zanzibar	640
New Guinea	305,000	Timor	11,527	Oahu	604
Borneo	290,000	Sicily	9,926	Guadeloupe	583
Baffin	265,949	Somerset	9,370	Ahvenanmaa (Aland Is.)	564
Madagascar	226,400	Sardinia	9,301	Kauai	551
Sumatra	164,000	New Caledonia	7,335	Shetland Islands	551
Philippines	115,830	Shikoku	7,244	Rhodes	542
New Zealand: North and South Islands	103,736	Fiji Islands	7,015	Martinique	425
Honshu	88,946	New Hebrides	5,700	Tahiti	402
England-Scotland-Wales	88,764	Kuril Islands	5,700	Pemba	380
Victoria	83,896	Falkland Islands	4,618	Orkney Islands	376
Ellesmere	75,767	Bahama Islands	4,404	Madeira Islands	308
Celebes	72,986	Jamaica	4,232	Dominica	290
Java	48,842	Hawaii	4,036	Tonga	270
Newfoundland	43,359	Cape Breton	3,970	Caroline Islands	267
Cuba	43,036	New Ireland	3,800	Molokai	261
Luzon	41,765	Cyprus	3,473	St. Lucia	238
Iceland	39,768	Puerto Rico	3,435	Corfu	229
Mindanao	36,537	Corsica	3,368	Bornholm	227
Ireland	32,059	Crete	3,218	Isle of Man	227
Novaya Zemlya	31,900	Galápagos Islands	3,042	Singapore	226
Hokkaido	30,305	Hebrides	3,000	Guam	212
Molucca Islands	30,168	Wrangel	2,819	Isle Royale	210
Hispaniola	29,398	Canary Islands	2,808	Virgin Islands	192
Sakhalin	28,215	Kerguélen	2,700	Curaçao	182
Tasmania	26,215	Prince Edward	2,184	Barbados	166
Ceylon	25,332	Trinidad and Tobago	1,980	St. Vincent	150
Svalbard (Spitsbergen)	23,958	Balearic Islands	1,936	Isle of Wight	147
Banks	23,230	Madura	1,752	Lanai	141
Devon	20,861	South Georgia	1,600	Grenada	133
Bismarck Arch.	18,770	Cape Verde Islands	1,557	Maltese Islands	122
Tierra del Fuego	18,500	Long I., New York	1,401	Tobago	116
Melville	16,369	Socotra	1,400	Seychelles	109
Kyushu	16,200	Gotland	1,225	Martha's Vineyard	109
Southampton	15,700	Isle of Pines	1,180	Channel Islands	75
Solomon Islands	15,580	Samoa	1,173	Nantucket	57
New Britain	14,098	Réunion	969	St. Helena	47
Taiwan (Formosa)	13,948	Azores	893	Ascension	34
Hainan	13,000	Fernando Po	786	Hong Kong	29
Prince of Wales	12,830	Tenerife	785	Manhattan, New York	22
		Maui	728	Bermudas	20
		Mauritius	709		

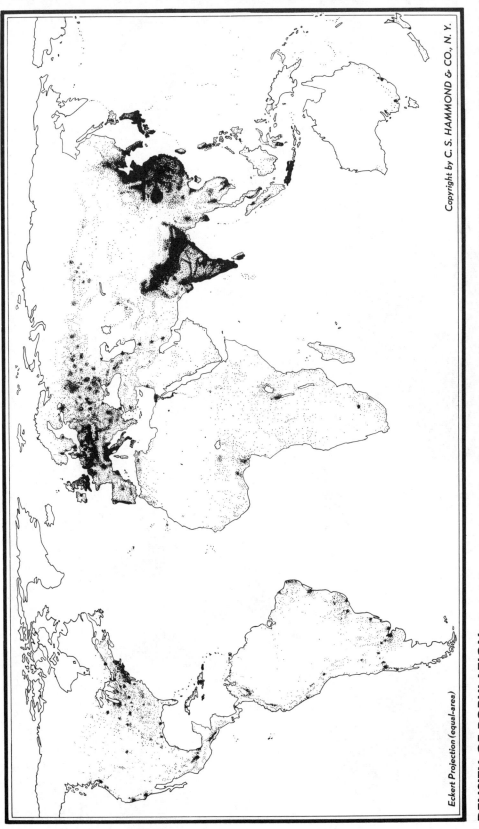

Eckert Projection (equal-area)

Copyright by C. S. HAMMOND & CO., N. Y.

DENSITY OF POPULATION. One of the most outstanding facts of human geography is the extremely uneven distribution of people over the Earth. One-half of the Earth's surface has less than 3 people per square mile, while in the lowlands of India, China, Java and Japan rural density reaches the incredible congestion of 2000-3000 per square mile. Three-fourths of the Earth's population live in four relatively small areas; Northeastern United States, North-Central Europe, India and the Far East.

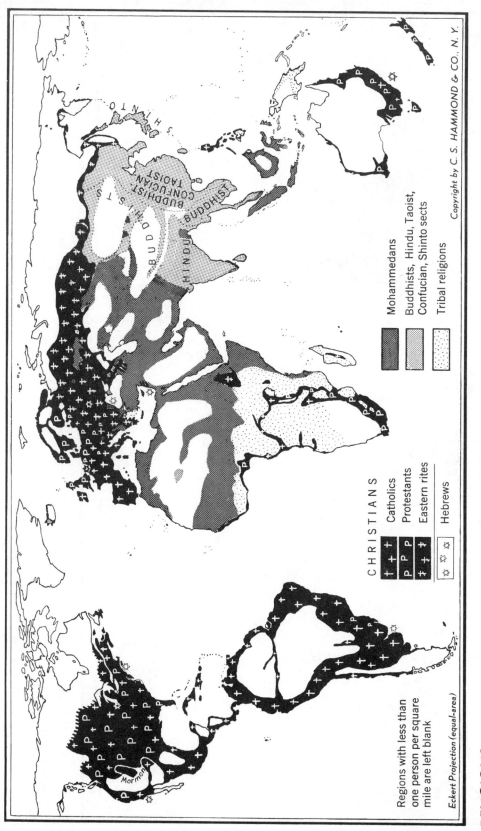

RELIGIONS. *Most people of the Earth belong to four major religions: Christians, Mohammedans, Brahmans, Buddhists and derivatives. The Eastern rites of the Christians include the Greek Orthodox, Greek Catholic, Armenian, Syrian, Coptic and more minor churches. The lamaism of Tibet and Mongolia differs a great deal from Buddhism in Burma and Thailand. In the religion of China the teachings of Buddha, Confucius and Tao are mixed, while in Shinto a great deal of ancestor and emperor worship is added. About 11 million Hebrews live scattered over the globe, chiefly in cities and in the state of Israel.*

CHRISTIANS

Catholics

Protestants

Eastern rites

Hebrews

Mohammedans

Buddhists, Hindu, Taoist, Confucian, Shinto sects

Tribal religions

Regions with less than one person per square mile are left blank

Eckert Projection (equal-area)

Copyright by C. S. HAMMOND & CO., N. Y.

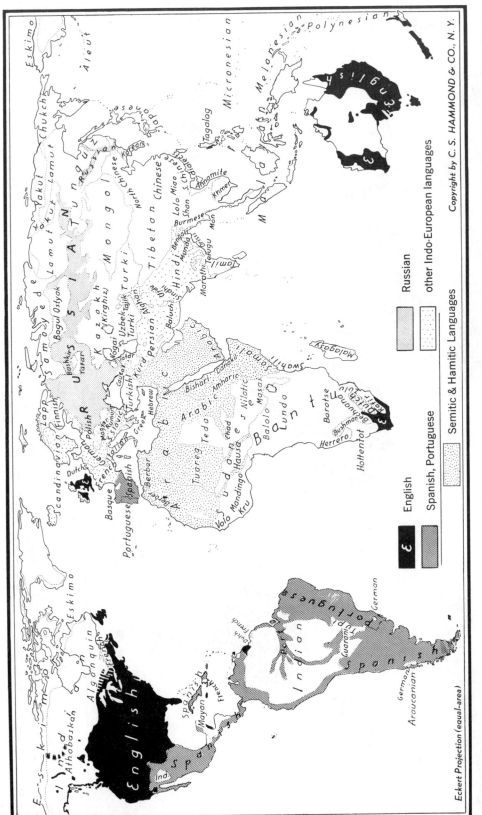

LANGUAGES. Several hundred different languages are spoken in the World, and in many places two or more languages are spoken, sometimes by the same people. The map above shows the dominant languages in each locality. English, French, Spanish, Russian, Arabic and Swahili are spoken by many people as a second language for commerce or travel.

Copyright by C. S. HAMMOND & CO., N. Y.

Eckert Projection (equal-area)

Ɛ English

Spanish, Portuguese

Russian

other Indo-European languages

Semitic & Hamitic Languages

203

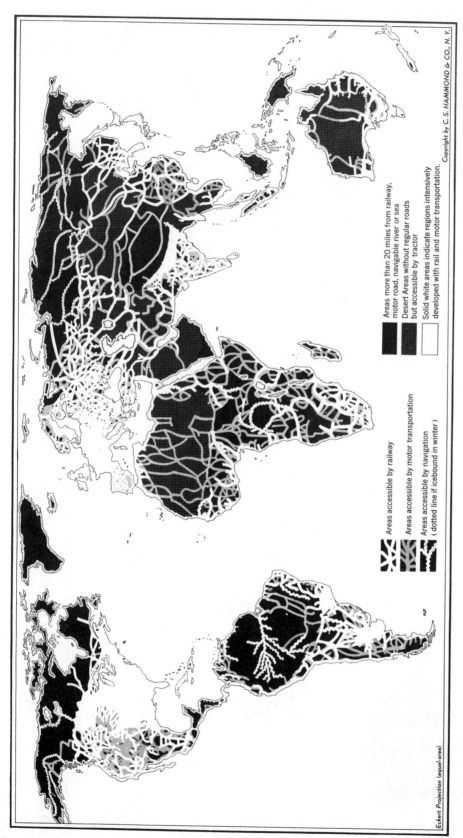

Areas accessible by railway

Areas accessible by motor transportation

Areas accessible by navigation
(dotted line if icebound in winter)

Areas more than 20 miles from railway, motor road, navigable river or sea

Desert Areas without regular roads but accessible by tractor

Solid white areas indicate regions intensively developed with rail and motor transportation.

Copyright by C. S. HAMMOND & CO., N. Y.

Eckert Projection (equal-area)

ACCESSIBILITY. Many regions in the world are far from railways, roads, navigable rivers or the seas. Their economic development is retarded because their products can be brought to the world's markets only at great expense. Such areas are in the tundra (alpine), the boreal forest and in the equatorial rain forest regions. Desert areas, if not too mountainous, can be crossed by tractors. The largest inaccessible area is in Tibet, on account of high mountains, the alpine climate and isolationist attitude of the people. Airplane transportation is helping to bring these inaccessible areas into the orbit of civilization.

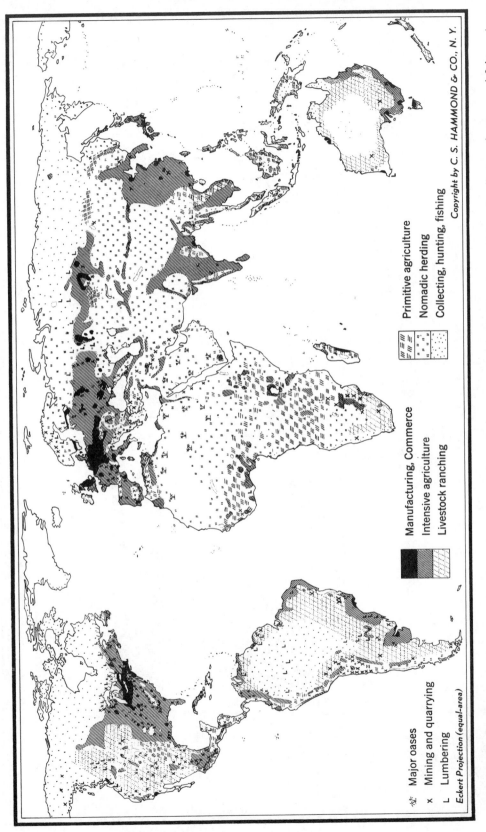

Major oases

x Mining and quarrying

L Lumbering

Eckert Projection (equal-area)

Manufacturing, Commerce

Intensive agriculture

Livestock ranching

Primitive agriculture

Nomadic herding

Collecting, hunting, fishing

Copyright by C. S. HAMMOND & CO., N. Y.

OCCUPATIONS. *Correlation with the density of population shows that the most densely populated areas fall into the regions of manufacturing and intensive farming. All other economies require considerable space. The most sparsely inhabited areas are those of collecting, hunting and fishing. Areas with practically no habitation are left blank.*

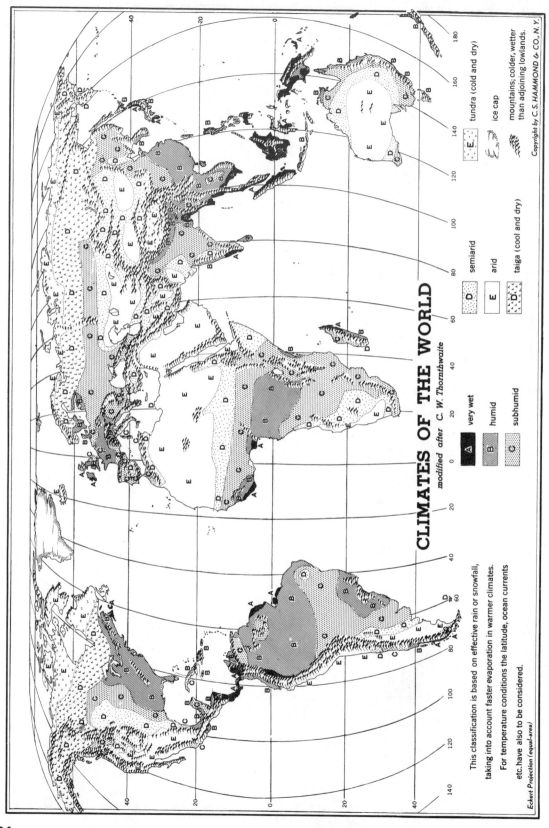

CLIMATES OF THE WORLD

modified after C. W. Thornthwaite

This classification is based on effective rain or snowfall,
taking into account faster evaporation in warmer climates.

For temperature conditions the latitude, ocean currents
etc. have also to be considered.

Eckert Projection (equal-area)

A	very wet	
B	humid	
C	subhumid	

D	semiarid	
E	arid	
D	taiga (cool and dry)	

E	tundra (cold and dry)
	ice cap
	mountains; colder, wetter than adjoining lowlands.

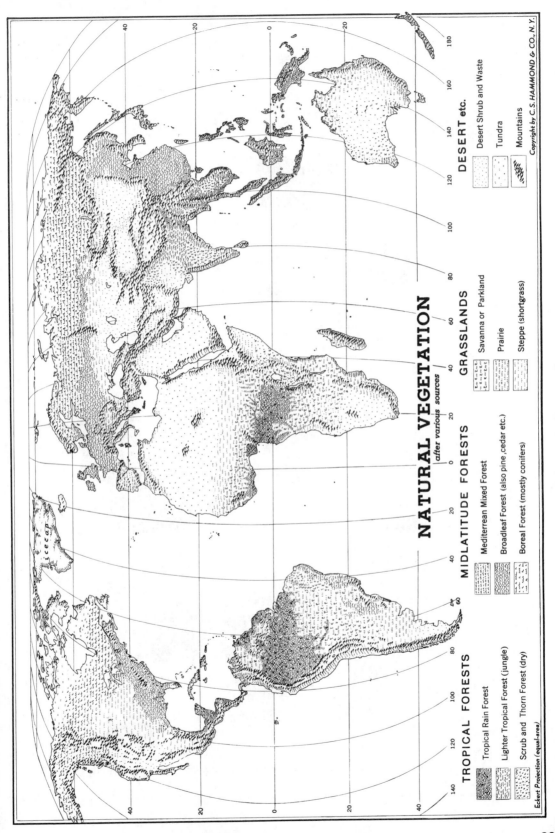

NATURAL VEGETATION
after various sources

TROPICAL FORESTS
- Tropical Rain Forest
- Lighter Tropical Forest (jungle)
- Scrub and Thorn Forest (dry)

MIDLATITUDE FORESTS
- Mediterranean Mixed Forest
- Broadleaf Forest (also pine, cedar etc.)
- Boreal Forest (mostly conifers)

GRASSLANDS
- Savanna or Parkland
- Prairie
- Steppe (shortgrass)

DESERT etc.
- Desert Shrub and Waste
- Tundra
- Mountains

Copyright by C. S. HAMMOND & CO., N. Y.

Eckert Projection (equal-area)

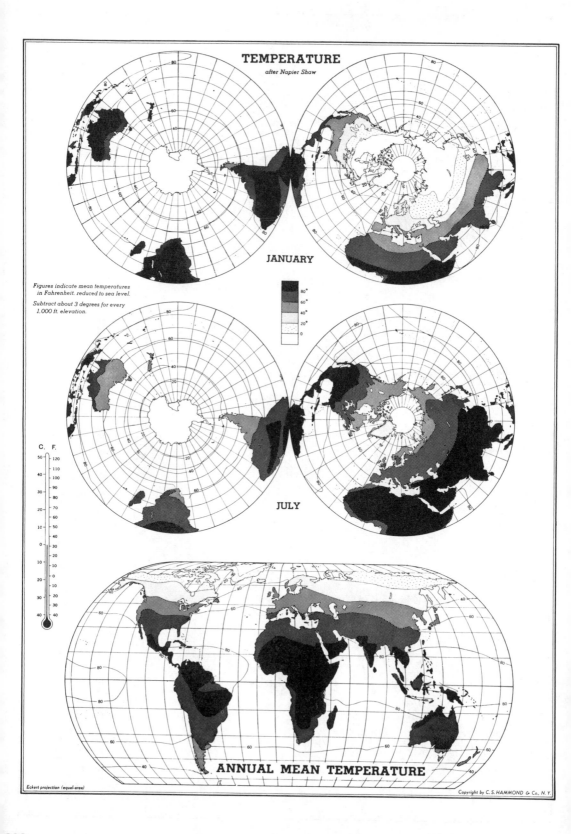

TEMPERATURE
after Napier Shaw

JANUARY

Figures indicate mean temperatures in Fahrenheit, reduced to sea level.

Subtract about 3 degrees for every 1,000 ft. elevation.

JULY

ANNUAL MEAN TEMPERATURE

Eckert projection (equal-area)

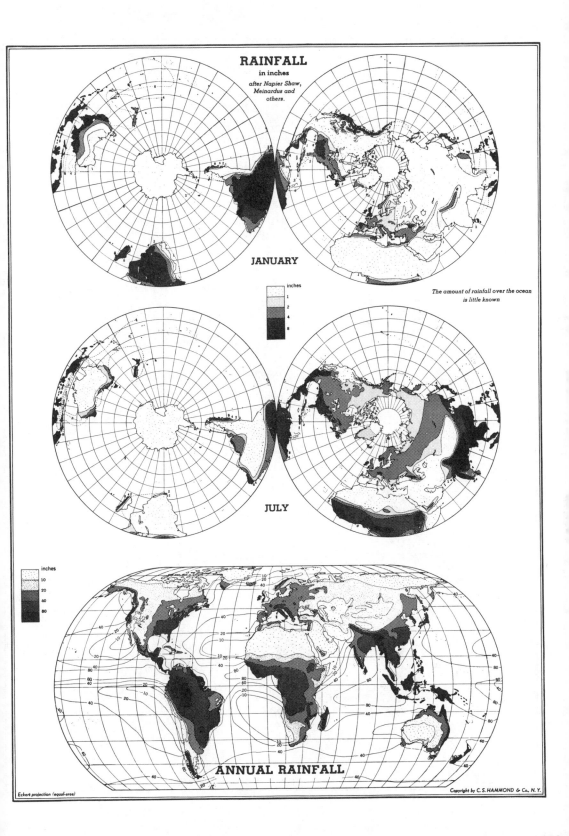

RAINFALL
in inches
*after Napier Shaw,
Meinardus and
others.*

JANUARY

inches
1
2
4
8

*The amount of rainfall over the ocean
is little known*

JULY

inches
10
20
40
80

40
20
10
40
20
10
40
80
80
40
20
10
80
40
80
40
20
10
40
80
80
40
40

ANNUAL RAINFALL

Eckert projection (equal-area)

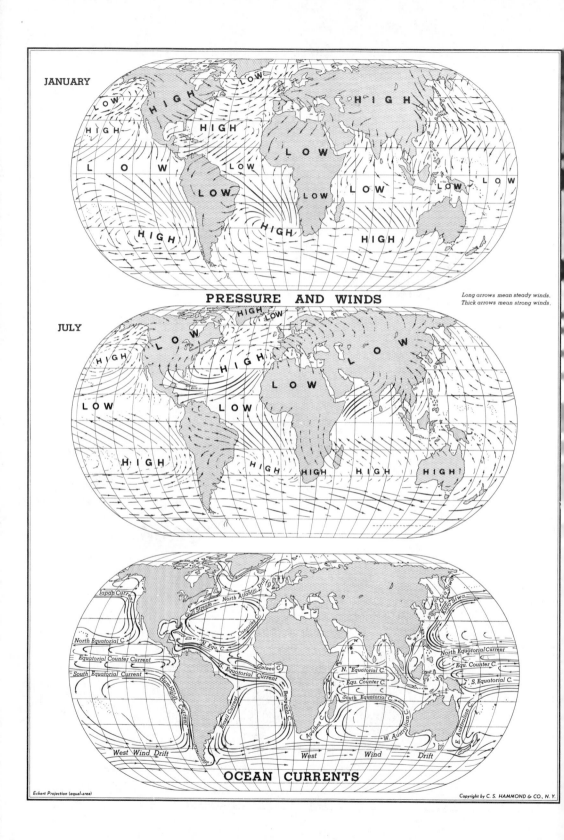

JANUARY

HIGH

LOW   LOW

LOW   HIGH   HIGH

HIGH   HIGH   LOW

LOW   W   LOW   LOW   LOW

LOW   LOW   LOW

HIGH   HIGH   HIGH

PRESSURE AND WINDS

Long arrows mean steady winds.
Thick arrows mean strong winds.

JULY

LOW   HIGH   LOW

HIGH   HIGH   LOW

LOW   LOW   LOW

HIGH   HIGH   HIGH   HIGH   HIGH

Japan Current

North Atlantic Drift

Gulf Stream

Kuro Siwo

North Equatorial C.

Canaries C.

North Equatorial Current

N. Equ. C.

Equatorial Counter Current

Guinea C.

S. Equatorial Current

N. Equatorial C.

Equ. Counter C.

South Equatorial Current

Equ. Counter C.

S. Equatorial C.

Humboldt Current

Brazil Current

Benguela C.

South Equatorial C.

Agulhas C.

W. Australian C.

E. Australian C.

West Wind Drift

West   Wind   Drift

OCEAN CURRENTS

Eckert Projection (equal-area)

Copyright by C. S. HAMMOND & CO., N. Y.

210

Illustrated
Social and Economic Tables
of the World

N.Y. State Dep't of Commerce

The headline events of the last half-century have made the average person acutely curious of the vast world beyond his country's borders. This new national concern for the external world and its problems is one of the hopeful signs pointing to a better future for mankind. However, no matter how well-intentioned our concern for international relations may be, it is of no value unless it is grounded on an intelligent appreciation of the great diversity of social, economic and political forms extant throughout the globe.

On the following pages the editors have presented information on the world's nations, products, peoples and governments arranged in easily-found tabular form. This arrangement by tables makes comparison between political units a simpler task. These data, used with the maps in this atlas, complete the story of the nations of the world.

Social and Economic Tables

POLITICAL DIVISION	GOVERNMENT	MONETARY UNIT	LANGUAGE	RELIGION
AFARS & ISSAS, TERR. OF THE	French overseas territory with a high commissioner, council of government and territorial assembly.	Djibouti franc	French Hamitic languages Arabic	Islam
AFGHANISTAN	Republic, at present under military rule, with a president, prime minister, appointed cabinet and a ruling central committee.	afghani	Pushtu (Afghan) Dari (Persian) Turkic languages	Islam
ALBANIA	Soviet-type republic with a head of state, cabinet and unicameral legislature, actually controlled by the Communist party.	lek	Albanian	Islam Eastern Orthodoxy Roman Catholicism
ALGERIA	Centralized republic under a president, prime minister, council of ministers, and a revolutionary council.	Algerian dinar	Arabic French Berber	Islam
AMERICAN SAMOA	U.S. territory with a governor and an elected bicameral legislature.	U.S. dollar	English Samoan	Protestantism
ANDORRA	Co-principality of the president of France and the Spanish bishop of Seo de Urgel, with an elected executive Syndic (manager) and a council general.	French franc and Spanish peseta	Catalan Spanish French	Roman Catholicism
ANGOLA	Portuguese overseas "state" with a governor-general and a legislative assembly.	Portuguese escudo	Portuguese Bantu languages	Tribal religions Roman Catholicism
ARGENTINA	A republic with a president, appointive cabinet, elective senate and house of deputies, at present under a military government.	Argentine peso	Spanish	Roman Catholicism
AUSTRALIA	Independent British Commonwealth member with a governor-general, prime minister, cabinet, and a bicameral parliament, composed of a senate and a house of representatives.	Australian dollar	English	Protestantism Roman Catholicism
AUSTRIA	A federal republic with a president, chancellor, cabinet, and a bicameral elective assembly.	schilling	German	Roman Catholicism
BAHAMAS	Independent British Commonwealth member, with a governor-general, prime minister, cabinet and bicameral legislature.	Bahamian dollar	English	Protestantism Roman Catholicism
BAHRAIN	Independent state with a sheikh, prime minister, cabinet, and a partly elected national assembly.	Bahrain dinar	Arabic	Islam
BANGLADESH	Independent republic in the British Commonwealth, with a president, prime minister, cabinet, and a unicameral legislature.	taka	Bengali English Urdu	Islam Hinduism Christianity Buddhism

of the World

MAJOR PRODUCTS

Boats, goats, sheep; hides; salt.

Wheat, barley, millet, corn, rice, sugar beets, vegetables and seeds, fruits, cotton, tobacco, sheep (karakul), camels, wool, skins; sheepskin, textiles, leather, carpets; chromite, iron, lapis lazuli, salt, copper, lead, silver, natural gas, talc.

Corn, tobacco, wheat, oats, rice, cotton, sugar beets, olives, fruits; livestock, poultry; fish; wool, hides; dairy products, paper, textiles, furs; bitumen, salt, lignite, petroleum, copper, iron, chromite, cement, timber.

Wheat, barley, oats, corn, grapes, olives, tobacco, dates, figs, citrus fruits, vegetables; sheep, goats, cattle, horses, camels; hides, skins; fish; timber; iron, phosphates, zinc, natural gas, coal, lead, petroleum; wine, olive oil, carpets, cotton weaving, tobacco products, wool, cork, cement, chemicals, machinery, refined petroleum.

Copra, taro, breadfruit, yams, bananas, arrowroot, pineapples, coconuts, oranges; mats; fish.

Tobacco, potatoes, oats, barley; sheep, cattle; lumber; iron ore, lead; dairy products, cigarettes, wood, wool products.

ALGERIA: A native letter writer in the streets of Constantine, the country's third largest city.
TWA–Trans World Airlines

Coffee, corn, sugarcane, peanuts, tobacco, wheat, palm products, cotton, sisal; iron ore, petroleum, diamonds; fish; timber; refined petroleum, cement, paper, tires, refined sugar.

Wheat, corn, oats, barley, rye, grapes, apples, cotton, sugarcane, potatoes, tobacco; yerba maté; cattle, sheep; quebracho, lumber; petroleum, zinc, silver, gold, lead, iron, tungsten; oils, wines, hides, wool, meats, textiles, metal products, steel, vehicles and machinery, chemicals, wood and paper products, leather, flour, dairy products, cement.

Wheat, oats, barley, fruits, vegetables, sugar; sheep, cattle; gold, coal, petroleum, copper, iron, lead, silver, bauxite, zinc; timber, iron and steel, wool, electrical and radio equipment, appliances, chemicals, petroleum products, optical and agricultural implements, machinery, textiles, leather, airplanes, engines, ships, processed meat, fruit and vegetables, oils, dairy products, building materials, vehicles.

Rye, wheat, oats, barley, potatoes, sugar beets, hops, grapes, flax, tobacco; iron, copper, lead, magnesite, graphite, coal, aluminum, petroleum, salt; timber, pulp, poultry, livestock; wine, steel, machinery, machine tools, chemicals, textiles, paper, processed foods, dairy products, leather.

Tomatoes, pineapples, sugarcane, vegetables, sponges, citrus fruits, bananas; crawfish, shells; lumber; salt; handcraft products, cement, pulpwood, processed fish, rum, refined petroleum, drugs.

Shrimping, petroleum, fishing; fruits, vegetables, dates, refined petroleum, processed aluminum, fish, shellfish, electrical goods, flour.

Rice, sugarcane, jute, cotton, oilseeds, tobacco, tea, fruit; timber; cattle, fish; natural gas, coal; textiles, hides, flour, cement, refined petroleum, steel, chemicals, refined sugar, handicrafts, paper, tools, leather goods.

AUSTRALIA: The country's first oil field at Moonie, Queensland, is in a sheep herding region.
Australian Government

Social and Economic Tables

POLITICAL DIVISION	GOVERNMENT	MONETARY UNIT	LANGUAGE	RELIGION
BARBADOS	Independent British Commonwealth member, with a governor-general, prime minister, cabinet and a bicameral legislature.	East Caribbean dollar	English	Protestantism
BELGIUM	Constitutional, hereditary monarchy, with a king, prime minister, cabinet, and a bicameral legislature.	Belgian franc	French (Walloon) Flemish	Roman Catholicism
BELIZE	Internally self-governing British colony with governor, prime minister, cabinet and bicameral legislature.	Belize dollar	English; Spanish Mayan; Creole	Roman Catholicism Protestantism
BERMUDA	Internally self-governing British colony with a governor, prime minister, house of assembly, and legislative and executive councils.	Bermuda dollar	English	Protestantism
BHUTAN	Monarchy with a king, cabinet, and an elected national assembly.	Indian rupee; tikchung	Tibetan dialects Nepali	Buddhism Hinduism
BOLIVIA	Centralized constitutional republic, with a president, cabinet and bicameral legislature, at present under a military junta.	Bolivian peso	Spanish Quechua Aymará	Roman Catholicism
BOTSWANA	Constitutional republic within the British Commonwealth, with a president, cabinet, a unicameral national assembly and an advisory house of chiefs.	South African rand	English Setswana Sindebele Bushman Afrikaans	Tribal religions Protestantism
BRAZIL	Federal republic with a president, vice-president, appointive cabinet and a bicameral legislature.	cruzeiro	Portuguese	Roman Catholicism
BRUNEI	Internally self-governing British protected sultanate, with a chief minister, cabinet, and executive and legislative councils.	Brunei dollar	Malay English	Islam
BULGARIA	Soviet-type republic with a cabinet, state council and unicameral assembly, which elects a presidium whose chairman is the chief of state. Actual control is by the Communist party.	lev	Bulgarian	Eastern Orthodoxy Islam
BURMA	One-party socialist republic with a national congress, prime minister and council, and a state council with its chairman the president.	kyat	Burmese Karen Shan; Chin English	Buddhism Tribal religions
BURUNDI	One-party republic with a president, cabinet, and a political bureau.	Burundi franc	French; Kirundi Kiswahili	Tribal religions Roman Catholicism
CAMBODIA	Khmer Republic, at present under president who rules by decree, cabinet, council and assembly.	riel	Khmer French	Buddhism
CAMEROON	One-party republic, with a president, cabinet, and unicameral assembly.	CFA franc	French; English Sudanese and Bantu languages	Tribal religions Islam Christianity

of the World

Sugarcane, cotton; fish; manjak (asphalt); sugar, molasses, rum, edible oil, margarine.

Wheat, rye, oats, barley, potatoes, sugar beets, flax, tobacco, fibers, vegetables, fruit, hops; livestock; fish; coal, iron, zinc, lead, dolomite; coke, iron and steel, machinery, textiles, lace, glass, chemicals, petroleum and uranium refining, sugar, vinegar, beer, paper, wine, wool, cut diamonds, dairy products, aircraft, cement, vehicles.

Rice, corn, bananas, coconuts, citrus fruits, cocoa, sugarcane; cattle; hard and softwoods; fish; rum, meat and food products.

Lily bulbs, onions, bananas, cabbage, tomatoes, beans; coral; poultry, fish; perfume, pharmaceuticals.

BELGIUM: The Grand' Place in Brussels, with its flower market surrounded by Gothic and Renaissance architecture.

Belgian Gov't Info. Ctr.

Rice, wheat, barley, millet, corn, fruits; timber; cattle, yaks; handicrafts, dairy products.

Potatoes, corn, wheat, cassava, sugar, fruits, vanilla, rubber, quinine; timber; tin, zinc, lead, copper, silver, antimony, tungsten, gold, sulphur, petroleum; cattle, sheep; textiles, cement, tobacco products, beer, chemicals.

Kaffir, cotton, peanuts, beans, fruit, wheat and wheatmeal; cattle, sheep, goats, pigs; hides; gold, asbestos, diamonds, silver, nickel, manganese; meat and dairy products.

Coffee, corn, rice, cotton, cacao, sugarcane, soybeans, cassava, fibers, carnauba wax, medicinal plants, fruits, balata, tobacco, oilseeds; livestock; timber; nuts; iron, manganese, mica, gold, diamonds, bauxite, quartz, beryllium, petroleum, chromite, tungsten, silver; meat products, textiles, chemicals, drugs, metal products, paper, wood products, hides, machinery, sugar, iron and steel, vehicles, cement.

Rice, sago, rubber, jelutong, cutch, tapioca, bananas; timber; poultry, buffalo, pigs, cattle; petroleum, natural gas; boat building, cloth, brass and silverware.

Wheat, corn, barley, oats, tobacco, fruit, grapes, oilseeds, cotton, sugar beets, potatoes; livestock, silk; fish; coal, copper, iron, lead, manganese, zinc, natural gas, tobacco products, perfume, sugar, flour, textiles, leather goods, refined minerals and petroleum, beer, wine, chemicals, iron and steel, electrical goods, machinery.

Rice, pulses, peanuts, corn, wheat, cotton, jute, tobacco, sugarcane, fruit, spices, coconuts, oilseeds, rubber; teak, timber; livestock, fish; petroleum, lead, zinc, tin, tungsten, precious stones, coal, amber, salt; textiles, hides, chemicals, cement, steel, sugar, food and tobacco products, apparel, refined petroleum, drugs, electrical goods, paper.

Agricultural products, coffee, tea, cotton, quinine; cattle; fish; hides, textiles, cement, beer, food products.

Rice, tobacco, oilseeds, cotton, corn, fruit, rubber; timber; cattle; fish; silk, cotton, textiles, pottery; precious stones, gold, petroleum, paper, glass, cement, plywood, sugar.

Cocoa, nuts, bananas, caoutchouc (rubber), cacao, coffee, cotton, palm kernels and oil; timber; cattle, sheep; gold, tin; aluminum; rubber, tobacco, cotton products, hides, beer.

BRAZIL: Baling cotton for export by rail and sea in the state of São Paulo.

Pan American Union

Social and Economic Tables

POLITICAL DIVISION	GOVERNMENT	MONETARY UNIT	LANGUAGE	RELIGION
CANADA	Federated independent British Commonwealth member, with a governor-general, prime minister, cabinet and a bicameral parliament, composed of a senate and a house of commons.	Canadian dollar	English French	Protestantism Roman Catholicism
CAPE VERDE ISLANDS	Portuguese overseas territory under a governor and a legislative assembly.	Portuguese escudo	Portuguese	Roman Catholicism
CENTRAL AFRICAN REPUBLIC	One-party republic of the French Community, at present under a president and an appointed cabinet.	CFA franc	French; Sangho Sudanese and Bantu languages	Tribal religions Christianity Islam
CHAD	One-party republic of the French Community, with a president and a national assembly.	CFA franc	Arabic, French Bantu and Sudanese languages	Tribal religions Islam Roman Catholicism
CHILE	Constitutional republic, at present ruled by a military junta.	Chilean escudo	Spanish	Roman Catholicism
CHINA (PEOPLE'S REPUBLIC) (COMMUNIST)	In theory, governmental power resides in the National People's Congress and the State Council. In practice, power resides in the Communist party's Central Committee and its chairman.	yuan	Chinese Mongol Turkic languages	Confucianism Buddhism Taoism Islam
CHINA (REPUBLIC OF): TAIWAN (NATIONALIST)	Constitutional republic with an elected national assembly, which elects the president and vice-president. Legislative powers reside with the legislative yuan.	Taiwan dollar	Chinese	Confucianism Buddhism Taoism Christianity Tribal religions
COLOMBIA	A centralized federal republic with a president, vice-president, appointive cabinet, and elective bicameral legislature.	Colombian peso	Spanish	Roman Catholicism
COMORO ISLANDS	Internally self-governing French overseas territory, with a prime minister, high commissioner, council, and an elected chamber of deputies.	CFA franc	Arabic French	Islam
CONGO	One-party republic of the French Community, with a president, prime minister, cabinet, and national assembly.	CFA franc	French Sudanese and Bantu languages	Tribal religions Roman Catholicism
COOK ISLANDS	Internally self-governing state associated with New Zealand with a commissioner, prime minister, cabinet and legislative assembly.	New Zealand dollar	Polynesian dialects English	Protestantism
COSTA RICA	Constitutional republic with president, cabinet and unicameral legislature.	colón	Spanish	Roman Catholicism

of the World

CHILE: Bathers and cabanas on the Pacific sands of Las Salinas, a popular beach at Viña del Mar.

Hamilton Wright

MAJOR PRODUCTS

Wheat, oats, barley, rye, potatoes, vegetables, sugar beets, tobacco, fruits, oilseeds; livestock; fish; timber; furs; gold, copper, nickel, zinc, lead, silver, cadmium, magnesium; platinum, iron ore, titanium, cobalt, radium, uranium, petroleum, natural gas, coal, asbestos, salt, gypsum, fluorspar, sulphur; hydro-electric power; foods, beverages, meat products, transportation equipment, iron and steel, aluminum, metal products, pulp, paper and wood products, textiles, electrical goods, chemicals, motor vehicles, dairy products, cement.

Coffee, bananas, nuts, castor beans, corn; goats, oxen, pigs; hides, skins; preserved fish, salt, lime, sugar, cement.

Coffee, cotton, sisal, peanuts, tobacco, corn, rice, millet, sorghum; timber; livestock; gold, diamonds, uranium; rubber; palm products, beeswax, textiles, flour, soap.

Millet, sorghum, wheat, sesame, cotton, rice, sugarcane, cassava, peanuts, vegetables, gum arabic; livestock, hides; fish; natron, ivory, ostrich feathers; meat products, dates, textiles.

Wheat, potatoes, oats, rice, barley, corn, potatoes, vegetable seeds, sugar beets, tobacco, fruits; fish; livestock; copper, silver, nitrates, iodine, iron ore, gold, molybdenum, manganese, coal; foods, textiles, leather, wood products, cement, chemicals, pharmaceuticals, wines, wool, iron and steel, petroleum, paper, pulp.

Rice, wheat, potatoes, corn, barley, millet, kaoliang, soybeans, oilseeds, cotton, nuts, tea, sugarcane, tobacco, opium, tung, silk; livestock, poultry; timber; fish; iron, coal, tungsten, tin, antimony, mercury, copper, lead, zinc, silver, bauxite, manganese, gold, petroleum, molybdenum; foodstuffs, textiles, chemicals, machinery, metal work, metallurgical products, cement, clothing, ceramics, iron and steel, vehicles.

Rice, tea, sugar, sweet potatoes, pineapples, bananas, tobacco, vegetables, soybeans, camphor; pigs; buffalo, cattle, goats, horses; fish; canned foods, metal products, machinery, textiles, wood products, apparel, electrical & electronic goods, chemicals, cement, glass, plastics.

Coffee, sugarcane, rice, cotton, bananas, cacao, wheat, tobacco, cinchona; cattle; rubber, fibers; petroleum, gold, silver, platinum, emeralds; textiles, beer, sugar, cement, flour, tobacco products, iron and steel, chemicals, machinery.

Sugarcane, vanilla, rice, sweet potatoes, yams, copra, sisal, coffee, essential oils, cloves, cacao, perfume plants; timber; rum distilling.

Palm products, rice, sugarcane, hardwoods, veneers, peanuts, coffee, cocoa, bananas, rubber, tobacco; tin, gold, petroleum, diamonds, potash; livestock; cement, textiles, food processing.

Citrus fruits, coconuts, copra, oilseeds, tomatoes, arrowroot, pineapples, breadfruit, taro, kumaras, plantains, yams; mother-of-pearl, textiles.

Coffee, bananas, cocoa, abacá, sugarcane, rice, tobacco; cattle; tuna; gold, bauxite; tobacco products, textiles, furniture, sugar, electric goods, beef.

COLOMBIA: One of the country's principal products, coffee, drying under the tropical sun.

Pan American Union

Social and Economic Tables

POLITICAL DIVISION	GOVERNMENT	MONETARY UNIT	LANGUAGE	RELIGION
CUBA	Nominal republic with an appointed cabinet, dictatorial powers being held by the prime minister.	Cuban peso	Spanish	Roman Catholicism
CYPRUS	British Commonwealth republic, with a president (Greek), vice-president (Turkish), cabinet, and Greek and Turkish communal chambers.	Cyprus pound	Greek Turkish English	Greek Orthodoxy Islam
CZECHOSLOVAKIA	Soviet-type republic with a president, cabinet, bicameral legislature, and Czech and Slovak National Councils, with actual power residing in the Communist party presidium.	koruna	Czech and Slovak	Roman Catholicism Protestantism
DAHOMEY	Republic, at present under a head of state and national revolutionary council.	CFA franc	French Sudanese languages	Tribal religions Christianity Islam
DENMARK	Constitutional, hereditary monarchy with a queen, a bicameral elective legislature and an appointed cabinet.	krone	Danish	Protestantism
DOMINICAN REPUBLIC	Republic with a president, vice-president, appointed cabinet, and bicameral legislature.	peso oro (Dominican peso)	Spanish	Roman Catholicism
ECUADOR	Constitutional republic at present under the rule of a military junta.	sucre	Spanish Indian languages (Quechua, etc.)	Roman Catholicism
EGYPT	One-party Arab republic with a president (with supreme powers), cabinet, and a partly elected unicameral assembly.	Egyptian pound	Arabic	Islam Christianity
EL SALVADOR	Republic with a president, cabinet, and unicameral legislature.	colón	Spanish	Roman Catholicism
ENGLAND AND WALES	Integral part of the United Kingdom, with executive power nominally residing in the Crown, but actually exercised by the prime minister, cabinet and bicameral parliament, composed of a house of lords and a house of commons.	pound sterling	English Welsh	Protestantism Roman Catholicism
EQUATORIAL GUINEA	One-party centralized republic with a president and a national assembly.	ekowele	Spanish Bantu languages	Tribal religions Roman Catholicism
ETHIOPIA	Hereditary constitutional monarchy with an emperor, prime minister, council and bicameral legislature.	Ethiopian dollar	Amharic Hamitic languages English	Coptic Christianity Islam Tribal religions
FALKLAND ISLANDS	British colony with a governor, and executive and legislative councils.	pound sterling	English	Protestantism Roman Catholicism

of the World

MAJOR PRODUCTS

Sugarcane, tobacco, coffee, rice, fruits, henequen; cattle; timber; fish; chromite, iron, manganese, copper, nickel; sugar, textiles, alcohol, refined petroleum, cement, chemicals, tobacco products, electrical goods, food products, steel.

Wheat, barley, grapes, raisins, olives, potatoes, carobs, citrus fruits, cotton, tobacco, hemp, flax, vegetables, corn, melons; sponges, fish; livestock; copper, iron pyrites, asbestos, chromite, copper concentrates; tobacco products, buttons, wine, false teeth, textiles, cement, leather goods, dried fruits, cheese, refined petroleum.

Wheat, rye, barley, oats, corn, hops, sugar beets, grapes, potatoes; poultry, livestock; timber; coal, mercury, aluminum, iron, garnets, silver, natural gas, lead, salt, manganese, zinc; beverages, malt, metals, munitions, machinery, iron and steel, cement, porcelain, shoes, textiles, wood products, pulp and paper, sugar, leather, foods, chemicals, rubber products, glassware, aircraft.

Palm products, tobacco, peanuts, cotton, corn, copra, coffee, castor oil, kapok, millet; livestock; fish; gold, diamonds, bauxite, iron ore; oilseed milling, textiles.

Barley, oats, rye, wheat, potatoes, sugar beets; livestock, poultry, fish; clay; ships and transportation equipment, butter, bacon, eggs, cheese, milk, meat; textiles, machines, chemicals, tobacco products, metal goods, leather goods, beverages, stone, earthenware, glassware, electrical goods, ship building, cement.

Sugarcane, cacao, coffee, tobacco, bananas, rice, corn; cattle; lumber; gold, bauxite; starch, alcohol, molasses, chocolate, sugar, meat, cigars, cigarettes, leather, rum.

Rice, cacao, coffee, bananas, rubber, kapok, cotton, nuts, cinchona; poultry, livestock; fish; gold, petroleum, silver, lead, balsa wood; textiles, toquilla (panama) hats, sugar, flour, chemicals, pharmaceuticals, cement, soap, candles, beer.

Cotton, barley, wheat, rice, sugarcane, corn, millet, fruits, vegetables; sheep, goats, cattle, buffalo, camels; fish; petroleum, phosphates, salt, iron ore, manganese, asbestos, limestone; cotton ginning, milling, iron and steel, refined petroleum, food processing, textiles, chemicals, cement, petrochemicals.

Coffee, cotton, corn, tobacco, sorghums, beans, henequen, sugarcane, rice; shellfish, fish, livestock; balsa and other woods; gold, silver; cotton textiles, sugar, pharmaceuticals.

Potatoes, turnips, beets, oats, wheat, barley, rye, hay, beans, peas, cabbage, vetches, hops, fruits; sheep, cattle, pigs, horses, poultry; fish; coal, coke, gas, iron, copper, lead, nickel, tin, clay; dairy products, wool, cotton and linen textiles; electrical goods, vehicles, steel, scientific instruments, cutlery, foods and beverages, tobacco products, clothing and shoes, chemicals, pottery, china, machinery, locomotives, carpets, knitwear, lace, pharmaceuticals.

Cocoa, cacao, coffee, bananas, sugarcane, tobacco, vanilla, palm oil and kernels, copra; timber, cabinet woods; fish.

Coffee, teff, barley, durra, wheat, cotton, oilseeds, fruits, vegetables, chat, civet, wax, spices, gum arabic, sugarcane; livestock; hides, skins; gold, platinum, rocksalt; meat products, cement, beverages, textiles, food processing.

Forage crops, sheep; wool, skins, tallow, animal and vegetable oil, whalemeat meal.

DENMARK: Amalienborg Palace in Copenhagen, the queen's residence, and the statue of King Frederik V.

Danish Nat'l Travel Office

FRANCE: Fresh fruits and vegetables occupy a market in Paris, near the right bank of the Seine.

TWA—Trans World Airlines

Social and Economic Tables

POLITICAL DIVISION	GOVERNMENT	MONETARY UNIT	LANGUAGE	RELIGION
FIJI	Independent British Commonwealth member, with a prime minister, cabinet, and a bicameral legislature.	Fiji dollar	English; Fijian Hindi; Chinese Polynesian dialects	Protestantism Roman Catholicism Hinduism Islam
FINLAND	Constitutional republic with a president, cabinet, and a unicameral legislature.	(new) markka	Finnish Swedish	Protestantism
FRANCE	A constitutional republic with a president, a bicameral elective legislature and appointive council of ministers.	franc	French	Roman Catholicism
FRENCH GUIANA	Overseas department of France governed by a prefect with an elective council-general.	French franc	French	Roman Catholicism
FRENCH POLYNESIA	Overseas territory of France, with a governor, government council, and an elected territorial assembly.	CFP franc	Polynesian dialects French	Protestantism Roman Catholicism
GABON	One-party republic of the French Community with a president, vice-president and national assembly.	CFA franc	French Bantu languages	Roman Catholicism Tribal religions Islam
GAMBIA	Republic of the British Commonwealth, with a prime minister, cabinet and unicameral legislature.	dalasi	English Sudanese languages	Islam Tribal religions Protestantism
GERMANY	Country is divided between two governments — a democratic Federal Republic of Germany in the west and a Soviet-dominated German "Democratic" Republic in the east. Federal Republic has an elected federal diet and council who jointly elect the president. German "Democratic" Republic has a communist-controlled legislative branch which selects the president, cabinet and prime minister.	West German Deutsche mark East German Ostmark	German	Protestantism Roman Catholicism
GHANA	Republic of the British Commonwealth at present under a military council and cabinet.	cedi	English Sudanese languages	Tribal religions Protestantism Islam
GIBRALTAR	Partly self-governing British colony, with a governor, cabinet, house of assembly and local council.	pound sterling	English Spanish	Roman Catholicism
GILBERT AND ELLICE ISLS.	Self-governing British colony, with a governor and local councils.	Australian dollar	English Gilbertese Ellice	Protestantism Roman Catholicism
GREAT BRITAIN	See: England and Wales, Northern Ireland, Scotland.			
GREECE	Nominal republic, at present ruled by military decree under a president.	drachma	Greek	Greek Orthodoxy
GREENLAND	Integral part of the Danish kingdom, with representation in Parliament and a provincial council.	Danish krone	Danish Greenlandic Eskimo	Protestantism
GRENADA	Independent British Commonwealth member with a premier, cabinet, and bicameral legislature.	East Caribbean dollar	English French patois	Roman Catholicism Protestantism

MAJOR PRODUCTS

Sugarcane, coconuts, rice fruits, cotton, rubber, ginger, oilseeds, vegetables, groundnuts, corn, tobacco, cattle, pigs; fish, bêche-de-mer, trochus shell; gold, silver, copper, manganese; sugar, copra, coconut oil, molasses, butter, ghee, candlenut oil, cement, beer; meat products.

Hay, potatoes, wheat, oats, barley, rye, sugar beets; livestock, poultry, reindeer; timber; fish; copper, iron, titanium, silver; lumber, plywood, furniture, pulp, paper, cardboard, textiles, dairy products, meat, flour, leather, chemicals, china, glass, foodstuffs, machinery, ships, transportation equipment, electrical goods.

Sugar beets, potatoes, wheat, oats, barley, rye; corn, turnips, fruits, nuts, grapes, buckwheat; cattle, sheep, pigs, horses; fish; coal, iron ore, lignite, salt, bauxite, pyrites; potash salts, sulphur, natural gas, iron and steel, chemicals; silk, cotton, rayon, wool and linen, textiles; clothing, lace, perfumes and cosmetics, automobiles, machinery, dairy products, beet sugar, wines, porcelain, aluminum, foods, leather, lumber, spirits.

Rice, cacao, bananas, sugarcane, corn, cassava, woods; gold; hides, rosewood essence, shoes, rum, fish glue.

Coconuts, tropical fruits, sugarcane, coffee, bamboo, pearls; phosphates; mother-of-pearl, sugar, rum, copra.

Cocoa, rubber, coffee; corn, plantains; tropical woods; gold, manganese, iron ore, petroleum, natural gas, uranium; fish; oil refining, manganese and uranium processing.

Peanuts, rice, cotton, limes, palm kernels; hides and skins; fish; beeswax, textiles, peanut oil refining, fish processing.

Wheat, rye, barley, oats, potatoes, sugar beets, fruits, hops; pigs, cattle, poultry, horses; fish; forest products; coal, lignite, iron, copper, potash, sulphur, salt, uranium, lead, zinc, fluorspar, gypsum, vanadium, aluminum; automobiles, steel, cement, diesel oil, gasoline, cotton yarn, woolen yarn, rayon fiber, beet sugar, beer, wines, optical instruments, sulphuric acid, sodium bicarbonate, chemicals, machinery, electrical equipment, aircraft, metal and electronic products.

Cocoa, palm products, fruits, tobacco, coffee, peanuts, rubber, cotton; livestock, fish; timber; gold, diamonds, manganese, bauxite; aluminum, refined petroleum.

Fish for export and processing of commodities for local consumption.

Coconuts, copra, phosphate of lime; pearl shell, fish; hats, mats.

Wheat, barley, corn, oats, rye, tobacco, cotton, currants, citrus fruits, olives, figs, grapes; sheep, goats, cattle, pigs, horses, mules; fish; iron ore, sulphur, emery, magnesite, zinc, lead, lignite, marble, silver, bauxite; textiles, olive oil, foods, wines, chemicals, leather, wood and paper, metal products, machinery, petroleum and aluminum refining.

Grass for fodder; cod and other fish; sheep, furs; cryolite; processed fish, hides.

Cocoa, nutmeg, mace, limes, bananas, sugarcane, coconuts, vegetables, cotton; fish; livestock; sugar refining, cotton ginning, copra, lime oil, rum.

GREECE: An "evzone," one of the uniquely uniformed guards at the palace in Athens.

J. Walter Thompson

GUATEMALA: Removing the nuts from the pods at a cacao "finca," or plantation, is the first stage of processing chocolate.

I.I.A.A.

Social and Economic Tables

POLITICAL DIVISION	GOVERNMENT	MONETARY UNIT	LANGUAGE	RELIGION
GUADELOUPE	Overseas department of France with a prefect and elective general council.	French franc	French French Patois (Creole)	Roman Catholicism
GUAM	U.S. territory with a governor, advisory staff, and an elected unicameral legislature.	American dollar	English Chamorro Spanish	Roman Catholicism
GUATEMALA	Republic with a president, cabinet and one-house legislature.	quetzal	Spanish	Roman Catholicism
GUINEA	One party republic with a president, cabinet, prime minister and national assembly.	sily	French Sudanese languages	Islam Tribal religions Roman Catholicism
GUYANA	"Co-operative" republic within the British Commonwealth, with president, prime minister, cabinet, and unicameral legislature.	Guyana dollar	English	Christianity Hinduism Islam
HAITI	Nominal republic with president, cabinet, and a unicameral legislature.	gourde	French Creole	Roman Catholicism
HONDURAS	Republic with a president, council of ministers and unicameral legislature.	lempira	Spanish	Roman Catholicism
HONG KONG	British colony ruled by a governor assisted by executive and legislative councils.	Hong Kong dollar	English Chinese (Cantonese)	Confucianism Buddhism Taoism Christianity
HUNGARY	Soviet-type republic with a president, two vice-presidents, and council selected by the national assembly. Actual power is in the hands of a politburo, highest organ of the Communist party.	forint	Hungarian	Roman Catholicism Protestantism
ICELAND	A republic with a president, prime minister, an elective, bicameral legislature and an appointive cabinet.	króna (crown)	Icelandic	Protestantism
INDIA	An independent republic within the British Commonwealth with a president, vice-president, prime minister, cabinet and a bicameral parliament.	Indian rupee	Hindi; English Assamese, Bengali, Gujarati, Kannada, Kashmiri, Malayalam, Marathi, Oriya, Panjabi, Sanskrit, Tamil, Telugu, Urdu	Hinduism Islam Buddhism Animism Christianity Sikhism Jainism Zoroastrianism Lamaism
INDONESIA	Republic headed by a president, appointed cabinet, and consultative legislature.	rupiah	Bahasa Indonesia (Indonesian Malay) Papuan	Islam Christianity Hinduism Buddhism Tribal religions
IRAN	Constitutional monarchy governed by a shah, an appointed prime minister & cabinet, and a partly elective bicameral legislature.	rial	Persian (Farsi) Kurdish Arabic Turkic languages	Islam Zoroastrianism Christianity Judaism

of the World

MAJOR PRODUCTS

Sugarcane, bananas, pineapples, mangoes, avocados, coffee, cocoa, vanilla, cassava; fish; alcohol, rum.

Coconut products, corn, taro, bananas, citrus fruits, mangoes, papayas, breadfruit, sweet potatoes, cocoa, cassava, sugar cane, pineapples; cattle, pigs, poultry, buffalo.

Coffee, bananas, sugarcane, yams, pumpkins, plantains, rubber, cotton, wheat, corn, rice, chicle, cacao, abacá, cattle; mahogany; essential oils; nickel, gold; textiles, chemicals, drugs, wood and leather goods, food processing, meat products.

Rice, peanuts, palm oil and kernels, wax, honey, pineapples, bananas, indigo, kola nuts, coffee; cattle, sheep, goats; hides and skins; bauxite, iron ore, diamonds; timber; aluminum, textiles, wood products, cigarettes, food products.

Sugarcane, rice, coconuts, coffee, citrus fruits, cacao; balata, rubber; timber; livestock; shrimp; bauxite, diamonds, gold; textiles, milled rice, beer and rum, lime rum and oil, sugar, woods, molasses, charcoal, matches, aluminum.

Coffee, sugarcane, bananas, sisal, cotton, rice, cocoa, logwood; bauxite, copper; molasses, sisal products, handicrafts.

Bananas, coffee, coconuts, tobacco, corn, beans, sugar cane, cotton, grapefruit, rice, henequen; mahogany; cattle; fish; gold, silver; meat products.

Rice, sugar, ginger; fish; poultry, pigs; lead, iron, wolfram; shipbuilding, enameled ware, textiles, wood and plastic products, jewelry, toys, radios, electronic goods, cement.

Wheat, corn, rye, oats, sugar beets, tobacco, grapes, fruits, peppers, flax; pigs, cattle, poultry; fish; coal, petroleum, natural gas, iron ore, bauxite, manganese; flour, sugar, brewing, iron and steel, wines, textiles, chemicals, leather, metal products, wood and paper products, machinery, tools, transportation equipment, drugs, aluminum.

Hay, potatoes, turnips, hothouse fruits and vegetables; sheep, poultry, horses, cattle; fish; dairy products, meats, animal and vegetable oils, hides, skins, leather, clothing, textiles, frozen fish, herring oil, herring meal, aluminum.

Rice, wheat, legumes, peanuts, oilseeds, tea, tobacco, jute, cotton, rubber, coffee, sugarcane, barley, millet, corn; cattle, goats, buffalo, sheep, pigs; fish; coal, manganese, gold, petroleum, salt, mica, iron, copper, chromite, ilmenite, diamonds, silver, bauxite; textiles, shawls, carpets, jute manufactures, wood-carving and metal work, leather, chemicals, shipbuilding, petroleum refining, sugar refining, cotton ginning, iron and steel, glass, soap, matches, transportation equipment, aircraft, typewriters, cement, machinery.

Rice, sugarcane, rubber, palm oil, tobacco, corn, coconuts, copra, spices, sweet potatoes, groundnuts, tea, beans, cotton, kapok, coffee, taro, fish, cinchona, cocoa, pepper, fruits, vegetables; pigs, poultry, cattle, buffalo; timber; tin, coal, iron ore, petroleum, bauxite, nickel, copper, manganese; rubber goods, chemicals, shipyards, textiles, paper.

Wheat, cotton, gums, opium, fruits, rice, barley, sugar beets, rye, tobacco, tea, corn, millet, vegetables, nuts; timber; livestock; fish; petroleum, copper, sulphur, coal, salt, manganese, lead, zinc, cobalt, turquoise, iron ore; hides, carpets, textiles, leather products, chemicals, petrochemicals, iron and steel, jute, tobacco products, refined petroleum, processed foods, tires, drugs, automobiles, appliances, oils, aluminum.

INDIA: A typical scene in one of the busy streets of the native section in Bombay.

TWA–Trans World Airlines

INDONESIA: Educational progress—a mother and daughter attending school together.

Indonesian Info. Office

Social and Economic Tables

POLITICAL DIVISION	GOVERNMENT	MONETARY UNIT	LANGUAGE	RELIGION
IRAQ	Nominal republic headed by a revolutionary council and an appointed cabinet.	Iraqi dinar	Arabic Kurdish	Islam Christianity Judaism
IRELAND	Republic with a president, prime minister, cabinet, and a bicameral parliament.	Irish pound	Irish English	Roman Catholicism Protestantism
ISRAEL	Republic with a president, prime minister, cabinet and elective unicameral parliament.	Israeli pound	Hebrew Arabic English	Judaism Islam Christianity
ITALY	Constitutional republic with a president, a bicameral elective legislature and an appointive cabinet.	lira	Italian	Roman Catholicism
IVORY COAST	One-party republic, with a president, cabinet, and a unicameral national assembly.	CFA franc	French Sudanese languages	Tribal religions Islam Christianity
JAMAICA	Independent member of the British Commonwealth, with a governor-general, prime minister, cabinet, and bicameral parliament.	Jamaican dollar	English Jamaican Creole	Protestantism Roman Catholicism
JAPAN	Constitutional monarchy with the executive power vested in prime minister and cabinet, the legislative power residing in a bicameral parliament. The duties of the emperor are merely ceremonial.	yen	Japanese	Buddhism Shintoism Christianity
JORDAN	Constitutional monarchy with king, prime minister, cabinet and bicameral national assembly.	Jordanian dinar	Arabic English	Islam
KENYA	One-party republic of the British Commonwealth, with a president, vice-president, cabinet, and unicameral national assembly.	Kenyan shilling	English Kiswahili Bantu, Hamitic and Sudanese languages	Tribal religions Christianity Islam
KOREA	Divided by Armistice Line of August 1953: North Korea — a communist "people's republic" ruled by the politburo; South Korea — a republic with a president, cabinet, & a unicameral national assembly.	won	Korean	Buddhism Confucianism Christianity
KUWAIT	Constitutional state with a sheikh, cabinet and an elected unicameral national assembly.	Kuwaiti dinar	Arabic	Islam
LAOS	Constitutional monarchy with a king, prime minister, cabinet and a bicameral legislature.	kip	Lao French	Buddhism Tribal religions
LEBANON	Republic with a president, an appointed prime minister and cabinet, and an elected unicameral parliament.	Lebanese pound	Arabic French Armenian	Christianity Islam

of the World

MAJOR PRODUCTS

Dates, fruits, barley, wheat, rice, tobacco, cotton, beans, corn, sorghum, sesame; sheep, goats, asses; camels, horses, buffalo; petroleum; salt, wool, textiles, cigarettes, distilling, hides, petroleum products, cement.

Hay, potatoes, turnips, beets, sugar beets, oats, wheat, barley, rye, flax; cattle, sheep, pigs; fish; coal, peat, gypsum; tobacco, dairy products, foodstuffs, beer, malt, machinery, meats, textiles, clothing, shoes, wood and paper products.

Vegetables, eggs, fruits, wheat, barley, peanuts, cotton, corn; goats, sheep, cattle, camels; fish; textiles, clothing, tobacco, diamond polishing, shoes, metal and wood products, rubber goods, leather, electrical products, paper, pharmaceuticals, chemicals, dyes, radios, oil refining, wines, food products, refined petroleum, transportation and electronic equipment, aircraft.

Wheat, corn, oats, sugar beets, potatoes, tomatoes, rice, olives, grapes, citrus fruits, hemp, tobacco, nuts; timber; fish; sheep and goats, cattle, pigs; natural gas, sulphur, zinc, bauxite, lead, mercury, marble, manganese; textiles, chemicals, wines, automobiles, machinery, electrical goods, sugar, olive oil, clothing, processed foods, petrochemicals, typewriters.

Coffee, cocoa, sugarcane, bananas, pineapples, rice, palm oil, peanuts, kola nuts, rubber, cotton, tobacco; tropical woods; livestock, fish; diamonds, iron ore; textiles, food products, wood products.

Sugarcane, bananas, tobacco, coconuts, cacao, pimentos, citrus fruits, coffee, ginger; bauxite; honey; logwood; rum, textiles, cigars, copra, aluminum, chemicals, paper and rubber products, clothing, flour.

Rice, wheat, barley, potatoes, fruits, vegetables, oats, tobacco, soybeans, tea, flax, camphor; timber, bamboo; horses, cattle, sheep, goats, pigs; fish, pearl oysters; silkworms; coal, pyrites, gold, copper, pyrethrum, magnesium, silver, sulphur, chromite, zinc, salt, tin, lead, iron, petroleum; textiles, steel, coke, wood pulp, metal products, paper, porcelain, earthenware, vegetable oil, toys, shoes, machinery, automobiles, electric and electronic goods, instruments, chemicals, clothing, fish products.

Wheat, barley, legumes, vegetables, fruits, olives; sheep, goats, camels; salt, phosphates, potash; wool, tobacco products, flour milling, olive oil, leather goods; refined petroleum.

Sisal, wheat, tea, coffee, pyrethrum, cotton, corn, sugarcane, sesame, peanuts, wattle; hides and skins; livestock; timber; gold, kyanite, salt, silver, flourspar; bags, butter, sugar, sisal products, petroleum products, meat and dairy products.

Rice, barley, millet, wheat, soya beans, cotton, tobacco, hemp, ginseng, fruit; timber; draft cattle, pigs, sheep; fish; gold, iron ore, coal, tungsten, copper, silver, graphite, salt, kaolin, bismuth, fluorite; textiles, fertilizer, cement, silkworms, chemicals, machinery, metal, rubber, wood, paper and tobacco products.

Petroleum, natural gas; pearls, skins, wool; fish; refined petroleum, ammonia, fertilizers, cement, beverages, fish products, chemicals.

Rice, coffee, tea, citrus fruits, corn, cinchona, gum, benzoin, tobacco, cardamon; stick-lac; teak; tin; wool products.

Wheat, barley, corn, potatoes, fruits, onions, olives; vegetables, tobacco; livestock; iron, lignite; textiles, cement, olive oil, tobacco products, soap, matches, petroleum refining, gasoline, leather, food processing.

ITALY: A gondolier and his craft on one of the many waterways in Venice.

TWA—Trans World Airlines

LUXEMBOURG: La Place Guillaume, in the heart of the grand duchy's picturesque capital city.

Office Nat'l du Tourisme

Social and Economic Tables

POLITICAL DIVISION	GOVERNMENT	MONETARY UNIT	LANGUAGE	RELIGION
LESOTHO	Nominal monarchy presently ruled by a prime minister, cabinet, and an appointed national assembly.	South African rand	Sesotho English	Tribal religions Christianity
LIBERIA	One-party republic, with a president, cabinet, and a bicameral legislature.	Liberian dollar	English Sudanese languages	Tribal religions Christianity Islam
LIBYA	Arab republic ruled by a revolutionary council and an appointed premier and cabinet.	Libyan dinar	Arabic; Berber English Italian	Islam
LIECHTENSTEIN	Constitutional monarchy with a prince and a unicameral legislature.	Swiss franc	German	Roman Catholicism
LUXEMBOURG	Constitutional monarchy with a grand duke, minister of state, cabinet, and a bicameral parliament.	Luxembourg franc	Letzeburgisch (German dialect) French	Roman Catholicism
MACAO	Portuguese overseas territory under a governor and a legislative assembly.	pataca	Chinese (Cantonese) Portuguese	Buddhism Taoism Confucianism Christianity
MALAGASY REPUBLIC	Republic of the French Community, at present under a military government.	ariary	Malagasy; French Bantu languages	Tribal religions Christianity Islam
MALAWI	One-party republic of the British Commonwealth, with president (for life), cabinet, and unicameral legislature.	Malawi kwacha	Chichewa English Bantu languages	Tribal religions Christianity Islam
MALAYSIA	Constitutional monarchy of the British Commonwealth, with a paramount ruler, cabinet and bicameral parliament.	Malaysian dollar	Malay English Chinese Hindi, Tamil	Islam Confucianism Buddhism Hinduism; Taoism Christianity Tribal religions
MALDIVES	Republic with a president, cabinet & a unicameral legislature.	Maldivian rupee	Divehi Arabic	Islam
MALI	One-party republic at present under a revolutionary committee and a consultative cabinet. The president rules by decree.	Malian franc	French Sudanese and Hamitic languages	Islam Tribal religions
MALTA	An independent member of the British Commonwealth, with a prime minister, a cabinet and a unicameral parliament.	Maltese pound	Maltese English	Roman Catholicism
MARTINIQUE	Overseas department of France, with a prefect and elective general council.	French franc	French Creole	Roman Catholicism
MAURITANIA	One-party republic, with a president, appointed cabinet, and a national assembly.	ouguiya	French; Arabic Sudanese and Hamitic languages	Islam
MAURITIUS	Independent member of the British Commonwealth, with a governor, premier, cabinet, and unicameral parliament.	Mauritian rupee	English; French Creole Hindi; Urdu Chinese	Hinduism Christianity Islam Buddhism
MEXICO	Constitutional federative republic with a president, council of ministers and a bicameral congress.	Mexican peso	Spanish	Roman Catholicism

of the World

MAJOR PRODUCTS

Corn, wheat, sorghum, barley, oats, beans, peas; cattle, sheep, goats, horses, donkeys, pigs, mules; diamonds; wool, mohair, hides and skins, textile products, processed foods.

Rubber, rice, coffee, cassava, sugar cane, cacao, palm oil and kernels, piassava, peanuts; timber; fish, shrimp; iron ore, diamonds; petroleum products, cement, processed foods.

Barley, wheat, olives, grapes, dates, tomatoes, figs, peanuts, citrus fruits, tobacco, esparto; goats, sheep, camels; sponge and tuna fishing; hides and skins; petroleum; matting, carpets, leather articles, embroidered fabrics, olive oil.

Grain, potatoes, grapes, wood; cattle; textiles, wine, leather, dairy products, ceramics, instruments, drugs, canned foods, postage stamps.

Oats, potatoes, wheat, rye, grapes; livestock; iron ore, slate, gypsum; iron and steel, metal products, chemicals, beverages, tobacco, leather, wine, dairy products, rubber products, fertilizers, plastic goods.

Rice, vegetables; fish; cement, metal work, lumber, tobacco (processed), matches, wine, textiles, fireworks.

Cassava rice, corn, potatoes, vanilla, cloves, coffee, sugarcane, beans, peanuts, sisal, castor oil, tobacco, raffia; timber; livestock; fish, shrimp; graphite, mica, chromite, phosphates; textiles, processed foods, refined petroleum, paper, cement.

Tobacco, tea, cotton, pulses, tung oil, sisal, corn, sugarcane; cassava, wheat, rice, millet, peanuts, rubber, beeswax, timber; goats, cattle, pigs, sheep; gold, mica, corundum; hides, skins, meat, ghee, soap, sugar.

Rubber, rice, coconuts, coffee, pineapples, pepper, sugar, tobacco, fibers, vegetables, tea; timber; buffalo, swine, oxen, goats; fish; tin, iron ore, bauxite, petroleum, antimony, gold, manganese; copra, palm oil, rubber products, petroleum and wood products, textiles.

Coconuts, fruits, nuts; fish, cowries; cloth, mats, boats, fish products, handicrafts, copra, coir, ambergris.

Millet, rice, sorghum, peanuts, corn, cotton, tobacco, nuts, sisal; livestock; fish; salt, gold; hides and skins; ceramics, jewelry, leather, rice mills, soap, processed fish and foods, textiles, sugar, tobacco products, cement.

Wheat, barley, potatoes, onions, grapes and other fruits, cumin seed, cotton; goats, sheep, pigs, cattle; fish; lace, filigree, wine, footwear, beer, cigarettes, buttons, pipes, gloves; textiles, flowers, ceramics, rubber goods.

Sugarcane, cocoa, mangoes, avocados, pineapples, bananas, coffee; rum, sugar.

Millet, gum, sorghum, rice, corn, watermelons, wheat, dates, gum arabic, henna; sheep, goats, cattle, camels, asses, horses; fish; salt, copper, iron ore; hides and skins, fish products.

Sugarcane, aloe fiber, corn, coffee, vanilla beans, hemp, sisal, peanuts, tea, yams, manioc, pineapples, tobacco, coconuts; alcohol, molasses, rum, copra, refined sugar; dairy products, tea and tobacco products, processed fruits.

Corn, wheat, sugar cane, bananas, barley, cotton, coffee, tomatoes, vegetables; cattle; henequen; fish; silver, petroleum, lead, gold, sulfur, manganese, coal, iron ore, zinc, copper; textiles, sugar, alcohol, metal products, oil refining, chemicals, aluminum, cement, petrochemicals, paper, meat, fibers, pharmaceuticals.

MEXICO: The Pyramid of the Sun at San Juan Teotihuacán, not far from Mexico City.

J. Walter Thompson

MOROCCO: Downtown Casablanca, the chief port, with the Place Lyautey in the foreground.

French Gov't Tourist Office

Social and Economic Tables

POLITICAL DIVISION	GOVERNMENT	MONETARY UNIT	LANGUAGE	RELIGION
MONACO	Constitutional hereditary principality, with elected national and communal councils.	French franc	French	Roman Catholicism
MONGOLIA	Communist republic, ruled by chairman of the party politburo, with a unicameral legislature.	tughrik	Mongolian Turkic languages	Lamaism Tribal religions
MOROCCO	Constitutional monarchy, with a king, an appointed prime minister and cabinet, and a unicameral legislature.	dirham	Arabic Berber French Spanish	Islam Judaism Christianity
MOZAMBIQUE	Portuguese overseas "state" under a governor-general and a legislative assembly.	Portuguese escudo	Portuguese Bantu languages	Tribal religions Roman Catholicism Islam
NAURU	Republic with a president, cabinet, and unicameral parliament.	Australian dollar	English Nauruan	Protestantism
NEPAL	Constitutional monarchy, with king, prime minister, cabinet, and a unicameral legislature.	Nepalese rupee	Nepali; Newari Hindi English	Hinduism Buddhism Christianity
NETHERLANDS	A constitutional, hereditary monarchy governed by the queen, a cabinet, ministers and a bicameral partly elected states general.	guilder	Dutch	Roman Catholicism Protestantism
NETHERLANDS ANTILLES	Self-governing part of Netherlands Union with governor, cabinet and unicameral legislature.	Dutch guilder	Dutch Papiamento Spanish	Roman Catholicism Protestantism
NEW CALEDONIA	French overseas territory with a governor, a government council and a territorial assembly.	CFP franc	Melanesian and Polynesian dialects French	Roman Catholicism Tribal religions
NEW GUINEA, TERR. OF	Australian U.N. trusteeship, governed jointly with Papua by a high commissioner, chief minister, executive council and an elected house of assembly.	Australian dollar	Papuan Pidgin English English	Tribal religions Roman Catholicism Protestantism
NEW HEBRIDES	British and French condominium administered by British and French high commissioners, with a partly elected advisory council.	Australian dollar New Hebrides franc	Melanesian dialects Pidgin English English; French	Tribal religions Protestantism Roman Catholicism
NEW ZEALAND	An independent member of the British Commonwealth governed by a governor-general, a prime minister, a cabinet and a unicameral assembly.	New Zealand dollar	English Maori	Protestantism Roman Catholicism
NICARAGUA	Republic at present ruled by a presidential triumvirate, with a bicameral legislature.	córdoba	Spanish	Roman Catholicism
NIGER	One-party republic, with a president, cabinet, and a unicameral national assembly.	CFA franc	French Sudanese and Hamitic languages Arabic; Berber	Islam Tribal religions

of the World

Principal revenue derived from Monte Carlo gambling casino and the tourist trade. Tobacco, postage stamps, perfume, liqueurs, olive oil, oranges.

Stock raising (sheep, goats, cattle, horses, camels); coal, lead, gold; dairy products, wool, hides, skins, horns, bricks, machinery, meat, furs.

Wheat, barley, olives, nuts, citrus fruits, dates, grapes, vegetables, linseed; hides & skins; timber; livestock; fish; phosphates, iron ore, anthracite, manganese, zinc, cobalt, lead, petroleum, antimony; leather, carpets, olive oil, wine, wool, fish products, textiles, cement.

Sugarcane, corn, cotton, copra, cashew nuts, bananas, sisal, coffee, tea, tobacco; timber; livestock; gold, coal, iron ore, copper, bismuth, bauxite; sugar, textiles, flour, rice milling, cement, vegetable oil milling, processed foods and fish.

Phosphates.

Rice, wheat, corn, jute, sugarcane, tea', vegetables, oil seeds, tobacco, cotton, potatoes, medicinal herbs; timber; cattle, hides, skins, ghee; iron, coal, copper; paper, rice and oil milling, sugar, cigarettes, textiles, cement, bricks, tools.

Potatoes, sugar beets, rye, wheat, oats, barley, flax, legumes, flower bulbs, seeds, vegetables, fruit; livestock; fish; coal, petroleum, natural gas, salt; leather, rubber, footwear, metal products, textiles, paper, dairy products, chemicals, foods and beverages, clothing, shipbuilding, ceramics, cement, tobacco products, petroleum products, machinery, electric and electronic products, transportation equipment.

Fish; dividi (tannin); crude salt, phosphates; refined petroleum, petroleum products.

Coconuts, copra, coffee, cotton, manioc, corn, tobacco, bananas, pineapples, vegetables, rice; timber; livestock; guano, trochus shell; nickel, chrome, manganese, iron ore, cobalt, copper, lead, silver, gold; canned meat, nickel processing.

Coconuts, coffee, copra, cocoa, rubber, dairying; fish; timber; gold, silver, copper; boat making, tobacco products, brewing.

Coconuts, copra, cocoa, coffee, bananas, yams, taro, manioc, fruits; sandalwood, kauri pine; cattle, pigs; fish, trochus shells; manganese; meat and fish products.

Wheat, oats, barley, seeds, kauri, gum; sheep, cattle, pigs, horses; hides, skins; timber; fish; gold, silver, coal, copper, petroleum, natural gas, manganese, iron, tungsten; dairy products, meats, wool, clothing, lumber, woodwork, furniture, electrical and radio goods, motor assembly, printing, publishing, biscuits, confections, footwear, rubber products, chemicals, fertilizers, tobacco products, brewing.

Coffee, sugarcane, sesame, corn, bananas, rice, cacao, tobacco, cotton, beans; cattle; hardwoods; gold, copper, silver; sugar, wood products, meat products.

Millet, peanuts, rice, wheat, cotton, gum arabic, corn, beans, sorghum, dates, sugarcane; livestock; hides and skins, leather; natron, limestone, cassiterite, uranium, salt; meat products, cement, tanning, peanut oil milling.

NEW ZEALAND: Mt. Cook, the country's highest peak, and the Southern Alps are seen across Lake Matheson, on the South Island.

Nat'l Publicity Studios

NORWAY: The popular resort of Balestrand, on the Sogne Fjord in western Norway.

Scandinavian Travel Comm'n

Social and Economic Tables

POLITICAL DIVISION	GOVERNMENT	MONETARY UNIT	LANGUAGE	RELIGION
NIGERIA	Federal republic of the British Commonwealth, now under a supreme military council and a federal executive council.	Nigerian pound	English Sudanese languages	Islam Tribal religions Christianity
NIUE	New Zealand dependency, with a resident commissioner, cabinet & a legislative assembly.	New Zealand dollar	Melanesian and Polynesian dialects; English	Protestantism
NORTHERN IRELAND	Executive power vested in appointed governor and cabinet responsible to a unicameral assembly.	pound sterling	English	Protestantism Roman Catholicism
NORWAY	A constitutional, hereditary monarchy with a king, a council of ministers, a cabinet, and unicamerally elected but bicamerally operating legislature.	krone (crown)	Norwegian	Protestantism
OMAN	An independent sultanate and an absolute monarchy.	rial saidi	Arabic Hindi	Islam Hinduism
PACIFIC ISLANDS, TRUST TERR.	United States U. N. trusteeship, with a high commissioner and a bicameral Congress of Micronesia.	U.S. dollar	English Micronesian dialects	Roman Catholicism Protestantism
PAKISTAN	Federal republic with a president, prime minister, cabinet and a bicameral legislature.	Pakistani rupee	Urdu English Panjabi, Pushtu Sindhi, Baluchi	Islam
PANAMA	Nominal republic presently ruled by a military junta by decree.	balboa	Spanish	Roman Catholicism
PAPUA	(For Government, see New Guinea, Terr. of)	Australian dollar	Papuan; English Pidgin English	Tribal religions Protestantism Roman Catholicism
PARAGUAY	A centralized republic with a president, an appointed cabinet and a bicameral congress.	guaraní	Spanish Indian (Guaraní)	Roman Catholicism
PERU	Nominal republic, presently ruled by a military junta.	sol	Spanish Indian (Quechua, Aymará)	Roman Catholicism
PHILIPPINES	Republic governed by a president, prime minister, a cabinet and a unicameral national assembly.	Philippine peso	Pilipino (Tagalog) English; Spanish	Roman Catholicism Protestantism Islam Tribal religions
PITCAIRN ISLANDS	British colony, with a governor (in New Zealand) and an island magistrate.	New Zealand dollar	English	Seventh Day Adventist
POLAND	A Soviet-type "People's Republic" headed by a unicameral parliament which elects two ruling councils. Actual power in the hands of politburo, highest organ of Communist party.	zloty	Polish	Roman Catholicism

of the World

PERU: The beginning of festivities in the bull ring in Lima, the capital city.

Pan American World Airways

MAJOR PRODUCTS

Palm oil and kernels, cocoa, spices, cacao, peanuts, cotton, rubber, bananas, corn, rice, fruits, millet, coffee; livestock; fish, shrimp; timber; tin, coal, iron ore, limestone, columbite, lead, petroleum, marble; cigarettes, soap, sugar, cement, textiles, plywood, refined petroleum, hides and skins.

Copra, sweet potatoes, bananas; hats, baskets.

Potatoes, oats, flax, barley, hay; cattle, sheep, pigs; basalt and igneous rocks, sand and gravel; linen, rayon, cotton and woolen textiles, carpets, hosiery, clothing, shipbuilding, aircraft, machinery, tobacco, whiskey, electronic equipment.

Hay, potatoes, oats, barley, wheat, rye, fruits, vegetables; dairy products, livestock; fish; iron, copper, zinc, nickel, molybdenum; timber; pulp, cellulose, paper, canned foods, metal and electro-chemical products, transportation equipment, salted, dried and canned fish, leather, textiles, fertilizers, shipbuilding, aluminum, furs.

Dates, pomegranates, limes and other fruits, vegetables, coconuts, tobacco, sugarcane; dried fish; cattle, sheep, goats, camels; petroleum, dried fish, ghee.

Copra, vegetables, fish, tropical fruits, coconuts, trochus shell; poultry, livestock.

Rice, wheat, corn, cotton, sugarcane, citrus fruits, oilseeds, tobacco; cattle, goats, sheep, horses, camels; hides, skins, wool; fish; salt, coal, petroleum, chromite, natural gas, antimony; textiles, flour, cement, iron and steel, sugar, leather, chemicals, glass, sports equipment, handicrafts, surgical instruments, refined petroleum.

Bananas, cacao, abacá, coconuts, rice, sugarcane, coffee, pineapples; fish, shrimp; cattle; hardwoods; gold; hides, sugar, wood products, textiles, leather products, oil refining.

Coconuts, rubber, sago, rice, bananas, coffee, kapok, bamboo, sisal, copra; fish, shells; cattle, goats, poultry; gold, copper; tobacco products, brewing, boat making.

Cotton, tobacco, sugarcane, rice, yerba maté, corn, coffee, citrus fruits; cattle, hides; lumber, quebracho; iron, manganese, copper; canned meats, meat products, vegetable oils, cigarettes.

Cotton, sugarcane, potatoes, barley, corn, rice, wheat, cacao, tobacco, coffee, quinine, flax, rubber, guano; fish; livestock; petroleum, lead, zinc, copper, silver, gold, iron ore; textiles, foodstuffs, fish products, sugar, cement, leather, wool, pharmaceuticals, paper products, clothing, metal.

Rice, sugarcane, copra, manila hemp (abacá), corn, tobacco, vegetables, maguey, rubber, bananas, pineapples, citrus fruits; hogs, carabaos, cattle, horses; fish; timber, gum resins; gold, iron ore, copper, chromite, silver, manganese, gypsum, nickel, coal, petroleum; sugar, textiles, desiccated coconuts, tobacco products, rice milling, cocoa, coconut oil, fruit canning, wood products, handicrafts, paper, automobiles, chemicals, steel, cement, glass.

Fruits, vegetables, goats, poultry; handicrafts.

Potatoes, rye, sugar beets, wheat; livestock; fish; zinc, lead, coal, sulphur, copper, iron ore, petroleum, natural gas, phosphates; iron and steel, coke, textiles, cement, chemicals, wood, timber, paper, leather products, glass, machinery, petrochemicals, tools, electric & electronic equipment, shipbuilding, aluminum, fertilizers.

PORTUGAL: The Praça dos Restauradores in Lisbon, with the monument dedicated to the seventeenth century restorers of Portuguese independence.

Photo "Sni-Yan"

Social and Economic Tables

POLITICAL DIVISION	GOVERNMENT	MONETARY UNIT	LANGUAGE	RELIGION
PORTUGAL	Constitutional republic, at present ruled by a military junta.	escudo	Portuguese	Roman Catholicism
PORTUGUESE GUINEA	Portuguese overseas territory under a governor and a legislative assembly.	Portuguese escudo	Portuguese Sudanese languages	Tribal religions Islam Roman Catholicism
PORTUGUESE TIMOR	Portuguese overseas territory under a governor and a legislative assembly.	Portuguese escudo	Portuguese Indonesian Malay	Islam Tribal religions Roman Catholicism
PUERTO RICO	Self-governing "free state" associated with the United States, with a governor, advisory council, and a bicameral congress.	U.S. dollar	Spanish English	Roman Catholicism
QATAR	Independent sheikhdom, ruled by a prime minister and cabinet.	Qatar riyal	Arabic	Islam
RÉUNION	French overseas department, with a prefect and general council.	French franc	French	Roman Catholicism
RHODESIA	Constitutional republic, with a president, cabinet, and bicameral parliament. Unilateral independence from Britain declared in 1965.	Rhodesian dollar	English Bantu languages	Tribal religions Protestantism
RUMANIA	A Soviet-type "People's Republic" with a president, a state council, a cabinet of ministers and a unicameral national assembly. Supreme power resides in Communist party politburo.	leu	Rumanian Hungarian	Rumanian Orthodoxy Roman Catholicism
RWANDA	Nominal republic, at present under military rule.	Rwanda franc	Kinyarwanda French; English Kiswahili	Roman Catholicism Tribal religions Islam
ST. HELENA	British colony with a governor, legislative and executive councils.	pound sterling	English	Protestantism
ST. PIERRE AND MIQUELON	French overseas territory with a governor, privy council and elective general council.	CFA franc	French	Roman Catholicism
SAN MARINO	Republic with two regents, a cabinet, and a unicameral legislature.	lira	Italian	Roman Catholicism
SÃO TOMÉ AND PRÍNCIPE	Portuguese overseas territory under a governor and an assembly.	Portuguese escudo	Bantu languages Portuguese	Tribal religions Roman Catholicism
SAUDI ARABIA	Absolute monarchy, with king, prime minister and cabinet. All authority is exercised by the king.	Saudi riyal	Arabic	Islam
SCOTLAND	A secretary of state for Scotland, in the British cabinet controls agriculture, education, health and home. Authority in other matters is exercised by other members of the British cabinet.	pound sterling	English Gaelic	Protestantism Roman Catholicism
SENEGAL	One-party republic in the French Community, with a president, a prime minister, cabinet and unicameral assembly.	CFA franc	French Sudanese languages	Islam Tribal religions Roman Catholicism
SEYCHELLES	British colony with a governor, cabinet and legislative assembly.	Seychelles rupee	French Creole English; French	Roman Catholicism

of the World

MAJOR PRODUCTS

Wheat, corn, oats, rice, potatoes, tomatoes, citrus fruits, grapes, olives; livestock; cork, lumber, resin; fish; coal, copper, tin, sulphur, tungsten, iron ore; wines, olive oil, canned seafood, textiles, porcelain, embroideries, machinery, food products, automobiles, electronic equipment, cordage, cement.

Rice, palm kernels and oil, wax, peanuts, coconuts; hides and skins; timber.

Coffee, copra, rubber, sandalwood, wax, cocoa; livestock, hides, shells.

Sugarcane, tobacco, fruits, pineapples, grapefruit, coconuts, coffee, cotton, livestock, vegetables; sand and gravel; molasses, embroideries, rum, canned fruit and juice, alcohol, cordials, tobacco products, sugar, cement.

Dates, fruit, tomatoes; shrimp, fish; camels; natural gas, limestone, petroleum; fish products, cement, flour, ammonia.

Sugarcane, tea, tobacco, vanilla, corn, manioc; livestock; essences, fruit and vegetable preserves, rum, sugar.

Corn, tobacco, peanuts, wheat, potatoes, cotton, tea, sugarcane, citrus fruits; livestock; copper, gold, asbestos, chromite, coal; textiles, apparel, cigarettes, flour, wood and rubber products, meat products, refined sugar, iron, vehicles, electrical goods, metal products, chemicals.

Wheat, barley, rye, corn, oats, potatoes, sugar beets, hemp, flax, grapes, fruits, tobacco; timber; sheep, cattle, pigs, horses; petroleum, natural gas, salt, coal, lignite, iron and copper ores, gold, silver, bauxite, lead, manganese, zinc; food products, iron and steel, metal products, textiles, wood and paper products, chemicals, machinery.

Coffee, cotton, rice, tea, corn, peanuts, pyrethrum, vegetables; livestock; hides; cassiterite, tungsten, tantalite, beryl, wolfram; textiles, handicrafts, processed foods.

Hemp, fruit, vegetables, lily bulbs, potatoes; sheep, goats, cattle, donkeys, poultry; cordage, fibers, lace.

Fish; sienna earth, yellow ocher; fish products, furs.

Cattle, hides; textiles, tiles, ceramics, wine, stone, postage stamps.

Cacao, coffee, coconuts, cinchona, bananas; livestock; palm oil, copra.

Dates, corn, wheat, rice, alfalfa, coffee, grapes, nuts, vegetables, gum, sesame oil; fish; livestock; petroleum, gold, copper, lead, silver; petrochemicals, hides, wool, pottery, refined petroleum, cement, meat and dairy products.

Turnips, potatoes, wheat, barley, sugar beets, flax, vegetables, fruits; sheep, cattle, horses; fish; coal, iron ore, granite, slate, lead, clay; steel, machinery, tools, locomotives, electronic equipment, shipbuilding, watches, textiles, hosiery, thread, lace, yarn, chemicals, whiskey, paper, clay products, preserves, boots and shoes, furniture.

Millet, peanuts, sorghum, rice, corn, cotton, gum arabic, palm nuts; livestock; fish; titanium, phosphates; brick, pottery, weaving, jewelry, oil cakes, fish products.

Coconuts, cinnamon, patchouli, vanilla, corn; fish; tortoise shell, calipee, copra, coconut oil, dried fish, fibers.

PUERTO RICO: One of the island's chief products, pineapples, on their way to the cannery.

Hamilton Wright

SCOTLAND: Loch Garten, a highland lake in the eastern part of Inverness.

British Travel Ass'n

Social and Economic Tables

POLITICAL DIVISION	GOVERNMENT	MONETARY UNIT	LANGUAGE	RELIGION
SIERRA LEONE	One-party republic of the British Commonwealth, with a president, vice-president, prime minister, cabinet & unicameral legislature.	leone	English Sudanese languages Pidgin (Krio)	Tribal religions Islam Christianity
SINGAPORE	Republic in the British Commonwealth, with a president and advisory council, cabinet, prime minister and unicameral parliament.	Singapore dollar	Chinese (Mandarin) Malay Tamil; Hindi English	Confucianism Buddhism Taoism; Hinduism Islam Christianity
SOLOMON ISLANDS PROT.	British protectorate, with high commissioner and partly elected governing council.	Australian dollar	English Pidgin English Melanesian dialects	Tribal religions Protestantism Roman Catholicism
SOMALIA	Republic, at present under a revolutionary council, with a president, several vice-presidents, and a Council of Secretaries (cabinet).	Somali shilling	Somali Arabic English Italian	Islam
SOUTH AFRICA	Republic with a state president, prime minister, executive council (cabinet) & bicameral parliament.	rand	Afrikaans English Bantu languages Bushman	Protestantism Roman Catholicism Islam Hinduism Buddhism Judaism
SOUTH-WEST AFRICA	South African territory with an administrator and legislative assembly, with representation in the South African legislature.	South African rand	Afrikaans English; German Bantu languages Bushman	Tribal religions Protestantism
SPAIN	Nominal monarchy governed by a chief of state and cabinet, prime minister, and unicameral parliament. A king is to be sworn in as chief of state upon death or incapacitation of the chief of state.	peseta	Spanish (Castilian) Catalan Basque Galician	Roman Catholicism
SPANISH SAHARA	Overseas Spanish province, with a governor general and a unicameral assembly.	Spanish peseta	Spanish Arabic Tachelt (Berber)	Islam Roman Catholicism
SRI LANKA (CEYLON)	Independent republic in the British Commonwealth with a president, a prime minister, a cabinet and a unicameral national assembly.	Ceylon rupee	Sinhala Tamil English	Buddhism Hinduism Christianity Islam
SUDAN	Republic with a president & revolutionary council, aided by an assembly. Local autonomy has been granted the southern provinces.	Sudanese pound	Arabic English Sudanese and Hamitic languages	Islam Tribal religions Christianity
SURINAM	Self-governing part of the Netherlands Union, with governor, cabinet and unicameral legislature.	Surinam guilder	Dutch Creole English	Christianity Islam Hinduism
SWAZILAND	Monarchy within the British Commonwealth, with a prime minister, cabinet and bicameral parliament, at present under rule by decree.	South African rand	English Siswati Afrikaans	Tribal religions Christianity
SWEDEN	A constitutional hereditary monarchy with a titular king, prime minister, cabinet and a unicameral parliament.	krona (crown)	Swedish	Protestantism

of the World

MAJOR PRODUCTS

Palm oil and kernels, rice, coffee, kola nuts, ginger, cassava, piassava, peanuts, cocoa; diamonds, iron ore, bauxite, rutile.

Rubber, coconuts, fruits, vegetables, rice, coffee, tapioca, tobacco, sweet potatoes, pepper, pineapples; pigs, poultry, cattle; fish; tin; tin smelting, rubber milling, coconut milling, soap, beer, pineapple canning, biscuits, brick making, shipping, textiles, palm oil, cigarettes, gasoline, kerosene.

Coconuts, rice, sorghum, cocoa, pigs, poultry; trochus and turtle shell, bêche-de-mer; timber; copra.

Sugarcane, cotton, sorghum, corn, peanuts, sesame, tobacco, bananas, grains, beans; livestock; skins, hiles; fish, shellfish, mother-of-pearl; zinc, salt; fish and meat products, refined sugar, textiles.

Corn, wheat, potatoes, oats, barley, tobacco, sugarcane; tea, fruits, rye, peanuts, grapes, pineapples; livestock; fish, lobsters; gold, coal, diamonds, copper, asbestos, manganese, limestone, platinum, chrome ore, iron ore, tungsten, mercury, vanadium, tin, antimony, silver, uranium; hides; timber; chemicals, wool, rubber, machinery, clothing, textiles, food, vehicles, printing, furniture, iron and steel, sugar, aluminum, wood and metal products.

Cattle, horses, sheep, goats; fish, shellfish; diamonds, copper, lead, zinc, salt, tin, manganese, vanadium, iron ore, cadmium, silver, fluorspar, tantalite, phosphate, sulfur, germanium; karakul wool, fish processing.

Wheat, barley, potatoes, oranges, olives, oats, rye, rice, corn, peas, beans, grapes, onions, sugar beets, esparto, flax hemp, pulse, cork, nuts; livestock and poultry; fish; coal, lignite, iron ore, lead, iron pyrites, potash, zinc, mercury, sulphur, copper; textiles, wines, olive oil, paper, cement, hides, leather, chemicals, machinery, vehicles, iron and steel, furniture, shoes, shipbuilding, oil refining, apparel.

Barley, corn; goats, sheep, camels; fish; phosphates.

Tea, coconuts, rubber, rice, millet, tobacco, cacao, cinnamon, nuts, sugar cane, citronella, cloves, fruits, palmyra, fish; cattle, buffalo, goats, swine; graphite, plumbago, ilmenite, gem stones, silver, titanium, monazite; salt, pearls, copra, plywood, leather, shoes, glass, steel, acetic acid, ceramics, quinine, strychnine, coconut oil, textiles, cement, beer, refined petroleum, tobacco products, paper, apparel.

Cotton, cottonseed, sorghum (durra), castor beans, gum arabic, senna, resins, peanuts, sesame, millet, dates, dom nuts, wheat, shea nuts; livestock; mahogany; hides and skins, ivory, gold, salt, trochus shell, mother-of-pearl, iron and manganese ore; textiles, cement, tanning.

Rice, citrus fruits, coconuts, coffee, bananas, sugarcane, cacao, balata, corn, tobacco; timber; gold, bauxite; sugar, rum, plywood, molasses, aluminum, food processing.

Tobacco, corn, peanuts, sugarcane, wheat, cotton, rice, pineapples, citrus fruits; cattle; timber; hides, skins; asbestos, gold, tin, iron ore, coal; meat and dairy products, refined sugar, wood pulp, canned citrus fruits.

Hay, sugar beets, potatoes, oats, wheat, rye, barley; timber; cattle, pigs, sheep, horses; fish; iron ore, sulphur, arsenic, zinc, copper, silver, gold, lead, manganese; wood products, machinery, textiles, iron and steel, metal goods, chemicals, dairy products, tobacco products, porcelain, glass, shipbuilding, matches, automobiles, munitions, liquor, instruments.

SOUTH AFRICA: Commissioner Street, in the downtown part of Johannesburg, the country's largest city.
South African Gov't Info. Office

SWITZERLAND: Milk still being delivered by dog cart in a rural section of the republic.
TWA–Trans World Airlines

Social and Economic Tables

POLITICAL DIVISION	GOVERNMENT	MONETARY UNIT	LANGUAGE	RELIGION
SWITZERLAND	Federal republic with a president, vice-president, an executive federal council and a bicameral elective federal assembly.	Swiss franc	German French Italian Romansh	Protestantism Roman Catholicism
SYRIA	Arab republic with a president, prime minister, and legislative people's council, under presidential decree.	Syrian pound	Arabic Turkish; Kurdish French; English	Islam Christianity
TANZANIA	One-party united republic of the British Commonwealth, with a president, two vice-presidents, cabinet, and unicameral national assembly proportionately representing Tanganyika and Zanzibar.	Tanzanian shilling	Kiswahili English Bantu languages Arabic Gujarati	Tribal religions Islam Christianity Hinduism
THAILAND (SIAM)	Constitutional monarchy, at present under a prime minister and cabinet.	baht	Thai Khmer; Malay Chinese	Buddhism Islam Confucianism
TOGO	One party republic with a president and an appointed council of ministers.	CFA franc	French Sudanese languages	Tribal religions Roman Catholicism Islam
TOKELAU ISLANDS	An island territory of New Zealand with a high commissioner.	New Zealand dollar	Samoan	Protestantism Roman Catholicism
TONGA	Constitutional monarchy of the British Commonwealth, with cabinet and unicameral assembly.	pa'anga	Tongan English	Protestantism Roman Catholicism
TRINIDAD AND TOBAGO	Independent British Commonwealth member, with prime minister, cabinet, & a bicameral parliament.	Trinidad and Tobago dollar	English	Protestantism Roman Catholicism Hinduism; Islam
TUNISIA	A republic with a president, an appointed cabinet, a prime minister, and an elective unicameral assembly.	Tunisian dinar	Arabic French Berber	Islam Roman Catholicism
TURKEY	Constitutional republic with a president, prime minister, cabinet, and a bicameral parliament.	Turkish lira	Turkish Kurdish Arabic	Islam
UGANDA	Nominal republic of the British Commonwealth, at present under a president and a military government.	Ugandan shilling	English; Kiswahili Sudanese, Bantu, and Hamitic languages	Christianity Tribal religions Islam
U.S.S.R.	A federation of 15 socialist republics with an elected bicameral — house legislature (Supreme Soviet) which elects the executive presidium and council of ministers. The policy of the state is largely defined by the Politburo and Secretariat of the Central Committee of the Communist party, the only legal party.	ruble	Russian, Ukrainian, White Russian, Uzbek, Tatar, Azerbaidzhani, Georgian, Lithuanian, Armenian, Yiddish, Latvian, Mordvinian, Chuvash, Tadzhik, Estonian, Kazakh, etc.	Russian Orthodoxy Islam Roman Catholicism Judaism
UNITED ARAB EMIRATES	Constitutional Arab federation of seven sheikhdoms, with a president, vice-president, cabinet and national council.	dirham	Arabic	Islam
UNITED KINGDOM	See: England and Wales, Northern Ireland, Scotland.			

of the World

MAJOR PRODUCTS

Wheat, potatoes, sugar beets, rye, oats, barley, fruits, tobacco; livestock; salt, iron, manganese; dairy products, textiles, watches and clocks, chemicals, foods, wines, dyes, drugs, machinery, precision instruments, chocolate.

Wheat, barley, sorghum, cotton, vegetables, olives, grapes, tobacco; sheep, goats, cattle, camels, horses; petroleum, gypsum; leather, textiles, cement, wine, flour, oil refining, wool, meat, hides and skins, food processing.

Sisal, kapok, copra, coconuts, cotton, cloves; pyrethrum, gum arabic, coffee, bananas, tobacco, vegetables, peanuts, cashew nuts, tea, oilseeds, beeswax, sugarcane; livestock; hides and skins; diamonds, gold, phosphates, mica, salt, camphor, tungsten, lead, silver; cement, textiles, petroleum products, refined sugar, wood products, shoes, cordage, rolled iron and aluminum.

Rice, rubber, coconuts, sugarcane, tobacco, tapioca, cotton, corn, kenaf, beans; teak and other woods; bullocks, buffalo, horses, elephants; fish; tin, wolfram; lac, jute.

Palm oil and kernels, tapioca, copra, kapok, cocoa, yams, coffee, plantains, corn, peanuts, cotton, kola, cassava, rubber; fish; livestock; phosphates; textiles, fertilizers.

Coconuts, fiber, taro; pigs, chickens; fish; hats, mats, copra.

Coconuts, bananas, yams, breadfruit, taro, papayas, pineapples, melons, tobacco, corn, peanuts, fungus, candlenuts; fish; pigs, cattle, goats, chickens; copra.

Coffee, cocoa, sugarcane, citrus fruits; cattle; petroleum, natural gas, asphalt; rum, canned grapefruit juice, sugar, chemicals, textiles, plastic products, oil refining.

Wheat, barley, alfalfa, oats, corn, sorghum, beans, grapes, olives, vegetables, nuts, citrus fruits, dates, oranges; cork, timber; livestock; fish, sponges; phosphates, petroleum, iron ore, lead, zinc; flour milling, oil refining, wine, olive oil, wool spinning, pottery, leather, silk weaving, textiles, food processing, fertilizers, iron and steel, paper.

Tobacco, cereals, olives, cotton, figs, opium, nuts, fruits; cattle, livestock; fish; chromium, iron ore, copper, coal, lignite, meerschaum, manganese; textiles, iron and steel, paper, rugs, olive oil, cement, petroleum products.

Cotton, coffee, tea, plantains, sisal, peanuts, millet, tobacco, sugarcane, rubber; livestock; hides and skins; copper, gold, phosphates, tin; cigarettes, shoes, cement, fertilizers, copper smelting, food processing, textiles.

Wheat, rye, oats, barley, corn, sugar beets, linseed, sunflower seeds, cotton, forage crops, flax, hemp, potatoes, tobacco; cattle, sheep, goats, pigs, horses; timber, furs; fish; coal, peat, petroleum, iron, lignite, copper, lead, zinc, nickel, aluminum, diamonds, mercury, phosphates, manganese, gold, sulphur, potash, asbestos, platinum, salt, chromite; steel, machinery, textiles, sugar, flour, meats, automobiles, paper, synthetic rubber, foods, wines, chemicals, lumber and wood products, tools and metal products, transportation equipment, fertilizers, apparel.

Dates, grains, vegetables; sheep, goats; fish, pearl fishing; petroleum; cement refined petroleum, petrochemicals, postage stamps, dried fish.

THAILAND: The heroine and hero in costume for a classical dance in the Asian kingdom.

Gov't of Thailand

TURKEY: The Galata Bridge, spanning the Golden Horn in Istanbul, one of the most heavily traveled bridges in the world.

Turkish Info. Office

Social and Economic Tables

POLITICAL DIVISION	GOVERNMENT	MONETARY UNIT	LANGUAGE	RELIGION
UNITED STATES	Federal republic with a president, vice-president, and bicameral congress (senate and house of representatives), and an appointed cabinet. It consists of 50 states, each with a governor and state legislature.	U.S. dollar	English	Protestantism Roman Catholicism Judaism
UPPER VOLTA	Republic with a president, a unicameral assembly, and a military cabinet.	CFA franc	French Sudanese languages	Tribal religions Islam
URUGUAY	A republic governed by a president, cabinet and a legislative council of state.	Uruguayan peso	Spanish	Roman Catholicism
VATICAN CITY	The Pope, elected for life by cardinals of the Roman Catholic Church, exercises absolute legislative, executive and judicial power.	Italian lira	Italian Latin	Roman Catholicism
VENEZUELA	Constitutional republic with a president, appointive cabinet, and an elective bicameral congress.	bolívar	Spanish	Roman Catholicism
VIETNAM	Divided in two parts by Armistice Line Sept. 1954. North of 17th parallel is communist-controlled "republic." South is a republic with a president and a bicameral elective legislature.	South: piaster North: dong	Vietnamese Khmer Lao French Chinese	Buddhism Taoism Confucianism Roman Catholicism
VIRGIN ISLANDS (BR.)	British colony with an administrator, chief minister and executive and legislative councils.	B. W. I. dollar; U.S. dollar	English Creole	Protestantism
VIRGIN ISLANDS (U.S.)	U.S. territory with an elected governor, local executive departments and a local unicameral legislature.	U.S. dollar	English Creole	Roman Catholicism Protestantism
WESTERN SAMOA	Independent member of the British Commonwealth, with a head of state, prime minister, cabinet and legislative assembly.	tala (dollar)	Samoan English	Protestantism Roman Catholicism Tribal religions
YEMEN ARAB REP.	Arab republic, with a president, cabinet, prime minister and a consultative assembly.	Yemeni riyal	Arabic	Islam
YEMEN, PEOPLES DEM. REP. OF	"People's" republic with president, prime minister, and ruling supreme council.	dinar	Arabic	Islam
YUGOSLAVIA	A Soviet-type federal republic with a president, federal executive council and five-chambered elective assembly. Actually ruled by Communist party.	Yugoslav dinar	Serbian-Croatian Slovenian Macedonian	Eastern Orthodoxy Roman Catholicism Islam
ZAIRE	One-party republic, with a president and prime minister, ruled by decree.	zaire	Bantu languages French	Tribal religions Roman Catholicism
ZAMBIA	One-party republic of the British Commonwealth, with a president, vice-president, an appointed prime minister, cabinet and a unicameral assembly.	Zambian kwacha	Bantu languages English	Tribal religions Christianity

of the World

MAJOR PRODUCTS

Corn, hay, tobacco, wheat, cotton, oats, soy beans, potatoes, barley, sorghums, peanuts, rye, rice, citrus fruits, fruits, sugar beets, sugarcane, vegetables, tree nuts, feed grains and hay; livestock; fish; lumber; petroleum, coal, cement, iron, natural gas, copper, sand and gravel, zinc, lead, stone, gold, silver, molybdenum, bauxite, phosphates, mica, sulphur; foods, transportation equipment, machinery, primary metal products, electrical machinery, textiles, chemicals, paper and wood products, beverages, dairy products.

Millet, sweet potatoes, peanuts, sugarcane, cassava, corn, karite, shea nuts and butter, vegetables, rice, cotton, sisal, sesame, sorghum, tea; livestock; gold, manganese, bauxite, copper, silver; hides and skins, meat products, refined sugar, flour, textiles, processed foods and oils.

Wheat, corn, oats, seeds, peanuts, barley, rice, fruits, grapes, vegetables, tobacco; sheep, cattle; gold; meat, hides, wool, textiles, leather, shoes, wines, chemicals, metallurgy.

UNITED STATES: The American Falls at Niagara Falls, New York, a major tourist attraction.

N.Y. State Dep't of Commerce

Coffee. cacao, sugar cane, corn, rice, cotton, tobacco, yucca, coconuts, bananas, rubber; livestock; fish, pearls; petroleum, natural gas, iron ore, gold, coal, copper, phosphates, nickel, asphalt, salt, diamonds; textiles, leather, sugar, cement, wood products, chemicals, vehicles, food products, meats, refined petroleum, dairy products, apparel, rubber products, paper, steel.

Rice, corn, sugar, tobacco, coffee, fruits, nuts, tea; cotton, manioc, rubber, copra, groundnuts, sweet potatoes, cinnamon; bamboo, silk; livestock; fish; lumber; gold, tin, copper, coal, zinc, iron ore, cement, chromite, tungsten, manganese, phosphate, lead, bauxite; paper, textiles, chemicals, sugar, food processing, steel, wood products, handicrafts.

Poultry and livestock, fish; fruit, vegetables; handicrafts.

Vegetables, sugar cane, citrus fruits, coconuts; cattle; fish; rum, bay rum, bay oil, molasses, handicrafts, sugar, lime juice, hides, bitters.

Breadfruit, yams, pawpaws, cocoa, bananas, taro; fish; timber; pigs, poultry; copra.

Coffee, barley, wheat, cotton, fruits, qat, millet, sesame; cattle, hides; fish; rock salt; textiles.

Dates, gums, tobacco, cotton, fruit, salt, fish oil; wheat, barley, sesame, millet, sorghum; goats, sheep, camels, cattle; fish; dhow building, ship bunkering, oil refining.

Wheat, barley, rye, oats, corn, sugar beets, hops, tobacco, flax, vegetables, fruits; timber; livestock; coal, lignite, iron, copper, lead, natural gas, salt, zinc, mercury, antimony, petroleum, bauxite, chrome, cement; lumber, textiles, foods, beverages, sugar, wood products, wines, machinery, chemicals, shipbuilding, meat.

Palm oil and kernels, cotton, coffee, tea, cocoa, rice, peanuts, rubber; livestock; ivory; timber; copper, coal, silver, tin, diamonds, gold, cobalt, radium, uranium; tantalum, zinc, manganese, bauxite, cassiterite; flour, textiles, processed foods.

Corn, wheat, tobacco, sorghum, millet, peanuts, cassava, rice, beans, cotton; timber; fish; cattle; copper, lead, manganese, zinc, cobalt, tin; iron and steel, metal products, textiles, chemicals, refined oil and copper, processed foods, dairy products.

VENEZUELA: Avenida Bolívar and the thirty story office buildings of downtown Caracas.

Hamilton Wright

ECUADOR: Independence Plaza in Quito, with the Cathedral, the center of tourist activity in the country.
Hamilton Wright

ENGLAND: Trafalgar Square and the famous pillar dedicated to Lord Nelson, in London.
British Info. Services

AUSTRALIA: A view of Sydney Harbour, with the botanical gardens at Farm Cove in the foreground.
Qantas

INDIA: The Hawa Mahal at Jaipur, in the state of Rajasthan, with old and new forms of transportation.
Gov't of India Info. Bur.

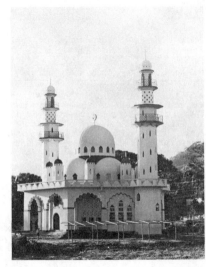

TRINIDAD & TOBAGO: A typical mosque in Port of Spain.
Trinidad & Tobago Tourist Board

INDEX OF PRINCIPAL CITIES OF THE WORLD

This alphabetical list of cities and towns gives statistics of population based on the latest official census reports or most recent reliable estimates. Each line begins with the name of a place, followed by the name of the country or state, the population, the index reference and plate number. This index reference gives the location of the city or town name on ,the accompanying map plates. The name is found within the square formed by the two lines of latitude or longitude which enclose each of the co-ordinates—i.e. the marginal letters and numbers. In the case of maps consisting entirely of insets, the name is found near the intersection point of imaginary lines'connecting the co-ordinates.

Where space on the map has not permitted giving the complete form of a name, the extended form is shown in the index. Where a place may be known under different names or by various spellings of the same name, the different forms have been included, to a large extent, in the index. Where an alternative spelling in parentheses is shown on the map itself, the first name gives the local official form, the conventional form following in parentheses.

* Capitals of countries, states and provinces. † Population figure includes suburbs or subdivision.

Lipetsk, U.S.S.R., 290,000 ....E 4 37
Lisbon (Lisboa),* Port.,
  828,000 ....A 1 26
Lisichansk, U.S.S.R., 117,000 ......E 5 37
Litoměřice, Czechoslovakia,
  18,000 ....C 1 32
Little Rock,* Ark., 132,483 ....F 4 110
Liuchow, China, 190,000 ....G 7 51
Liverpool, England, 677,450 ....F 2 16
Livingstone, Zambia, †43,000 ......L15 65
Livonia, Mich., 110,109 ....F 6 143
Livorno (Leghorn), Italy,
  152,517 ....C 3 28
Ljubljana, Yugoslavia,
  183,000 ....B 3 34
Llanelly, Wales, 27,570 ....D 5 17
Locarno, Switzerland, 12,200 ....G 4 31
Łódź, Poland, 750,400 ....D 3 21
Logroño, Spain, 58,545 ....E 1 27
Loja, Ecuador, 26,785 ....E 4 68
Lokeren, Belgium, 26,654 ....C 5 20
Lomas de Zamora, Arg.,
  †275,219 ....O12 71
Lomé,* Togo, 90,600 ....G10 62
London,* England,
  7,703,410 ....B 5 17
London, Ontario, 223,222 ....C 5 90
Londonderry, Northern Ireland,
  55,000 ....C 3 16
Long Beach, Calif., 358,633 ....C11 113
Longueuil, Quebec, 97,590 ....J 4 89
Longwy, France, 21,052 ....F 3 24
Lorain, Ohio, 78,185 ....F 3 166
Lorient, France, 66,023 ....B 4 24
Los Alamos, N. Mex., 11,310 ......C 3 158
Los Angeles, Calif., 2,809,596 .....C10 113
Lota, Chile, †51,548 ....F11 70
Louisville, Ky., 361,958 ....F 4 132
Lourdes, France, 17,627 ....C 6 25
Lourenço Marques,* Mozambique,
  65,716 ....N17 65
Louvain, Belgium,
  32,125 ....E 6 20
Lowell, Mass., 94,239 ....J 2 141
Lower Hutt, New Zealand,
  58,700 ....L 6 59
Lowestoft, England, 50,730 ....G 4 17
Loyang, China, 500,000 ....H 5 51
Luanda,* Angola, 400,000 ....J13 64
Lubbock, Tex., 149,101 ....C 4 180
Lübeck, Germany, 242,191 ....D 2 22
Lublin, Poland, 211,900 ....F 3 21
Lubumbashi, Zaire, 318,000 ....M14 65
Lucca, Italy, 45,398 ....C 3 28
Lucena, Philippines, 56,000 ....G 3 55
Lucerne, Switzerland, 73,000 ......F 2 31
Luchow, China, 130,000 ....F 6 51
Lucknow, India, 750,512 ....E 3 48
Lüdenscheid, Germany,
  80,096 ....B 3 23
Ludhiana, India, 401,124 ....D 2 48
Ludwigsburg, Germany, 79,538 ....C 4 23
Ludwigshafen, Germany,
  174,698 ....C 4 23
Lugano, Switzerland, 21,100 ....G 4 31
Lugansk, U.S.S.R., 382,000 ....F 5 37
Lugo, Spain, 45,497 ....C 1 26
Lugoj, Rumania, 35,388 ....F 3 34
Luimneach (Limerick), Ireland,
  50,786 ....B 4 17
Luleå, Sweden, 36,428 ....N 4 18
Lund, Sweden, 50,494 ....H 9 19
Lüneburg, Ger., 59,944 ....D 2 22
Lünen, Germany, 72,195 ....B 3 22
Lunéville, France, 22,961 ....G 3 24
Lusaka,* Zambia, †238,200 ....M15 65
Lüshun (Port Arthur), China,
  126,000 ....K 4 51
Lüta, China, 1,590,000 ....K 4 51
Luton, England, 156,690 ....F 5 17
Luxembourg,* Lux., 77,458 ....H 8 20

Luzern (Lucerne), Switzerland,
  73,000 ....F 2 31
Lvov, U.S.S.R., 553,000 ....B 4 37
Lyallpur, Pakistan, 425,248 ....C 2 48
Lynchburg, Va., 54,083 ....F 6 184
Lynn, Mass., 90,294 ....D 6 140
Lyon, France, 524,500 ....F 5 25
Maastricht, Netherlands,
  †93,927 ....G 6 20
Macao,* Macao, 262,000 ....H 7 51
Macclesfield, England, 41,870 .....E 4 17
Maceió, Brazil, 242,867 ....N 5 69
Machida, Japan, 154,000 ....H 2 52
Macon, Ga., 122,423 ....E 5 120
Madinat ash Sha'b, Peoples Dem.
  Rep. of Yemen, 29,897 ....E 7 44
Madison,* Wis., 172,007 ....H 9 191
Madiun, Indon., 152,000 ....J 2 55
Madras, India, 2,470,288 ....E 6 49
Madrid,* Spain, 2,850,631 ....E 2 27
Madurai (Madura), India,
  548,298 ....D 7 49
Maebashi, Japan, 225,000 ....E 3 52
Magdeburg, Germany, 268,269 ....D 2 22
Magelang, Indon., 119,000 ....J 2 55
Magnitogorsk, U.S.S.R.,
  364,000 ....G 4 38
Magog, Quebec, 13,281 ....E 4 89
Maidenhead, England, 46,050 .....F 5 17
Maidstone, England, 67,400 ....G 5 17
Maiduguri, Nigeria, 139,965 ....J 9 62
Mainz, Germany, 176,720 ....C 4 23
Majunga, Malagasy Rep.,
  47,654 ....R15 65
Makeyevka, U.S.S.R., 393,000 .....E 5 37
Makhachkala, U.S.S.R., 186,000....G 6 37
Malabo,* Equat. Guinea, †37,237..H11 62
Malacca, Malaysia, 69,848 ....C 5 54
Málaga, Spain, 259,245 ....D 4 26
Malang, Indon., 419,000 ....K 2 55
Malatya, Turkey, 104,428 ....H 3 40
Malden, Mass., 56,127 ....D 6 140
Maldonado, Uruguay, 15,005 ......K11 71
Male,* Maldives, 13,336 ....C 8 49
Malegaon, India, 191,784 ....C 4 48
Malines, Belgium, 65,728 ....E 5 20
Malmö, Sweden, 256,064 ....H 9 19
Manado, Indon., 160,000 ....G 5 55
Managua,* Nicaragua,
  262,047 ....D 4 78
Manama,* Bahrain, 79,098 ....E 4 44
Manaus, Brazil, 284,118 ....H 4 68
Manchester, England,
  593,770 ....G 2 16
Manchester, N.H., 87,754 ....B 4 155
Mandalay, Burma, 195,348 ....B 2 53
Mangalore, India, 171,759 ....C 6 49
Manila, Philippines, 1,499,000.....G 3 55
Manisa, Turkey, 69,711 ....B 3 46
Manizales, Colombia, 267,543 .....E 2 68
Mannheim, Germany, 330,920 .....C 4 23
Manresa, Spain, 46,105 ....G 2 27
Mansa, Zambia, †5,700 ....M14 65
Mansfield, England, 56,210 ....F 4 17
Mansfield, Ohio, 55,047 ....F 4 166
Manta, Ecuador, 33,622 ....D 4 68
Mantua, Italy, 55,806 ....C 2 28
Manzanillo, Cuba, 91,200 ....C 3 76
Manzanillo, Mexico, †46,170 ......G 7 80
Maracaibo, Venezuela,
  625,101 ....F 1 68
Maracay, Venezuela, 185,655 .....G 1 68
Maraş, Turkey, 63,284 ....G 4 46
Marburg, Germany, 51,382 ....C 3 23
Marcinelle, Belgium, 25,992 ....D 7 20
Mar del Plata, Argentina,
  141,886 ....J11 71
Margate, England, 49,080 ....G 5 17
Marianao, Cuba, 454,700 ....A 2 76
Maribor, Yugoslavia, 89,000 ......B 2 34
Marília, Brazil, 73,165 ....K 8 69

Marion, Ind., 39,607 ....F 3 126
Marion, Ohio, 38,646 ....D 4 126
Marl, Germany, 75,779 ....B 3 22
Marrakech, Morocco, 295,000 .....E 5 62
Marseille, France, 880,527 ....F 6 25
Martin, Czech., 29,000 ....E 2 33
Maseru,* Lesotho, 18,797 ....M17 65
Mason City, Iowa, 30,379 ....G 2 129
Massa, Italy, 46,992 ....C 2 28
Massawa, Ethiopia, 25,000 ....O 8 63
Massillon, Ohio, 32,539 ....G 4 166
Masulipatnam, India, 112,636 .....E 5 49
Matagalpa, Nicaragua,
  15,030 ....E 4 78
Matamoros, Mexico, †182,887 ....L 4 81
Matanzas, Cuba, 84,100 ....B 2 76
Mathura, India, 131,813 ....D 3 48
Matosinhos, Portugal, 37,694 .....B 2 26
Matsue, Japan, 115,000 ....D 4 52
Matsumoto, Japan, 159,000 ....E 3 52
Matsuyama, Japan, 310,000 ....D 4 52
Maturín, Venezuela, 54,362 ....H 2 68
Mayagüez, Puerto Rico,
  69,485 ....F 1 77
Maykop, U.S.S.R., 111,000 ....F 6 37
Maywood, Ill., 29,019 ....A 2 124
Mazatlán, Mexico, †171,835 ......F 5 50
Mbabane,* Swaziland, 13,803 .....N17 65
Mecca,* Saudi Arabia,
  185,000 ....C 5 44
Mechelen (Malines), Belgium,
  65,728 ....E 5 20
McKeesport, Pa., 37,977 ....C 7 172
Medan, Indonesia, 590,000 ....B 5 54
Medellín, Colombia, 967,825 ......E 2 68
Medford, Mass., 64,397 ....C 6 140
Mediaş, Rumania, 46,396 ....G 2 34
Medicine Hat, Alberta, 26,518 ....E 4 97
Medina, Saudi Arabia, 72,000 .....D 5 44
Meerut, India, 271,325 ....D 3 48
Meissen, Germany, 47,166 ....E 3 23
Meknès, Morocco, 235,000 ....E 5 62
Melbourne,* Victoria,
  †2,110,168 ....H 7 59
Melilla, Spain, 77,000 ....F 4 62
Melitopol', U.S.S.R., 137,000 .....D 5 37
Melo, Uruguay, 28,673 ....K10 71
Melrose, Mass., 33,180 ....D 6 140
Melun, France, 33,345 ....E 3 24
Memel (Klaipėda), U.S.S.R.,
  140,000 ....B 3 36
Memphis, Tenn., 623,530 ....B 4 178
Mendoza, Argentina,
  109,122 ....G10 70
Menton, France, 23,401 ....G 6 25
Mercedes, Argentina, 35,449 ......G10 70
Mercedes, Uruguay, 31,325 ....J10 71
Mergui, Burma, 33,697 ....B 4 53
Mérida, Mexico, †253,856 ....P 6 81
Mérida, Venezuela, 46,339 ....F 2 68
Meriden, Conn., 55,959 ....D 2 116
Meridian, Miss., 45,083 ....G 6 147
Merseburg, Ger., 55,562 ....D 3 22
Mersin, Turkey, 86,692 ....F 4 46
Merthyr Tydfil, Wales,
  56,360 ....E 5 17
Merton, England, 183,570 ....B 5 17
Meshed, Iran, 409,616 ....H 2 45
Messina, Sicily, Italy,
  202,095 ....E 5 29
Mestre, Italy, 138,822 ....D 2 28
Metairie, La., 136,477 ....O 4 135
Metz, France, 105,533 ....G 3 24
Mexicali, Mexico, †390,411 ....B 1 80
Mexico City,* Mexico,
  †3,025,564 ....L 1 87
Miami, Fla., 334,859 ....B 5 119
Miami Beach, Fla., 87,072 ....C 5 119
Michigan City, Ind., 39,369 ....C 1 126
Middleton, Eng., 57,510 ....G 2 16
Middletown, Conn., 36,924 ....E 2 117